Vocabulary Workshop
Sixth Course

- **Words in Context**
- **Analogies**
- **Synonyms**
- **Prefixes, Suffixes, Roots**

HOLT, RINEHART AND WINSTON

A Harcourt Classroom Education Company

Austin · New York · Orlando · Atlanta · San Francisco · Boston · Dallas · Toronto · London

EDITORIAL
Director
Mescal Evler
Manager of Editorial Operations
Bill Wahlgren
Executive Editor
Emily G. Shenk
Project Editor
Cheryl L. Christian
Writing and Editing: Janis D. Russell
Editorial Assistant: Kim Soriano
Copyediting: Michael Neibergall, *Copyediting Manager;* Mary Malone, *Senior Copyeditor;* Joel Bourgeois, Elizabeth Dickson, Gabrielle Field, Julie A. Hill, Jane Kominek, Millicent Ondras, Theresa Reding, Dennis Scharnberg, Kathleen Scheiner, Laurie Schlesinger, *Copyeditors*
Project Administration: Marie Price, *Managing Editor;* Lori De La Garza, *Editorial Operations Coordinator;* Thomas Browne, Heather Cheyne, Diane Hardin, Mark Holland, Marcus Johnson, Jill O'Neal, Joyce Rector, Janet Riley, Kelly Tankersley, *Project Administration;* Gail Coupiand, Ruth Hooker, Margaret Sanchez, *Word Processing*
Editorial Permissions: Janet Harrington, *Permissions Editor*

ART, DESIGN AND PHOTO
Graphic Services
Kristen Darby, *Manager*
Image Acquisitions: Joe London, *Director;* Tim Taylor, *Photo Research Supervisor;* Rick Benavides, *Assistant Photo Researcher;* Elaine Tate, *Supervisor;* Erin Cone, *Art Buyer*
Cover Design
Sunday Patterson

PRODUCTION
Belinda Barbosa Lopez, *Senior Production Coordinator;* Simira Davis, *Supervisor;* Nancy Hargis, *Media Production Supervisor;* Joan Lindsay, *Production Coordinator;* Beth Prevelige, *Prepress Manager*

ELECTRONIC PUBLISHING
Carol Martin, *Senior Electronic Publishing Manager;* Robert Franklin, *Electronic Publishing Manager;* Indira Konanur, *Project Coordinator;* JoAnn Brown, Richard Chavez, Jim Gaile, Heather Jernt, Lana Kaupp, Christopher Lucas, Robin McKinney, Nanda Patel, *EP staff;* Emilie Keturakis, Katelijne Lefevere, Sally Williams, *Quality Control Coordinators*

MANUFACTURING
Michael Roche, *Supervisor of Inventory and Manufacturing*

Printed in the United States of America

ISBN 0-03-056296-1

1 2 3 4 5   095   04 03 02 01 00

Consultant

Norbert Elliot, the general editor of *Vocabulary Workshop,* has a Ph.D. in English from The University of Tennessee. He is a professor of English at New Jersey Institute of Technology. A former site director for the National Writing Project, he has directed summer language arts institutes for kindergarten through twelfth-grade teachers in the public schools. A specialist in test development and evaluation of writing, Norbert Elliot has written books and articles on writing assessment, communication, and critical thinking. Dr. Elliot is the father of five children and is married to Lorna Jean Elliot, under whose care, he says, "everything thrives."

CONTENTS

British Literature and Culture

MAKING NEW WORDS YOUR OWN 1

SKILLS AND STRATEGIES
- Context Clues
- Word Structure
- Sound Clues
- Dictionary Definitions
- Sentence Completion

CONTEXT: Literary Figures

CONTEXT: History and Society

CONTEXT: Science and Technology

CONNECTING NEW WORDS AND PATTERNS 123

SKILLS AND STRATEGIES
• Understanding Analogies
• Types of Analogies
• Solving Analogies

READING NEW WORDS IN CONTEXT 141

> SKILLS AND STRATEGIES
> • Reading Longer Passages
> • Finding Synonyms
> • Reading Strategically

CONTEXT: Literary Figures

CONTEXT: History and Society

CONTEXT: Science and Technology

The following tables list some common roots, prefixes, and suffixes. Use these tables to help you determine the meaning of a word by examining its structure.

GREEK ROOTS		
BASE	**MEANING**	**EXAMPLES**
anthropo	human being	**anthropo**logy, **anthropo**id, phil**anthrop**ic
aster, astro	star	**astro**nomy, **astro**nomical, **aster**isk
baro	pressure	**baro**meter, **baro**metric
biblio, bibli	book	**biblio**grapher, **biblio**mania, **bibli**cal
bio	life	**bio**logy, **bio**chemistry, **bio**degradable
chrom	color	**chrom**atic, **chrom**aticity
chrono	time	**chrono**logy, **chrono**meter, **chrono**scope
cosmo	world, order, universe	**cosmo**logy, **cosmo**naut, **cosmo**politan
crac, crat	rule, govern	aristo**crac**y, aristo**crat**ic, demo**crat**
dem	people	**dem**ocracy, **dem**agogue, epi**dem**ic
derm	skin	**derm**atitis, **derm**atology
ethno	nation	**ethn**ic, **ethno**centrism
eu	good, well	**eu**phoria, **eu**phony, **eu**phemism
gam	marriage	mono**gam**y, poly**gam**y, bi**gam**y
geo	earth	**geo**logy, **geo**centric, **geo**dynamics
gno, kno	to know	**kno**wledge, **gno**stic, a**gno**stic
graph, gram	to write, draw, record	auto**graph**, tele**gram**, para**graph**
gymno, gymn	athletic	**gymn**astics, **gymn**asium
hydro	water	**hydro**gen, **hydro**dynamics, **hydro**plane
hypno	sleep	**hypno**sis, **hypno**tic, **hypno**tize
hypo	under, below	**hypo**dermic, **hypo**tension, **hypo**thermia
lith	stone	mono**lith**, mega**lith**
logue, logo	idea, word, speech, reason	dia**logue**, mono**logue**, epi**logue**, **logo**cal
meter, metr	measure	dia**meter**, **metr**ic, milli**meter**
micro	small	**micro**scope, **micro**organism
mim	to copy, imitate	**mim**ic, **mim**e, **mim**eograph
miso	hatred of	**miso**neism, **miso**logy

GREEK ROOTS (continued)

BASE	MEANING	EXAMPLES
mono	one	**mono**logue, **mono**gamy, **mono**graph
mor	fool	**mor**on, **mor**onic
morph	form	pseudo**morph**, meso**morph**, meta**morph**osis
neur, nerv	nerve	**neur**ology, **nerv**ous, **neur**itis
nym, onym, onom	name	acro**nym**, hom**onym**, **onom**atopoeia
opt	eye	**opt**ic, **opt**ical, **opt**ician
ortho	straight	**ortho**dontics, **ortho**pedics
pan	all	**pan**genesis, **pan**gram, **pan**theism
path	feeling	a**path**y, sym**path**y, **path**etic
peri	around	**peri**meter, **peri**scope, **peri**phery
petr	rock	**petr**ify, **petr**oleum, **petr**oglyph
phe	speak, spoken about	eu**phe**mistic, pro**phe**t
phil, philo	love	**phil**odendron, **phil**ology, **phil**harmonic
phob	fear	**phob**ia, claustro**phob**ia, acro**phob**ia
phon	sound, voice	**phon**etics, **phon**ics, tele**phon**e
photo	light	**photo**graphy, **photo**flash, **photo**genic
pneu	breath	**pneu**monia, **pneu**matic
polis, polit	citizen, city, state	metro**polis**, **polit**ician, **polit**ical
poly	many	**poly**chromatic, **poly**ester
pseudo	false	**pseudo**nym, **pseudo**salt, **pseudo**morph
psych	mind, soul, spirit	**psych**ic, **psych**ology, **psych**oanalysis
pyr	fire	**pyr**omania, **pyr**otechnic
scope	to see	kaleido**scope**, tele**scope**, micro**scope**
soph	wise	philo**soph**er, **soph**isticated
syn, sym	together	**sym**phony, **syn**thesize
techn	art, skill	**techn**ical, **techn**ology, **techn**ique
tele	at a distance	**tele**scope, **tele**phone, **tele**commute
the, them, thet	to place, put	epi**thet**, anti**thes**is, **the**me
thea, theatr	to see, view	**thea**ter, **thea**trical, ampi**theatr**
theo	God	**theo**logy, **theo**cracy, **theo**centric
therm	heat	**therm**ometer, **therm**onuclear, **therm**al
topo	place	**topo**graphy, **topo**logy

LATIN ROOTS

BASE	MEANING	EXAMPLES
act	to do, drive	action, actor, react, transact, enact
alt	high	altitude, altimeter, altiplano
anima, anim	life, mind	animal, animated
ann, enn	year	annual, perennial, bicentennial
aqua	water	aquarium, aquamarine, aquanaut
arm	army, weapon	armory, armament
arbitr, arbiter	to judge, consider	arbitrator, arbritrary, arbiter
art	craft, skill	artist, artsy, artisan
aud	to hear	audience, auditorium, audible
bell	war	belligerent, bellicose
cede	to go; to yield	intercede, supercede, concede
cele	honor	celebrate, celebrities
cent	one hundred	percent, bicentennial, centennial
cept, capt, cip, cap, ceive, ceipt	to take hold, grasp	intercept, receive, receipt, capture
cert	to be sure, to trust	certain, ascertain, certifiable
cess, ced	to go; to yield	cessation, concession, accede, procession
cid, cis	to cut off, be brief; to kill	concise, homicide, genocide
circ, circum	around	circumference, circle, circular
clin	to lean, lie, bend	decline, incline, recline
cog	to think, consider	cognition, cognitive, recognize
comput	to compute	computer, computation
cor, cord, card	heart	cardiovascular, coronary
corp	body	corpse, corpulence, corporate
cred	to believe, trust	credibility, incredible, credit, credential
crit, cris	to separate; to discern, judge	criticism, critique, crisis
culp	fault, blame	culprit, culpable
curs, curr, corr	to run	current, occurrence, cursor, corral
custom	one's own	customized, customer, accustom
dent	tooth	dentist, dental, dentifrice
dic, dict	to say, to speak; to assert	diction, dictionary, dictate
duct, duc	to lead; to draw	aqueduct, abduct, conduct, reduce
dur	hard, lasting	duration, durable, durameter

LATIN ROOTS (continued)		
BASE	**MEANING**	**EXAMPLES**
ego	I	**ego**tistical, **ego**centric, **ego**ism
equ	equal, fair	**equ**ality, **equ**ation, **equ**ator
fac, fic, fect, fact	to make, do	**fac**simile, **fac**ility, de**fect**, ef**fic**ient
fer	to carry, bear, bring	of**fer**, trans**fer**, aqui**fer**
fid	trust, faith	**fid**elity, in**fid**el, in**fid**elity
fin	end, limit	**fin**ish, **fin**ite, in**fin**ite, **fin**al
flu	to flow	**flu**id, **flu**x, **flu**ctuate
form	shape, form	**form**al, **form**ative, in**form**
fort	strong	**fort**ress, **fort**ify, **fort**ification
frig	cool	**frig**id, re**frig**erate, **frig**orific
fum	smoke; scent	**fum**ing, **fum**igate, per**fum**e
gen	race, family, kind	**gen**ealogy, **gen**eral, **gen**eration
grad, gress	step, degree, rank	**grad**e, **grad**ual, re**gress**
grat	pleasing, thankful	con**grat**ulate, **grat**itude, **grat**ify
grav, griev	heavy	**grav**itate, **grav**ity, **griev**e
hab	to have, hold; to dwell	**hab**it, **hab**itat, in**hab**it
hom	man, human	**hom**age, **hom**icide
hosp	guest	**hosp**ital, **hosp**itality
host	enemy, stranger	**host**ile, **host**ility, **host**
init	to begin, enter upon	**init**ial, **init**iate, **init**iation
jur, jus, judic	law, right, judgment	**jur**ist, **jus**tify, **judic**ial
juven	young	**juven**ile, **juven**ility, re**juven**ate
labor	work	**labor**atory, **labor**er, **labor**ious
lat	lateral, side; wide	**lat**itude, **lat**itudinal
laud	praise	**laud**, **laud**able, **laud**atory
leg	law	**leg**al, **leg**islator, **leg**itimate
lev	to make light, to lift	e**lev**ator, **lev**er, **lev**itate
liber	free	**liber**al, **liber**ate, **liber**tarian
lingu, langu	tongue	**langu**age, sub**lingu**al
loc	place	**loc**al, **loc**alize, re**loc**ate, dis**loc**ate
locu, loqu, locut	word, speak	e**locut**ion, e**loqu**ent, **loqu**acious
luc, lumin	light	il**lumin**ate, **luc**ent, **luc**id

LATIN ROOTS (continued)

BASE	MEANING	EXAMPLES
manu	hand	**manu**al, **manu**facture
mar	sea	**mar**inate, **mar**ine, **mar**itime
med, medi	middle	**med**iate, **med**ieval, **medi**ocre
medic	physician, to heal	**medic**al, **medic**ine, **medic**inal
memor	mindful	**memor**ial, **memor**y
mon	to remind, advise, warn	ad**mon**ish, **mon**itor, pre**mon**ition
ment	mind	**ment**al, **ment**ally, **ment**ality
migr	to move, travel	im**migr**ant, **migr**ation, **migr**atory
mit, mis	to send	re**mis**sion, **mis**sive, trans**mit**
mort	death	**mort**al, **mort**ality, **mort**ify
mov, mob, mot	to move	**mob**, **mob**ile, re**mov**e, **mot**ion
mut	change, exchange	**mut**ant, **mut**ate, trans**mut**ate
necess	unavoidable	**necess**ary, **necess**itate, **necess**ity
noc, nox	harm	in**noc**ent, in**noc**uous, **noc**ent, ob**nox**ious
noc, nox	night	equi**nox**, **noc**turnal, **noc**turne
nomen, nomin	name	**nomin**al, **nomin**ate, **nomen**clature
null, nihil, nil	nothing, void	**nihil**ism, **nil**, **null**ify
ord, ordin	to put in order	**ord**er, **ord**inal, **ord**inary
par, pair	to arrange, get ready, set	**par**ade, pre**par**e, re**pair**
part, pars	portion, part	**part**ial , **part**icle, **part**ner
ped	foot	**ped**estal, **ped**estrian, **ped**al
pend, pond, pens	to weigh, pay; to consider	**pens**ion, **pens**ive, **pond**er
plic	to fold	**plic**able, **plic**ate, re**plic**ate
plur, plus	more	**plur**al, **plur**alistic, sur**plus**
port	to carry	im**port**, ex**port**, **port**able
pos	to place, put	**pos**ition, **pos**itive
pot	powerful	im**pot**ent, **pot**ent, **pot**ential
prim, prin	first	**prim**ary, **prim**e, **prim**itive, **prin**cipal
priv	separate	de**priv**e, **priv**ate, **priv**ilege
prob	to prove, test	**prob**ate, **prob**ation, **prob**e
reg, rig, rect	to rule; right, straight	**reg**al, **reg**ent, **reg**ion, **rect**ify
rupt	to break, burst	dis**rupt**, e**rupt**ion, **rupt**ure

LATIN ROOTS (continued)

BASE	MEANING	EXAMPLES
sacr, secr, sanct	sacred	desecrate, sacrifice, sacrilege, sanctify
sat, satis	enough	insatiable, satisfy, satiate
sci	to know	conscience, science, scientist
scrib, script	to write	inscribe, subscription, script
sed, sid, sess	to sit; to settle	sedate, sediment, subside, session
sent, sens	to feel	sense, sentimental, sentinel
sequ, secut	to follow; sequence	consequence, sequel, consecutive
simil, simul, sembl	like, similar	semblance, simulate, simile
sol, soli	alone, lonely	soliloquy, solo, solitary
somn	sleep	somnambulate, somnolent, somniloquy
son	sound	sonic, soniferous, sonnet
spec, spect, spic	to see, look at, behold	inspect, respect, spectacle, species
spond, spons	to pledge, promise	sponsor, sponsorship, respond
tac, tic	silent	tacit, taciturn
temp	time	temporary, temper
ten, tain, tent	to hold	contain, tenant, retention
tend, tens	to stretch, strive	tendon, tension, distend
termin	boundary, limit	terminal, terminate, determine
test	to witness, affirm	attest, contest, testify
tract	to pull, draw	attract, retract, traction
trib	to allot, give	attribute, tribute
vac	empty	evacuate, vacuous, vacuum
ven, vent	to come	advent, convene, revenue
ver	truth	veracity, verify, veritable
vers, vert	to turn	adverse, conversion, invert
vest	garment	vest, vestment
vestig	to track	investigate, vestige
via	way, road	via, viaduct
vir	manliness; worth	virile, virility, virtue
vis, vid	to see, look	revision, video, visible
viv, vit	life	vital, vivacious, vivid
voc, vok	voice, call	invocation, revoke, vocal

PREFIXES

PREFIX	MEANING	EXAMPLES
ab–	from; away from	**ab**normal, **ab**duct, **ab**sent, **ab**hor
ad–	to; motion toward; addition to	**ad**apt, **ad**dict, **ad**here, **ad**mit
aero–	air	**aero**bic, **aero**biology, **aero**space
amphi–	both; around	**amphi**bian, **amphi**theater
an–	not	**an**archy, **an**esthesia, **an**onymous
ante–	before	**ante**bellum, **ante**cede, **ante**date
anti–	against; opposite; reverse	**anti**aircraft, **anti**freeze, **anti**biotics
ap–	to; nearness to	**ap**proximate, **ap**point
auto–	self	**auto**matic, **auto**graph, **auto**biography
bene–	good	**bene**diction, **bene**factor, **bene**volent
bi–	two	**bi**facial, **bi**focal, **bi**ennial
circum–	around	**circum**navigate, **circum**ference
co–, con–	together	**co**author, **co**operate, **con**front, **con**found
contra–	against	**contra**dict, **contra**distinguish, **contra**ry
de–	opposite of; away from; undo	**de**activate, **de**form, **de**grade, **de**plete, **de**scend
dis–	opposite	**dis**agree, **dis**arm, **dis**continue, **dis**honest
ex–	out; beyond; away from; former	**ex**cel, **ex**clude, **ex**hale, **ex**ile
extra–	outside; beyond; besides	**extra**ordinary, **extra**curricular
for–	not	**for**bid, **for**get, **for**go
fore–	before	**fore**cast, **fore**word, **fore**stall, **fore**thought
hyper–	more than normal; too much	**hyper**active, **hyper**critical, **hyper**tension
il–	not	**il**legal, **il**legible, **il**literate, **il**logical
im–	into	**im**mediate, **im**merse, **im**migrate, **im**port
im–	not	**im**balance, **im**mature, **im**mobilize
in–	not; go into	**in**accurate, **in**active, **in**decisive, **in**habit
inter–	among; between	**inter**action, **inter**cede, **inter**change
intra–	within	**intra**mural, **intra**state, **intra**venous
ir–	not	**ir**redeemable, **ir**regular, **ir**responsible
mal–	wrong; bad	**mal**adjusted, **mal**function, **mal**ice
mis–	wrong; bad; no; not	**mis**fire, **mis**behave, **mis**conduct
non–	not; opposite of	**non**committal, **non**conductor, **non**partisan
ob–	against	**ob**stacle, **ob**stinate, **ob**struct, **ob**ject

PREFIXES (continued)		
PREFIX	**MEANING**	**EXAMPLES**
per–	through	**per**colate, **per**ceive
post–	after	**post**glacial, **post**graduate, **post**erior
pre–	before	**pre**amble, **pre**arrange, **pre**caution
pro–	before; for; in support of	**pro**gnosis, **pro**gram, **pro**logue, **pro**phet
pro–	forward	**pro**ceed, **pro**duce, **pro**ficient, **pro**gress
re–	back; again	**re**call, **re**cede, **re**flect, **re**pay
retro–	backward	**retro**active, **retro**spect, **retro**cede
se–	apart	**se**cure, **se**cede, **se**cession
self–	of the self	**self**-taught, **self**-worth, **self**-respect, **self**ish
semi–	half; partly	**semi**-circle, **semi**formal, **semi**trailer
sub–	under; beneath	**sub**contract, **sub**ject, **sub**marine, **sub**merge
super–	over	**super**abound, **super**abundant, **super**human
sur–	over; above	**sur**charge, **sur**face, **sur**mount, **sur**pass
trans–	across, over	**trans**atlantic, **trans**cend, **trans**cribe, **trans**fer
ultra–	extremely	**ultra**liberal, **ultra**modern, **ultra**sonic
un–	not; lack of; opposite	**un**able, **un**comfortable, **un**certain, **un**happy

SUFFIXES

SUFFIX	MEANING	EXAMPLES
–able, –ible	able to be; capable of being	intelligible, probable, inevitable
–ade	action or process	blockade, escapade, parade
–age	action or process	marriage, pilgrimage, voyage
–al, –ial	of; like; relating to; suitable for	potential, musical, national
–ance	act; process; quality; state of being	tolerance, alliance, acceptance
–ant	one who	assistant, immigrant, merchant
–ary	of; like; relating to	customary, honorary, obituary
–ate	characteristic of; to become	officiate, consecrate, activate
–cle, –icle	small	corpuscle, cubicle, particle
–cy	fact or state of being	diplomacy, privacy, relevancy
–dom	state or quality of	boredom, freedom, martyrdom
–ence	act or state of being	occurrence, conference
–ent	doing; having; showing	fraudulent, dependent, negligent
–er	one who; that which	boxer, rancher, employer
–ery	place for; act, practice of	surgery, robbery
–ess	female	goddess, heiress, princess
–esque	like	picturesque, statuesque
–ful	full of	careful, fearful, joyful, thoughtful
–ic	relating to; characteristic of	comic, historic, poetic, public
–ify	to make; to cause to be	modify, glorify, beautify, pacify
–ion	act, condition, or result of	calculation, action, confederation
–ish	of or belonging to; characterized by	tallish, amateurish, selfish
–ism	act, practice, or result of; example	barbarism, heroism, altruism
–ity	condition; state of being	integrity, sincerity, calamity, purity
–ive	of; relating to; belonging to; tending to	inquisitive, active, creative
–ize	make; cause to be; subject to	jeopardize, standardize, computerize
–less	without	ageless, careless, thoughtless, tireless
–let	small	islet, leaflet, owlet, rivulet, starlet
–like	like; characteristic of	childlike, waiflike
–logue	speech	dialogue, monologue, epilogue
–logy	study or theory of	biology, ecology, geology

SUFFIXES (continued)		
SUFFIX	**MEANING**	**EXAMPLES**
–ly	every	daily, weekly, monthly, yearly
–ly	in (a specified manner; to a specified extent)	officially, sincerely, kindly
–ment	action or process	development, government
–ment	state or quality of	amusement, amazement, predicament
–ment	product or thing	fragment, instrument, ornament
–ness	state or quality of being	kindness, abruptness, happiness
–or	one who	actor, auditor, doctor, donor
–ous	having; full of; characterized by	riotous, courageous, advantageous
–ship	state or quality of being	censorship, ownership, governorship
–some	like; tending to be	meddlesome, bothersome, noisome
–tude	state or quality of being	solitude, multitude, aptitude
–y	characterized by	thrifty, jealousy, frequency, sticky

CONTEXT

The words, phrases, or sentences around an unfamiliar word often provide clues to the word's meaning. In some cases, *signal words* can act as clues.

Restatement Clues

Words or phrases such as *in other words* or *that is* can signal the restatement of a word.

EXAMPLE The veterinarian treated every animal owner in an *affable* manner; **in other words**, she was gentle and friendly with them.

From the context, readers can tell that *affable* means "gentle and friendly." The phrase *in other words* signals that the words *gentle* and *friendly* restate the meaning of the word.

Restatement Signal Words		
in other words	that is	these

Example Clues

Words or phrases such as *such as, for example,* or *likewise* can indicate to readers that an unfamiliar word is being restated in more familiar terms.

EXAMPLE Many types of *fauna,* **for example** the javelina, the coyote, and the peregrine falcon, live in Big Bend National Park.

From the context, readers can tell that *fauna* are the animals of a particular region. The words *for example* signal that the animals listed are examples of the word *fauna.*

Example Signal Words		
for example	such as	in that
likewise	especially	

Contrast Clues

Words or phrases such as *but, by contrast,* or *although* indicate that an unfamiliar word contrasts with another word in the passage.

EXAMPLE Maria was *enthralled* by the new movie, **but** her friend found it dull and uninteresting.

From the context, readers can tell that *enthralled* means "fascinated." The word *but* signals that *enthralled* contrasts with the words *dull* and *uninteresting.*

Contrast Signal Words		
but	not	on the other hand
however	still	some . . . but others
although	despite	in contrast

Cause and Effect Clues

Words or phrases such as *lead to, cause,* and *because* show how one word may be a cause or effect related to an unfamiliar word.

EXAMPLE **Because** he wanted to marry a divorcée, Edward VIII chose to *abdicate* the British throne in 1936.

From the context, readers can tell that *abdicate* means "to formally give up power." The word **because** signals that abdicating is an effect of Edward VIII's wanting to marry a divorcée.

Cause and Effect Signal Words		
leads to	effect	reasons
cause	as a result	since
because	consequently	why

Definition/Explanation Clues

A sentence may actually define or explain an unfamiliar word.

EXAMPLE The title of F. Scott Fitzgerald's novel *Tender Is the Night* contains an *allusion,* or **reference,** to a poem by John Keats.

From the context, readers can tell that *allusion* means "reference." The appositive phrase "or reference" signals the meaning of the word.

INTRODUCING MAKING NEW WORDS YOUR OWN

How We Make New Words Our Own

Use the **Context Structure Sound Dictionary strategy (CSSD)** to improve your vocabulary, to make new words your own. Use one or more of the strategies to determine the meanings of each word you do not know. The exercises that follow will show you how to go about making new words your own.

HOW TO DO EXERCISE 1   *Wordbusting*

In these exercises, you will read the Vocabulary Word in a sentence. You will figure out the word's meaning by looking at its **context,** its **structure,** and its **sound.** Then you will look up the word in a **dictionary** and write its meaning *as it is used in the sentence.*

Here is an example of the Wordbusting strategy, using the word *transcribe.*

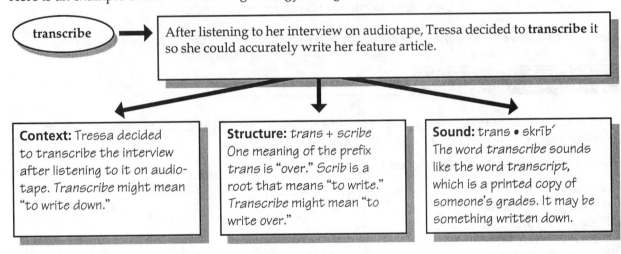

transcribe → After listening to her interview on audiotape, Tressa decided to **transcribe** it so she could accurately write her feature article.

Context: Tressa decided to transcribe the interview after listening to it on audiotape. *Transcribe* might mean "to write down."

Structure: *trans + scribe* One meaning of the prefix *trans* is "over." *Scrib* is a root that means "to write." *Transcribe* might mean "to write over."

Sound: *trans • skrīb´* The word *transcribe* sounds like the word *transcript,* which is a printed copy of someone's grades. It may be something written down.

Dictionary: "to write or type out a copy of, as from a speech or notes"

Hint #1   **Context:** Look for clues to the meaning of the word in the sentence. For example, *after* signals cause and effect and helps reveal the meaning of *transcribe.*

Hint #2   **Structure:** Examine the word parts for roots, prefixes, and suffixes that you know. Consult the word part tables on pages ix–xviii for meanings of parts you do not know.

Hint #3   **Sound:** Say the word aloud and listen for any word parts you know.

Hint #4   **Dictionary:** If you cannot determine a word's meaning from applying context, structure, and sound strategies, look up the unfamiliar word in a dictionary. Read all the definitions and choose one that best fits the given sentence.

Again, you will see the new word used in a sentence. This time, however, you're actually given a set of definitions, and you must match the new word with its meaning.

Here's an example of a context-clue exercise:

COLUMN A	COLUMN B
__G__ word: ___ecology___ *n.* the relationship between living things and their environments; the science of such relationships	(G) Aldo Leopold (1866–1948) learned to think like a mountain so that he could understand and preserve the **ecology** of nature. Nature's rights, he felt, must be respected.

Hint #1   Read Column B first, and look for clues to the meaning of the word. You might imagine that thinking like a mountain would give you strong opinions about how nature should be treated. For example, as part of the earth, you would make sure that the rights of the earth were respected.

Hint #2   You should scan Column A for a likely definition of the word. In this case, the idea of relationships suggests that the sample definition is the correct one.

Hint #3   As you write the word in the blank, say it to yourself to get a sense of the sound of the word.

HOW TO DO EXERCISE 3 *Sentence Completion* 👈

In the final part of **Making New Words Your Own,** you are asked to supply the missing Vocabulary Word or words in order to create a sentence that makes sense.

Here is an example of a sentence-completion exercise:

The science of _____ allows us to _____ our natural resources.
(A) zoology . . . diminish
(B) ecology . . . preserve
(C) cultivation . . . destroy
(D) zoology . . . ignore
(E) ecology . . . exhaust

Hint #1   Think about the logic of the sentence. You are looking for a type of science that deals with natural resources. You can assume that the ultimate aim of any science is some kind of improvement.

Hint #2   Substitute the words in choices (A) through (E) in the sentence to see which pair of words completes the logic of the sentence.
   • The pairs containing the word *zoology* can probably be ruled out, since *zoology* deals with animals in particular, not all natural resources.
   • Cultivation has something to do with natural resources, but it is unlikely that the aim of any science is to destroy.
   • Similarly, you can rule out answer E because the aim of ecology is not to exhaust but to preserve our natural resources. This conclusion leads to the correct answer, B.

As you complete these three types of exercises, you will develop the ability to make an educated guess about the meaning of a word by thinking about its context.

MAKING NEW WORDS YOUR OWN

Lesson 1 | CONTEXT: Literary Figures
British Poets

Over the last thousand years, the style and subject of British poetry have varied dramatically. Yet all great British poets hold this in common: They have contributed immeasurably to the beauty of the English language and to the richness of the world's literature.

In the following exercises, you will have the opportunity to expand your vocabulary by reading about some of Britain's poets. Below are ten Vocabulary Words that will be used in these exercises.

banal	finesse	lampoon	nefarious	pseudonym
bellicose	glib	lugubrious	nemesis	purloin

EXERCISE 1 *Wordbusting* ✍

Directions. Follow these instructions for this word and the nine words on the next page.
- Figure out the word's meaning by looking at its **context**, its **structure**, and its **sound.** Fill in at least one of the three **CSS** boxes. Alternate which boxes you complete.
- Then, look up the word in a dictionary, read all of its meanings, and write the meaning of the word as it is used in the sentence.
- Follow this same process for each of the Vocabulary Words on the next page. You will need to draw your own map for each word. Use a separate sheet of paper.

1.

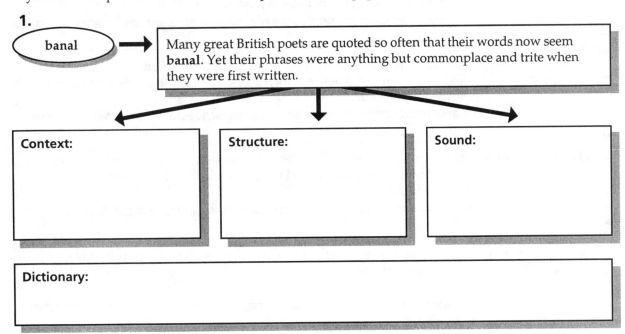

banal → Many great British poets are quoted so often that their words now seem **banal**. Yet their phrases were anything but commonplace and trite when they were first written.

Context:

Structure:

Sound:

Dictionary:

2.
bellicose ➔ A variety of colorful individuals have contributed to Britain's poetic heritage. One was Alexander Pope (1688–1744) who, although small and physically weak, was often aggressive and **bellicose** in his writing, using words almost as weapons.

3.
finesse ➔ The poet Sir Thomas Wyatt (1503–1542) handled relationships with **finesse**. He demonstrated such delicate skill in dealing with people that he served as a diplomat for King Henry VIII.

4.
glib ➔ No one would accuse Sir Francis Bacon (1561–1626) of being **glib**. He was a smooth talker, but his statements and his writing had substance.

5.
pseudonym ➔ It was not unusual for a British poet of the past to use a **pseudonym,** although most wrote under their own names.

6.
lampoon ➔ British poets who were somewhat cynical liked to **lampoon** the institutions of their day. They had to be careful, though: Satirists could be punished severely for making fun of those in power.

7.
lugubrious ➔ British poets have written in every conceivable tone. Some poems are so joyful that they are almost ecstatic; others are so sad that they could be considered **lugubrious**.

8.
nefarious ➔ This is in keeping with the variety of people who have written poetry. Some poets were basically good tempered and law abiding, while others were **nefarious**.

9.
nemesis ➔ These poets saw time as their **nemesis**. A recurring subject in their work is this unconquerable foe.

10.
purloin ➔ When poets use the ideas and styles of previous writers, their intention is not to **purloin** but to build on and reinterpret the past. Occasionally, however, a poet has been accused of stealing.

EXERCISE 2 *Context Clues* 👉

Directions. Scan the definitions in Column A. Then, think about how the boldface words are used in the sentences in Column B. To complete the exercise, match each definition in Column A with the correct Vocabulary Word from Column B. Write the letter of your choice on the line provided; then write the Vocabulary Word on the line before the definition.

COLUMN A	COLUMN B

COLUMN A

_____ **11.** word: _____

adj. done in a smooth, offhand manner; easily spoken; speaking too smoothly to be sincere

_____ **12.** word: _____

adj. sad or mournful, often to an exaggerated degree; doleful

_____ **13.** word: _____

n. delicate skill; subtlety; *v.* to bring about with skill; to evade

_____ **14.** word: _____

n. an avenger; an unbeatable rival; a person who punishes another for evil deeds

_____ **15.** word: _____

v. to steal

_____ **16.** word: _____

adj. commonplace; trite; stale from overuse

_____ **17.** word: _____

n. a fictitious name assumed by an author; a pen name

_____ **18.** word: _____

n. strongly satirical writing; *v.* to ridicule or satirize

_____ **19.** word: _____

adj. villainous; infamous; having a bad reputation

_____ **20.** word: _____

adj. quarrelsome; hostile; inclined to fighting

COLUMN B

(A) One of the greatest British poets was Alexander Pope, whose **finesse** with the English language is legendary. Few others have used words with such proficiency.

(B) One of Pope's most famous poems is *The Rape of the Lock,* a **lampoon** that makes fun of the petty daily lives of eighteenth-century English aristocracy.

(C) The title of the poem refers to the theft of a lock of hair, which an adventurous young man **purloins** from the fair Belinda.

(D) The action in the poem is based on an actual event. Pope wrote the poem, in part, to ridicule the people involved, who treated the **banal,** insignificant event as a major crisis.

(E) Pope himself was a fascinating individual. He was a literary success, yet he was often **lugubrious;** his sorrow and depression led him to refer to his life as a "long disease."

(F) Pope was also **bellicose.** He frequently attacked his contemporaries in his writings, often with great vigor and always with great skill.

(G) Those who suffered from his attacks considered Pope to be vicious, even **nefarious.** They called him the "Wicked Wasp of Twickenham," after the villa in which he lived.

(H) To his victims, Pope was a **nemesis;** his wit made him unbeatable.

(I) Pope's pride in his work is revealed by the fact that he never used a **pseudonym** but always published under his own name.

(J) Today we **glibly** use the expressions "To err is human, to forgive, divine," "Hope springs eternal in the human breast," and "For fools rush in where angels fear to tread." If you look these quotations up, you'll find that they are from Alexander Pope.

EXERCISE 3 *Sentence Completion* ✍️

Directions. For each of the following items, circle the letter of the choice that best completes the meaning of the sentence or sentences.

21. Almost all of us _____ phrases from British poets. However, our theft of their words may be considered a tribute to their genius.
    - (A) feign
    - (B) allay
    - (C) finesse
    - (D) revile
    - (E) purloin

22. A British poet who wished to remain anonymous could use a _____.
    - (A) banality
    - (B) pseudonym
    - (C) finesse
    - (D) nemesis
    - (E) mesmerism

23. Although some modern readers find his writing heavy-handed and lacking subtlety, others think poet and essayist John Milton (1608–1674) wrote with great _____.
    - (A) finesse
    - (B) banality
    - (C) bellicosity
    - (D) glibness
    - (E) nemesis

24. Satirist Jonathan Swift (1667–1745) was a master of the _____. His satires, which ridicule conventions of his day, are still considered to be among the best ever written.
    - (A) lampoon
    - (B) finesse
    - (C) nemesis
    - (D) propriety
    - (E) euphemism

25. William Wordsworth (1770–1850) was _____ after a failed love affair. With both care and _____, his friend and fellow poet Samuel Taylor Coleridge (1772–1834) helped Wordsworth move beyond his sadness and despair.
    - (A) glib . . . lampoon
    - (B) lugubrious . . . finesse
    - (C) banal . . . nemesis
    - (D) nefarious . . . glibness
    - (E) bellicose . . . finesse

26. Much of Robert Burns's (1759–1796) poetry is about the everyday, even _____, events experienced by ordinary people.
    - (A) glib
    - (B) nefarious
    - (C) banal
    - (D) lugubrious
    - (E) bellicose

27. The shy Alfred, Lord Tennyson (1809–1892) and the aggressive, almost _____, Arthur Henry Hallam (1811–1833) were friends. Hallam's early death left Tennyson _____ and heartbroken for years.
    - (A) bellicose . . . lugubrious
    - (B) glib . . . nefarious
    - (C) nefarious . . . banal
    - (D) banal . . . lugubrious
    - (E) banal . . . bellicose

28. Percy Bysshe Shelley (1792–1822) believed that the good could triumph over the _____. He himself worked as the _____ of evil in order to vindicate oppressed people.
    - (A) glib . . . finesse
    - (B) lampoon . . . pseudonym
    - (C) banal . . . lampoon
    - (D) bellicose . . . finesse
    - (E) nefarious . . . nemesis

29. Among the memorable characters created by William Shakespeare are the angry, _____ Tybalt and the witty, jovial Falstaff, whose ability to _____ people and situations help make him a comic figure.
    - (A) bellicose . . . lampoon
    - (B) nefarious . . . finesse
    - (C) glib . . . purloin
    - (D) lugubrious . . . lampoon
    - (E) bellicose . . . purloin

30. Tuberculosis was John Keats's (1795–1821) _____. Knowing that the disease was killing him, he wrote poetry that was sincere, not _____.
    - (A) nemesis . . . glib
    - (B) pseudonym . . . bellicose
    - (C) lampoon . . . lugubrious
    - (D) finesse . . . banal
    - (E) nemesis . . . nefarious

MAKING NEW WORDS YOUR OWN

Lesson 2 **CONTEXT:** Literary Figures

The Revolution of Mary Wollstonecraft

The late 1700s was a time of revolution, with freedom fighters struggling to overcome oppression in the British colonies and in France. In England, writer Mary Wollstonecraft (1759–1797) fought a revolution of her own—fought on behalf of women's rights. Wollstonecraft's most famous book is *A Vindication of the Rights of Woman* (1792). In this brief but forceful book, she argued that women should be men's equals in politics, economics, and law.

In the following exercises, you will have the opportunity to expand your vocabulary by reading about Mary Wollstonecraft. Below are ten Vocabulary Words that will be used in these exercises.

| abject | commensurate | euphemism | phlegmatic | prosaic |
| admonish | distraught | nebulous | propriety | revile |

EXERCISE 1 *Wordbusting*

Directions. Follow these instructions for this word and the nine words on the next page.
- Figure out the word's meaning by looking at its **context,** its **structure,** and its **sound.** Fill in at least one of the three **CSS** boxes. Alternate which boxes you complete.
- Then, look up the word in a dictionary, read all of its meanings, and write the meaning of the word as it is used in the sentence.
- Follow this same process for each of the Vocabulary Words on the next page. You will need to draw your own map for each word. Use a separate sheet of paper.

1.

abject → Wollstonecraft observed that many women lived **abject** lives; they were made miserable by men who treated them as members of an inferior class.

Context:

Structure:

Sound:

Dictionary:

2.
(prosaic) → Wollstonecraft said that society and men's attitudes toward women often kept women in **prosaic** or ordinary situations, when, in fact, they were capable of exceptional achievements.

3.
(propriety) → Conventional standards made women "weak and wretched," Wollstonecraft wrote. She criticized such forms of **propriety** and urged women to "acquire strength, both of mind and body."

4.
(revile) → Although she attacked men for treating women as inferior beings, Wollstonecraft did not **revile** men. Rather than resorting to name-calling, she attempted to explain what she thought they were doing wrong.

5.
(admonish) → In her writings, Wollstonecraft **admonished** men for not giving women the respect they deserve. Men were not used to such serious but polite scoldings from an educated woman.

6.
(commensurate) → Wollstonecraft believed that women should be treated in a way that was **commensurate** with their abilities. If she were alive today, she would support the idea that men and women who do the same work should be given the same wages.

7.
(phlegmatic) → Wollstonecraft had witnessed and experienced many injustices, and it was not her nature to remain **phlegmatic**. Far from indifferent, she tried to persuade women to stand up for their rights.

8.
(distraught) → Wollstonecraft suffered a series of difficult personal relationships. **Distraught** over these failures, she used the mental conflicts that arose from these experiences as material for her novels.

9.
(nebulous) → Whether or not they agree with her views, readers cannot accuse Wollstonecraft of being **nebulous**, for she clearly defines her ideas about society's tendency to glorify "feminine inferiority."

10.
(euphemism) → In the introduction to *A Vindication of the Rights of Woman*, Wollstonecraft states that she wants to avoid "flowery diction." Based on this information, one would not expect her writing to include **euphemisms**, but for her to call things what they are with honesty and directness.

Name _____ Date _____ Class _____

EXERCISE 2 *Context Clues*

Directions. Scan the definitions in Column A. Then, think about how the boldface words are used in the sentences in Column B. To complete the exercise, match each definition in Column A with the correct Vocabulary Word from Column B. Write the letter of your choice on the line provided; then write the Vocabulary Word on the line preceding the definition.

COLUMN A

_____ **11.** word: _____
n. a mild expression used in place of a harsh, crude, or distasteful expression

_____ **12.** word: _____
adj. hazy; vague; not clearly defined

_____ **13.** word: _____
adj. hopelessly low; wretched; miserable; without self-respect

_____ **14.** word: _____
n. acceptable behavior; conformity with conventional standards

_____ **15.** word: _____
v. to attack with abusive language; to call insulting names

_____ **16.** word: _____
adj. in a state of mental conflict; agitated; crazed

_____ **17.** word: _____
v. to reprove mildly and kindly, but seriously; to caution or warn; to urge

_____ **18.** word: _____
adj. matter-of-fact; ordinary; commonplace

_____ **19.** word: _____
adj. sluggish; indifferent; calm

_____ **20.** word: _____
adj. in proper proportion; having the same scale, measure, or size; proportionate

COLUMN B

(A) Wollstonecraft's early home life, which greatly influenced her views about men and women, was not a model of **propriety,** or respectability.

(B) As a child, Wollstonecraft was often **distraught**. She was especially distressed by her father's cruelty to her mother.

(C) Wollstonecraft's father physically abused her mother; probably he also **reviled,** or berated, her.

(D) You might say that Wollstonecraft's father was often "under the influence," which is a **euphemism** for "drunk."

(E) Wollstonecraft's passive, submissive mother was **phlegmatic** in her reaction to the abuse. Wollstonecraft, on the other hand, reacted quickly and tried to help her mother.

(F) Wollstonecraft's father made the family's **abject** home life even more pitiable by wasting an inherited fortune.

(G) Surely, no one would **admonish,** or express disapproval to Wollstonecraft for leaving home at the age of nineteen.

(H) Wollstonecraft needed a job that matched her abilities. Becoming a companion to a widow was **commensurate** with her limited experience at the time.

(I) Her physical circumstances may have been **prosaic,** but Wollstonecraft's independence was unusual for women of her time.

(J) Even if her overall plans for her life were **nebulous,** Wollstonecraft had one clear goal: to educate herself.

EXERCISE 3 *Sentence Completion* ✍

Directions. For each of the following items, circle the letter of the choice that best completes the meaning of the sentence or sentences.

21. Mrs. Epstein's plan for the seminar in our English literature class was _____ until she made a resolution to focus on Mary Wollstonecraft's feminist views.
   (A) nebulous
   (B) phlegmatic
   (C) distraught
   (D) abject
   (E) commensurate

22. When they heard what the topic was, students were at first _____, but they became actively interested when they learned more about Wollstonecraft's ideas.
   (A) commensurate
   (B) prosaic
   (C) omniscient
   (D) phlegmatic
   (E) abject

23. Each day our discussions grew more lively, becoming _____ with our increased knowledge of Wollstonecraft's writings.
   (A) abject
   (B) prosaic
   (C) commensurate
   (D) distraught
   (E) nebulous

24. "Wollstonecraft flew in the face of _____," Mrs. Epstein said, "for she openly criticized traditional ideas."
   (A) nebulousness
   (B) abjection
   (C) euphemism
   (D) commensuration
   (E) propriety

25. "Wollstonecraft was distressed, or _____, over injustices suffered by women she knew. Her pain was _____ with, or proportionate to, her awareness of inequalities."
   (A) distraught . . . commensurate
   (B) prosaic . . . abject
   (C) nebulous . . . phlegmatic
   (D) commensurate . . . distraught
   (E) nebulous . . . abject

26. "Look around," Mrs. Epstein said. "There are miserable people living in _____ poverty, and there are women whose jobs are not _____ with, or equal to, their abilities."
   (A) commensurate . . . nebulous
   (B) distraught . . . phlegmatic
   (C) phlegmatic . . . abject
   (D) abject . . . commensurate
   (E) euphemistic . . . distraught

27. One of our classmates, Ruben Paré, is idealistic and sensitive, which is really just a(n) _____ for "hopelessly romantic."
   (A) admonishment
   (B) euphemism
   (C) commensuration
   (D) propriety
   (E) abjection

28. Ruben was upset when Bruce, a true chauvinist, _____ Wollstonecraft for her feminist ideals. Ruben _____ Bruce for his narrow-minded views, politely censuring him.
   (A) reviled . . . absolved
   (B) admonished . . . inveigled
   (C) reviled . . . admonished
   (D) feigned . . . reviled
   (E) admonished . . . purloined

29. Bruce does not like to be reproved, but he accepted Ruben's _____ without becoming angry. However, I could tell that Ruben was _____ that such attitudes still exist.
   (A) propriety . . . nebulous
   (B) abjection . . . phlegmatic
   (C) euphemism . . . commensurate
   (D) revilement . . . prosaic
   (E) admonishment . . . distraught

30. "Whether people lead ordinary, _____ lives or extraordinary ones, they should be treated with respect. We should all care about women's rights," Ruben concluded.
   (A) phlegmatic
   (B) nebulous
   (C) prosaic
   (D) distraught
   (E) euphemistic

MAKING NEW WORDS YOUR OWN

Lesson 3 | CONTEXT: Literary Figures
A Gothic Story

Have you ever been part of a collaborative creative writing project, working with a group of students? One person starts a story, and then each group member in turn adds to it. Our literature class created a Gothic story in this way after studying the Romantic Movement of the late 1700s and early 1800s. Gothic stories involve mysterious, gloomy, remote settings, sometimes suggesting medieval times. Elements of the setting may include haunted castles, ruins, eerie landscapes, and ghostly visitors.

In the following exercises, you will have the opportunity to expand your vocabulary by reading excerpts from a Gothic story written by a group of students. Below are ten Vocabulary Words that will be used in these exercises.

assimilate	discursive	farcical	hyperbole	mesmerism
cognizant	ennui	fortuitous	incognito	omniscient

EXERCISE 1 | Wordbusting ✍

Directions. Follow these instructions for this word and the nine words on the next page.
- Figure out the word's meaning by looking at its **context,** its **structure,** and its **sound.** Fill in at least one of the three **CSS** boxes. Alternate which boxes you complete.
- Then, look up the word in a dictionary, read all of its meanings, and write the meaning of the word as it is used in the sentence.
- Follow this same process for each of the Vocabulary Words on the next page. You will need to draw your own map for each word. Use a separate sheet of paper.

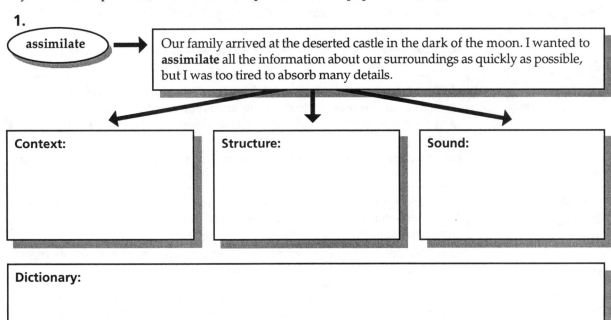

1.

assimilate ➝ Our family arrived at the deserted castle in the dark of the moon. I wanted to **assimilate** all the information about our surroundings as quickly as possible, but I was too tired to absorb many details.

Context:

Structure:

Sound:

Dictionary:

2.

 cognizant →

Suddenly, I was keenly aware of someone or something watching us. I do not know what made me **cognizant** of this; perhaps it was merely instinct. All I could see were huge trees, their branches swaying in the fierce wind.

3.

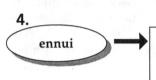 discursive →

Eric, my brother, started talking excitedly, rambling on about various subjects that nobody else cared about. I think he was trying to hide his fear with his **discursive** speech.

4.

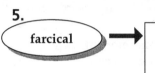 ennui →

Clearly, no one wanted to get out of the car. **Ennui** usually is a problem if we're stuck in the car too long on trips, but this time everyone stayed put not out of listlessness and boredom but out of uneasiness.

5.

 farcical →

My laughter startled all of us. "This is so **farcical,**" I said. "We must look ridiculous sitting out here in the middle of the night, lost and tired but afraid to get out of the car."

6.

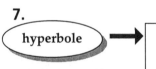 fortuitous →

"Well," my father said, "you have to admit it's **fortuitous** that we've found this house . . . or castle, or whatever it is. And it's also fortunate that someone inside appears to be awake. Look—there's a light on upstairs."

7.

 hyperbole →

I peered up through the darkness and saw a large figure at an upstairs window. Whoever it was seemed as big as a gorilla, and that's no **hyperbole**. I'm not exaggerating to scare you; I've really never seen anyone so massive.

8.

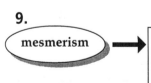 incognito →

I remembered an old horror movie I once saw about a man who disguised himself as an ape in order to carry out gruesome murders. Maybe the person at the window was similarly **incognito,** keeping his or her identity secret.

9.

 mesmerism →

I couldn't see the figure at the window very clearly, but I felt that it was exerting a strange **mesmerism** over me. I shuddered to think that it might be hypnotizing me.

10.

 omniscient →

The knowledge also suddenly came to me that the strange person—if the figure was indeed a person—was **omniscient** and knew everything about me and my family.

EXERCISE 2 *Context Clues* ✍

Directions. Scan the definitions in Column A. Then, think about how the boldface words are used in the sentences in Column B. To complete the exercise, match each definition in Column A with the correct Vocabulary Word from Column B. Write the letter of your choice on the line provided; then write the Vocabulary Word on the line preceding the definition.

COLUMN A	COLUMN B

COLUMN A

_____ **11.** word: _____
n. one who is in disguise or using an assumed name; *adj.* disguised; using a false name; *adv.* in disguise; under a fictitious name

_____ **12.** word: _____
adj. aware of or informed about something

_____ **13.** word: _____
adj. ridiculous; exaggeratedly comical

_____ **14.** word: _____
adj. wandering or shifting from one subject to another; rambling; long winded

_____ **15.** word: _____
n. an obvious exaggeration, made for effect and not meant to be taken literally

_____ **16.** word: _____
adj. knowing everything; having complete or infinite knowledge

_____ **17.** word: _____
adj. occurring by chance; accidental; fortunate

_____ **18.** word: _____
v. to absorb and incorporate food or knowledge; to absorb one group into a larger culture

_____ **19.** word: _____
n. discontent and listlessness from lack of occupation or interest

_____ **20.** word: _____
n. hypnotism; hypnotic appeal; intense fascination

COLUMN B

(A) There must have been a million lion heads carved on the castle door. Well, that may be **hyperbole,** but there certainly were many.

(B) Both the place and the man who answered the doorbell seemed to exert a power of **mesmerism** over all of us, although I can not explain this almost magnetic attraction.

(C) "Welcome, I am Rincent Brice," he said. I thought he must be **incognito** because that didn't sound like a real name.

(D) My father told our **farcical** story—the absurdity of errors, wrong turns, and late starts that resulted in our arriving there.

(E) "I am already **cognizant** of the details of your journey," Mr. Brice said, but he did not explain how he knew.

(F) Unlike my brother Eric, Mr. Brice was not **discursive.** He said as little as possible, and his speech was abrupt.

(G) Mr. Brice appeared to be aware of everything about us, even our future. "You will change your plans and stay here three weeks," our seemingly **omniscient** host announced.

(H) "Your arrival here was not **fortuitous,**" Mr. Brice said, sending shivers down my spine. "It was meant to be."

(I) Well, I thought, we surely won't have any problem with **ennui** here. Who could be bored under circumstances like these?

(J) "We want to **assimilate** you into our group," Mr. Brice said. "We have been waiting for you for a long time."

EXERCISE 3 *Sentence Completion* ✍️

Directions. For each of the following items, circle the letter of the choice that best completes the meaning of the sentence or sentences.

21. The longer we stayed, the more convinced I was that Mr. Brice was _____, masquerading as someone else.
    (A) cognizant
    (B) discursive
    (C) incognito
    (D) fortuitous
    (E) assimilated

22. We did not see anyone else for the next twenty-four hours, but I was _____ of presences and equally conscious that people were watching us.
    (A) discursive
    (B) cognizant
    (C) farcical
    (D) incognito
    (E) omniscient

23. You may think this merely _____, but I had goose bumps over every inch of my body.
    (A) ennui
    (B) incognito
    (C) mesmerism
    (D) assimilation
    (E) hyperbole

24. The next day, I wandered around the gloomy ruins behind the castle and wondered how my family could avoid being _____ into this strange place. Its eerie atmosphere made me think that we were all in danger of being absorbed by this strange community.
    (A) farcical
    (B) cognizant
    (C) omniscient
    (D) assimilated
    (E) discursive

25. Now my father had become _____, rambling in a disconnected way about how we had found ourselves here.
    (A) discursive
    (B) omniscient
    (C) fortuitous
    (D) farcical
    (E) cognizant

26. Eric was bored and complained of _____, so I told him to go outside. To use _____, he ran out as swiftly as a cheetah.
    (A) mesmerism . . . ennui
    (B) hyperbole . . . mesmerism
    (C) ennui . . . hyperbole
    (D) incognito . . . omniscience
    (E) discursiveness . . . incognito

27. It was lucky, or _____, that I happened to be outside just when Eric vanished into the woods. I ran after him but soon realized I was involved in a(n) _____, or preposterous, chase. Eric had vanished.
    (A) cognizant . . . discursive
    (B) fortuitous . . . farcical
    (C) farcical . . . incognito
    (D) incognito . . . cognizant
    (E) discursive . . . omniscient

28. I wished I were _____, able to know not only what was happening to Eric but to everyone else as well. I was afraid that my father had fallen under the hypnotic spell, or _____, of Mr. Brice.
    (A) farcical . . . ennui
    (B) incognito . . . hyperbole
    (C) discursive . . . ennui
    (D) omniscient . . . mesmerism
    (E) fortuitous . . . hyperbole

29. I wanted to be completely aware, fully _____ of our circumstances. That could help me figure out a way to get us out of this once _____ but now serious situation.
    (A) discursive . . . fortuitous
    (B) farcical . . . incognito
    (C) fortuitous . . . cognizant
    (D) assimilative . . . discursive
    (E) cognizant . . . farcical

30. If only I could be _____! If I were all-knowing, I could not be fooled by anyone, whether openly identified or _____.
    (A) omniscient . . . incognito
    (B) discursive . . . cognizant
    (C) farcical . . . omniscient
    (D) fortuitous . . . discursive
    (E) mesmerized . . . incognito

MAKING NEW WORDS YOUR OWN

Lesson 4 | CONTEXT: Literary Figures
Macbeth: Truth and Legend

Macbeth ruled Scotland from A.D. 1040 to 1057, and, from historical accounts, he was a good king. His reputation suffered, however, when his story became a folk legend that changed through many retellings. By the beginning of the 1600s, when Shakespeare wrote his play about the ruler, Macbeth had appeared in histories of Scotland as "a savage tyrant" who had met with witches and plotted King Duncan's murder. The histories themselves were as much legend as fact—and were all the more compelling for that reason. Shakespeare wove these tales and truths about Macbeth into one of his most powerful plays: *Macbeth*.

In the following exercises, you will have the opportunity to expand your vocabulary by reading about Shakespeare and Macbeth. Below are ten Vocabulary Words that will be used in these exercises.

adroit	blazon	choleric	despot	expatriate
allay	bravado	colloquy	dirge	feign

EXERCISE 1 | *Wordbusting* ✍

Directions. Follow these instructions for this word and the nine words on the next page.
- Figure out the word's meaning by looking at its **context,** its **structure,** and its **sound.** Fill in at least one of the three **CSS** boxes. Alternate which boxes you complete.
- Then, look up the word in a dictionary, read all of its meanings, and write the meaning of the word as it is used in the sentence.
- Follow this same process for each of the Vocabulary Words on the next page. You will need to draw your own map for each word. Use a separate sheet of paper.

1.

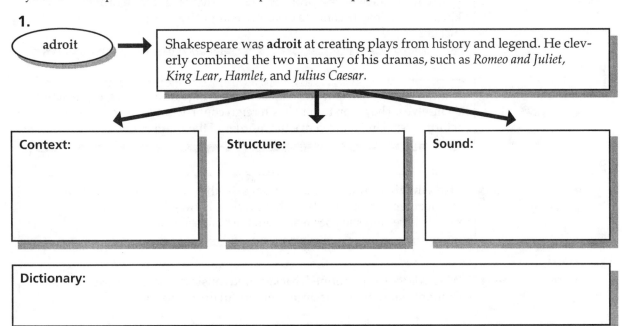

adroit → Shakespeare was **adroit** at creating plays from history and legend. He cleverly combined the two in many of his dramas, such as *Romeo and Juliet, King Lear, Hamlet,* and *Julius Caesar*.

Context:

Structure:

Sound:

Dictionary:

2.

allay → The lack of historical accuracy in Shakespeare's plays does not **allay,** or lessen, people's interest in them. In fact, the plays have remained popular for over four hundred years.

3.

blazon → Every year, Shakespeare's plays are performed all over the world. Audiences are attracted by posters that **blazon** information about performances.

4.

bravado → Shakespeare's plays appeal to people because they dramatize universal human characteristics, such as pride, envy, love, ambition, cowardice, courage, and false bravery, or **bravado**.

5.

choleric → Some of Shakespeare's characters are kind and good tempered, but some, like the **choleric** Macbeth, vent their bad tempers on all those around them. Macbeth's obsessive ambition drives him to react with quick anger.

6.

colloquy → When Macbeth and Banquo, generals in King Duncan's army, are returning from a victorious battle, they meet and speak with three witches. In this **colloquy** the witches prophesy that Macbeth will be king of Scotland.

7.

despot → When Duncan honors Macbeth by visiting his castle, Macbeth uses the occasion to fulfill the witches' prophecy. He murders Duncan in order to be king, and, in time, becomes a **despot,** a compulsive murderer, and a dictator.

8.

expatriate → Duncan's sons, Malcolm and Donalbain, fearing for their lives, **expatriate** themselves. They plan to stay in a foreign country until they can safely return to Scotland and avenge the murder of their father.

9.

feign → Macbeth **feigns** innocence of Duncan's death and puts the blame for the murder on others. Lady Macbeth, however, knows that her husband's story is false, and she goes mad from the guilt she feels.

10.

dirge → When *Macbeth* is performed, background music is sometimes used. After Duncan's murder, for instance, a mournful **dirge** sets the scene.

EXERCISE 2 *Context Clues*

Directions. Scan the definitions in Column A. Then, think about how the boldface words are used in the sentences in Column B. To complete the exercise, match each definition in Column A with the correct Vocabulary Word from Column B. Write the letter of your choice on the line provided; then write the Vocabulary Word on the line preceding the definition.

COLUMN A	COLUMN B

COLUMN A

_____ **11.** word: _____

n. a funeral hymn; a poetic or musical expression of grief

_____ **12.** word: _____

n. an absolute ruler; one in charge who acts like a tyrant

_____ **13.** word: _____

n. one who is exiled or who has withdrawn from his or her native land; *v.* to banish from one's native country; to withdraw from one's native land

_____ **14.** word: _____

n. a conversation or conference, usually formal

_____ **15.** word: _____

v. to lessen; to relieve; to calm

_____ **16.** word: _____

v. to pretend; to make up

_____ **17.** word: _____

v. to proclaim; to display publicly; *n.* a coat of arms; a banner

_____ **18.** word: _____

adj. having or showing a quick temper or irascible nature

_____ **19.** word: _____

adj. clever; skillful in a mental or physical way

_____ **20.** word: _____

n. a show of false bravery or confidence

COLUMN B

(A) Macbeth is afraid that his actions after Duncan's death will **blazon** his guilt for all to see.

(B) Apparently Macbeth's friendship with Banquo was not genuine, but **feigned**. In reality, Macbeth is willing to kill Banquo to secure the throne.

(C) Macbeth meets with underlings to decide on a plan. In true **despotic** fashion, he uses his unlimited powers to order them to kill Banquo and his son, Fleance. Fleance, however, escapes.

(D) When Banquo's ghost appears to Macbeth at a party, Macbeth's **bravado** is obvious; his pretended courage when he faces the ghost makes the guests suspicious.

(E) In another **colloquy,** the witches warn Macbeth to "beware Macduff." After this meeting with the witches, Macbeth orders Macduff's wife and children killed.

(F) The **choleric** witches prophesy Macbeth's doom, but he does not understand what these very irritable women mean until it is too late.

(G) Macduff leaves Scotland for England, becoming an **expatriate**. There he joins forces with Malcolm and Donalbain.

(H) Unlike her husband, Lady Macbeth is not **adroit,** or expert, at intrigue and murder. Her guilt leads to madness.

(I) Macbeth's fears increase when he realizes that what he considered impossible is coming true. Nothing can **allay** his fears; he cannot hope for relief.

(J) With all the deaths, including Macbeth's, there are many opportunities for **dirges** during a performance of the play.

EXERCISE 3   *Sentence Completion* ✍

Directions. For each of the following items, circle the letter of the choice that best completes the meaning of the sentence or sentences.

21. Shakespeare borrowed from other works and was ____, aptly combining stories from different sources.
    (A) choleric
    (B) blazoned
    (C) adroit
    (D) despotic
    (E) gratuitous

22. Shakespeare took the idea of the murder of Duncan from a historical account of the murder of King Duff by Donwald, an ambitious, angry, and ____ subject.
    (A) despotic
    (B) blazoned
    (C) choleric
    (D) expatriated
    (E) prosaic

23. In the play, Macbeth takes on some of the dark traits associated with the historical Donwald. Like Donwald, Macbeth pretends to be more courageous than he actually is; he uses ____ to hide his fears.
    (A) colloquy
    (B) blazon
    (C) conference
    (D) bravado
    (E) expatriation

24. The witches' prophecies stimulate, rather than ____, Macbeth's ambitious design to become king. No longer in doubt, he begins to plot.
    (A) blazon
    (B) expatriate
    (C) adroit
    (D) feign
    (E) allay

25. Shakespeare's witches ____ an interest in helping people, but actually they are expert, or ____, at deceiving those to whom they reveal their prophecies.
    (A) blazon . . . choleric
    (B) blazon . . . despotic
    (C) allay . . . choleric
    (D) expatriate . . . adroit
    (E) feign . . . adroit

26. Shakespeare's ____, inventive descriptions make it easy to picture armies proudly displaying their ____, or coats of arms.
    (A) choleric . . . bravado
    (B) adroit . . . blazons
    (C) despotic . . . expatriates
    (D) fortuitous . . . adroitness
    (E) sanguine . . . bravado

27. If King James I attended a play, it was a major event that would have been ____ throughout England. The king disliked long plays, so to ____ any criticism, Shakespeare kept *Macbeth* short.
    (A) feigned . . . expatriate
    (B) allayed . . . blazon
    (C) bravado . . . expatriate
    (D) blazoned . . . allay
    (E) feigned . . . despotic

28. Apparently the king, a ____ himself, did not object to plays about absolute monarchs whose rage leads them to commit murder. Nor, evidently was he depressed by the somber ____ played after death scenes.
    (A) dirge . . . bravado
    (B) despot . . . dirges
    (C) expatriate . . . blazons
    (D) colloquy . . . expatriates
    (E) despot . . . colloquies

29. Shakespeare may have held ____ with people who had been ____ from England for political reasons, learning much from these talks.
    (A) blazons . . . allayed
    (B) bravado . . . feigned
    (C) colloquies . . . expatriated
    (D) blazons . . . feigned
    (E) dirges . . . allayed

30. Scholars often hold ____ to discuss Shakespeare's writing. Some of these meetings are quite large.
    (A) colloquies
    (B) dirges
    (C) expatriates
    (D) blazons
    (E) bravados

MAKING NEW WORDS YOUR OWN

Lesson 5 | **CONTEXT:** Literary Figures
The Pre-Raphaelites: Painters and Poets

In the mid-1800s, a small group of artists who called themselves Pre-Raphaelites formed in England. Since *pre-* means "before" and the artist Raphael lived from 1483–1520, the term makes sense when you learn that the group's aim was to return to an artistic style that predated Raphael. One of the group's artists, Dante Gabriel Rossetti (1828–1882), was also a poet, and before long he formed a group of Pre-Raphaelite poets. What was it that these artists admired in the art styles that were popular three hundred years before they were born?

In the following exercises, you will have the opportunity to expand your vocabulary by reading about the Pre-Raphaelite Brotherhood of painters and poets. These ten Vocabulary Words will be used.

| amorphous | decorum | facile | proffer | sanguine |
| ascetic | doggerel | guile | protégé | seraphic |

EXERCISE 1 *Wordbusting*

Directions. Follow these instructions for this word and the nine words on the next page.
- Figure out the word's meaning by looking at its **context,** its **structure,** and its **sound.** Fill in at least one of the three **CSS** boxes. Alternate which boxes you complete.
- Then, look up the word in a dictionary, read all of its meanings, and write the meaning of the word as it is used in the sentence.
- Follow this same process for each of the Vocabulary Words on the next page. You will need to draw your own map for each word. Use a separate sheet of paper.

1.

amorphous → Dante Gabriel Rossetti, William Holman Hunt, and John Everett Millais were artists who detested the **amorphous** style of art of their time. They thought that art should conform to a definite type and should depict the true form of nature.

| Context: | Structure: | Sound: |

| Dictionary: |

Name _____ Date _____ Class _____

2.

guile

The Pre-Raphaelites wanted their works to be honest, totally lacking **guile**. They used bright, natural pigments and the simplicity of early Italian paintings in their works.

3.

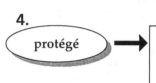
sanguine

Pre-Raphaelite paintings are filled with color and natural simplicity, and their models were beautiful young people. These **sanguine** subjects were a change from the dark, somber figures in other art of the day.

4.

protégé

Holman Hunt, whose works had been exhibited at the Royal Academy in London, helped and encouraged Dante Rossetti while Rossetti painted *The Girlhood of Mary*. Rossetti, who was at this time Hunt's **protégé,** was faithful to the ideas of the Pre-Raphaelites.

5.

facile

Dante Rossetti was a **facile** artist and poet who moved easily and skillfully from one art form to another. He is highly respected in both fields.

6.

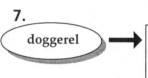
ascetic

Dante Rossetti's sister Christina, was an **ascetic** who lived a life of simplicity and seclusion. She denied herself marriage for religious reasons. Her poetry is more devotional than that of the other Pre-Raphaelites.

7.

doggerel

Christina Rossetti's poetry is simple but intense; it is concerned with the relationship between worldly and spiritual matters. Because it is very well written, it could never be regarded as **doggerel**.

8.

decorum

Her good manners and behavior made Christina Rossetti an ideal model for her brother's paintings. He wanted someone with **decorum** to pose for his painting of the Virgin Mary.

9.

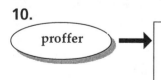
seraphic

Christ in the House of His Parents, by Millais, shows Christ as a healthy, normal boy, not as a **seraphic** figure in the clouds with other angelic creatures.

10.

proffer

When the Pre-Raphaelites first **proffered** their works to the public in 1850, they were rejected. Two years later, however, when the artists offered their paintings to the Royal Academy, the public and critics alike praised their works.

EXERCISE 2   *Context Clues*

Directions. Scan the definitions in Column A. Then, think about how the boldface words are used in the sentences in Column B. To complete the exercise, match each definition in Column A with the correct Vocabulary Word from Column B. Write the letter of your choice on the line provided; then write the Vocabulary Word on the line preceding the definition.

COLUMN A	COLUMN B

COLUMN A

_____ **11.** word: _____
n. craftiness; deceit; cunning

_____ **12.** word: _____
v. to offer; *n.* an offer

_____ **13.** word: _____
adj. angelic; of the highest order of angels

_____ **14.** word: _____
adj. shapeless; of no particular form or type; not organized

_____ **15.** word: _____
n. proper action, speech, and dress; good manners and behavior; polite behavior

_____ **16.** word: _____
n. someone whose welfare or career is guided and helped by a more influential person

_____ **17.** word: _____
adj. naturally cheerful and hopeful; confident; having a ruddy complexion

_____ **18.** word: _____
n. badly written or trivial verse, often with a singsong rhythm

_____ **19.** word: _____
n. a person who practices unusual self-denial or discipline, often for religious reasons; *adj.* self-denying

_____ **20.** word: _____
adj. easily done; performing or working with ease; adroit; not sincere or profound; superficial

COLUMN B

(A) Many Pre-Raphaelites were criticized for their sensual subject matter. The public expected them to be **ascetics** as artists and felt that neither their art nor their lives reflected sufficient strictness and severity.

(B) The painters were condemned for their informal lifestyles and what the public considered a lack of **decorum** in their actions, conduct, and attire.

(C) They were certainly not **seraphic,** or perfectly behaved, but they did not deserve to have their works condemned because of their personal lives.

(D) Because the Pre-Raphaelites believed strongly in portraying realistic detail, their works were never **amorphous**.

(E) After their works were criticized by the public, the Pre-Raphaelites were not very **sanguine** about their future as artists. Fortunately, they never lost their optimism or confidence.

(F) The poets of the group included the Rossettis, George Meredith, William Morris, and Algernon Swinburne. These writers may have addressed unconventional subjects, but their works were intelligent and well-crafted—far from **doggerel**.

(G) Their works were **proffered** to the public in various volumes. The Pre-Raphaelite poets, except for Christina Rossetti, tended to write overtly romantic verse.

(H) George Meredith was a **facile,** adept writer who wrote novels as well as poetry.

(I) Eventually, the openness and the lack of **guile** of Pre-Raphaelite art attracted the public to the movement.

(J) Other schools of art, such as Impressionism, were also attracting followers, and the Pre-Raphaelites had few **protégés**. A limited number of young artists sought their assistance.

EXERCISE 3 — *Sentence Completion* ✍

Directions. For each of the following items, circle the letter of the choice that best completes the meaning of the sentence or sentences.

21. It is a mark of _____ to know what kind of art or poetry a friend enjoys. It would be impolite to _____ a gift that would not please.
 (A) decorum . . . proffer
 (B) doggerel . . . blazon
 (C) guile . . . admonish
 (D) amorphousness . . . proffer
 (E) protégé . . . lampoon

22. Some people enjoy _____, since it takes little thought to read frivolous verse, and it can sometimes be humorous.
 (A) decorum
 (B) guile
 (C) doggerel
 (D) ascetic
 (E) seraphs

23. People who tend to be _____ probably prefer poetry about optimistic characters and events.
 (A) seraphic
 (B) ascetic
 (C) facile
 (D) sanguine
 (E) amorphous

24. Different people appreciate different kinds of art. Some prefer earthy, natural paintings; others like rather frilly, _____ scenes of floating cherubs.
 (A) sanguine
 (B) seraphic
 (C) ascetic
 (D) proferred
 (E) amorphous

25. Although the Pre-Raphaelite movement lasted only a few years, its open, natural style, its lack of _____, and its upbeat, _____ outlook strikes a happy note in the history of art.
 (A) decorum . . . guileful
 (B) doggerel . . . amorphous
 (C) guile . . . sanguine
 (D) ascetics . . . seraphic
 (E) protégés . . . guileful

26. Styles in art are constantly changing. Some modern art has moved so far from realism that it is _____, without definite shapes and outlines.
 (A) decorous
 (B) facile
 (C) sanguine
 (D) seraphic
 (E) amorphous

27. Writers and poets are often _____ of people who guide and advise them until they are ready to _____ their works to the public.
 (A) ascetics . . . sanguine
 (B) seraphs . . . ascetic
 (C) protégés . . . proffer
 (D) protégés . . . guileful
 (E) doggerel . . . seraphic

28. Writers can lose faith in their work and fear that it is _____ rather than profound. Eventually, however, most determined writers regain their self-assurance and feel _____ again.
 (A) guileful . . . seraphic
 (B) ascetic . . . amorphous
 (C) sanguine . . . guileful
 (D) facile . . . sanguine
 (E) amorphous . . . ascetic

29. Many artists and poets are poor and live _____ lives. Despite their financial condition, they can be _____ workers, able to exercise their talents easily.
 (A) sanguine . . . amorphous
 (B) ascetic . . . facile
 (C) facile . . . seraphic
 (D) seraphic . . . ascetic
 (E) amorphous . . . guileful

30. People with _____ know how to conduct themselves in galleries and museums. They speak quietly and don't touch the art works.
 (A) guile
 (B) decorum
 (C) protégés
 (D) ascetics
 (E) doggerel

MAKING NEW WORDS YOUR OWN

Lesson 6 CONTEXT: Literary Figures

The Space Stories of Doris Lessing

Doris Lessing (b. 1919), an important British novelist, has written a series of "space fiction" books: *Shikasta; The Marriages Between Zones Three, Four and Five; The Sirian Experiments; The Making of the Representative for Planet 8;* and *Documents Relating to the Sentimental Agents in the Volyen Empire.* A major premise of the series is that beings in space influence events on earth.

In the following exercises, you will have the opportunity to expand your vocabulary by reading about the space stories of Doris Lessing. Below are ten Vocabulary Words that will be used in these exercises.

dogma	implicit	nondescript	parsimonious	sundry
exhort	inveigle	nonentity	scurrilous	vociferous

EXERCISE 1 *Wordbusting*

Directions. Follow these instructions for this word and the nine words on the next page.
- Figure out the word's meaning by looking at its **context,** its **structure,** and its **sound.** Fill in at least one of the three **CSS** boxes. Alternate which boxes you complete.
- Then, look up the word in a dictionary, read all of its meanings, and write the meaning of the word as it is used in the sentence.
- Follow this same process for each of the Vocabulary Words on the next page. You will need to draw your own map for each word. Use a separate sheet of paper.

1.

dogma →

Dear Janet,
   I know that you have a strong set of personal beliefs, but I wish that you would read Doris Lessing's space series. Some of her ideas might conflict with your **dogma,** but I think you would enjoy them.

Context:

Structure:

Sound:

Dictionary:

2.

exhort → I **exhort** you to read at least one of Lessing's books. I'd like to know what you think of her science fiction. If you read just one book, you may not need further urging to read the others.

3.

implicit → My brother has also become a Lessing fan. We have never talked openly about borrowing and reading each other's books. We've just always had an **implicit** agreement to share our books.

4.

inveigle → I became so interested in the series that I **inveigled** my mother to buy the books for my birthday. "You're a great mom," I flattered her, "and you've always encouraged me to love reading." My trick worked—sort of. She ended up buying me three of the five books.

5.

nondescript → Frankly, I think some of the characters in the series are rather **nondescript,** but in spite of not being memorable for themselves, they serve important functions in the books.

6.

nonentity → I think that Lessing deliberately makes some of her characters **nonentities** because they are of little importance as individuals. She wants her readers to think about human destiny not personalities.

7.

parsimonious → I'd like to buy you a copy of *Shikasta,* but I can't right now. It's not that I am **parsimonious**—I'm usually generous with my money—but I just made a loan to my brother for a new bicycle.

8.

scurrilous → My brother can be rather **scurrilous**. I told him that I would lend him the money if he watched his language for two weeks. So far, he has kept his promise. It's been peaceful around here without his vulgar talk.

9.

sundry → Anyway, the story of my brother and his bicycle is only one of **sundry** things that I wanted to tell you about. Of all the items on my list, the most interesting is Lessing's science fiction.

10.

vociferous → Even my brother becomes **vociferous** about who gets to read the books. He shouts at me and tries to grab the book from my hands. He can be really loud and demanding at times.

EXERCISE 2 *Context Clues* 👈

Directions. Scan the definitions in Column A. Then, think about how the boldface words are used in the sentences in Column B. To complete the exercise, match each definition in Column A with the correct Vocabulary Word from Column B. Write the letter of your choice on the line provided; then write the Vocabulary Word on the line preceding the definition.

COLUMN A

____ **11.** word: _____
adj. implied; naturally involved though not obviously evident; unquestioning, absolute

____ **12.** word: _____
adj. not having individual characteristics; lacking in distinctive qualities; drab; hard to describe

____ **13.** word: _____
adj. various; miscellaneous

____ **14.** word: _____
v. to win over with trickery or flattery; to entice; to coax with deceitful talk; to dupe

____ **15.** word: _____
n. a belief or set of beliefs held to be true, especially by a church or other authority; a doctrine

____ **16.** word: _____
adj. given to the use of abusive or indecent language; foulmouthed

____ **17.** word: _____
adj. too economical; stingy; miserly

____ **18.** word: _____
v. to urge strongly; to advise or warn earnestly; to admonish

____ **19.** word: _____
n. a person or thing of little or no importance; something that does not exist or that exists only in the imagination

____ **20.** word: _____
adj. loud and noisy; clamorous; demanding

COLUMN B

(A) Request or **inveigle** the librarian to reserve for you a copy of *The Marriages Between Zones Three, Four and Five*. You may have to pretend that you need it for a class.

(B) You may not want my suggestions, but I **exhort** you to reserve a copy, since the book is so popular.

(C) Find a quiet place away from **vociferous** people and read about the romance of the queen from Zone Three and the king from Zone Four.

(D) The **nondescript** Providers, the colorless rulers of the cosmos, order these two to marry and unite the two zones.

(E) Zone Three is a lovely, peaceful place. Zone Four is a militaristic and crude place; its soldiers use **scurrilous** language. The contrast between civility and vulgarity is pretty jarring.

(F) Despite the **sundry** differences in their societies— and believe me, there are too many to count— the king and queen discover that they are compatible.

(G) A strong and **implicit** confidence develops between them.

(H) This is my favorite book in the series because it focuses on realistic characters rather than on **nonentities** who seem invented just to represent ideas.

(I) Problems develop, but they are not the usual domestic ones, such as conflicts between a generous and a **parsimonious** partner.

(J) All of these characters, however, live by a **dogma** that is foreign to our society. I can't imagine adopting their beliefs.

EXERCISE 3 *Sentence Completion*

Directions. For each of the following items, circle the letter of the choice that best completes the meaning of the sentence or sentences.

21. I don't find it difficult to consider _____ that are different from my own beliefs.
    (A) exhortations
    (B) nonentities
    (C) inveiglements
    (D) dirges
    (E) dogmas

22. Lessing tries to show that societies decay when people become too self-centered. I suppose that being _____ is a mark of self-centeredness, although thrift can be a valuable trait.
    (A) scurrilous
    (B) nondescript
    (C) parsimonious
    (D) vociferous
    (E) sundry

23. Among Lessing's _____ ideas is the belief that earth has lost the "substance-of-we-feeling." Sometimes she expresses the idea directly and sometimes _____.
    (A) sundry . . . implicitly
    (B) scurrilous . . . scurrilously
    (C) nondescript . . . parsimoniously
    (D) vociferous . . . dogmatically
    (E) parsimonious . . . scurrilously

24. The creatures in the fourth novel seem like _____. These imaginary beings are warned that their planet is dying and _____ to make plans to leave.
    (A) dogmas . . . exhorted
    (B) exhortations . . . inveigled
    (C) inveiglements . . . dogmatized
    (D) dogmas . . . inveigled
    (E) nonentities . . . exhorted

25. Is the dying planet _____? No, Lessing makes it a real and distinctive place with her assorted and _____ descriptions.
    (A) implicit . . . parsimonious
    (B) parsimonious . . . vociferous
    (C) scurrilous . . . nondescript
    (D) nondescript . . . sundry
    (E) vociferous . . . scurrilous

26. The fifth book, *Documents Relating to the Sentimental Agents in the Volyen Empire,* is about an older agent teaching a young one how to avoid becoming the victim of words, whether decent or _____.
    (A) nondescript
    (B) implicit
    (C) scurrilous
    (D) sundry
    (E) parsimonious

27. This book depicts a trial in which the Volyen state is accused of _____ the people, of completely misleading them.
    (A) dogmatizing
    (B) inveigling
    (C) broaching
    (D) exhorting
    (E) subjugating

28. The complicated plot deals with forms of tyranny and brings out the drama _____, or embodied, in the story.
    (A) nondescript
    (B) scurrilous
    (C) dogma
    (D) implicit
    (E) parsimonious

29. Lessing's fans can be quite vocal, even _____, in support of her. They're not at all _____ when it comes to buying her books.
    (A) parsimonious . . . scurrilous
    (B) vociferous . . . parsimonious
    (C) nondescript . . . sundry
    (D) sundry . . . implicit
    (E) vociferous . . . nondescript

30. I _____ you to read Lessing's science fiction, but others may implore you to read her realistic novels, such as *The Golden Notebook.* I hope you won't think I am trying to _____ you when I say that her books appeal to very intelligent people like you.
    (A) exhort . . . broach
    (B) inveigle . . . exhort
    (C) exhort . . . inveigle
    (D) broach . . . exhort
    (E) inveigle . . . broach

MAKING NEW WORDS YOUR OWN

| Lesson 7 | **CONTEXT:** Literary Figures
Old English: A Foreign Language

My grandparents live in England, and when they visit us, there is always good-natured talk about the English language. They contend that Americans don't speak real English at all. What *is* real English, and where did it come from? I decided to ask Dr. Hobson, a family friend who teaches the history of the English language at our local college. She told me that English has been spoken in England for only fifteen hundred years of the island's more than fifty-thousand-year history.

In the following exercises, you will have the opportunity to expand your vocabulary by reading about the languages of England before the English language evolved. Below are ten Vocabulary Words that will be used in these exercises.

broach	erudite	extol	immutable	truism
charlatan	etymology	gratuitous	predispose	venerate

| **EXERCISE 1** | *Wordbusting* ✍

Directions. Follow these instructions for this word and the nine words on the next page.
- Figure out the word's meaning by looking at its **context,** its **structure,** and its **sound.** Fill in at least one of the three **CSS** boxes. Alternate which boxes you complete.
- Then, look up the word in a dictionary, read all of its meanings, and write the meaning of the word as it is used in the sentence.
- Follow this same process for each of the Vocabulary Words on the next page. You will need to draw your own map for each word. Use a separate sheet of paper.

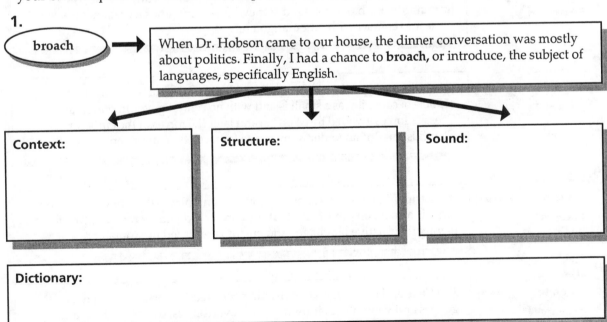

1.

broach → When Dr. Hobson came to our house, the dinner conversation was mostly about politics. Finally, I had a chance to **broach,** or introduce, the subject of languages, specifically English.

Context:

Structure:

Sound:

Dictionary:

2.
charlatan ➤ Dr. Hobson is no **charlatan**. She has expert knowledge of the history of the English language.

3.
erudite ➤ She was taught by **erudite** professors and has herself become a scholar. When I asked her about the origins of English, she told me that the language is closely related to German.

4.
etymology ➤ Dr. Hobson has spent years studying the **etymology** of the English language. Tracing languages to their origins can, at times, be very difficult and time consuming.

5.
extol ➤ My grandparents **extol** English as it is spoken in England, but the English they praise is actually a mixture of several languages, including Latin and French, according to Dr. Hobson.

6.
gratuitous ➤ The changes in the English language were not **gratuitous,** or without justification. They resulted from the island's conquests by Romans, Danes, Normans, and the Dutch, who drove out the native Celts, Picts, and Scots.

7.
immutable ➤ None of the languages brought to Britain by these invading groups was **immutable**. Each one changed somewhat—sometimes a great deal—as it came into contact with other languages.

8.
predispose ➤ Britain seemed **predisposed** to conquest by seafaring adventurers. It was susceptible because it was a small island with no central government. Julius Caesar's forces invaded three times, and later the forces of the emperor Claudius put Britain under Roman rule for more than three centuries.

9.
truism ➤ It is a **truism** that the Romans improved many places that they conquered, but it is also an obvious truth that the conquered people rarely appreciated having their native languages and customs replaced by Roman ones.

10.
venerate ➤ The Celts and others native to Britain preferred to speak their own languages and **venerate** their own gods. Nevertheless, by the third century A.D. some became Christians and worshiped as the Romans did.

Name _____ Date _____ Class _____

EXERCISE 2 *Context Clues* ✍

Directions. Scan the definitions in Column A. Then, think about how the boldface words are used in the sentences in Column B. To complete the exercise, match each definition in Column A with the correct Vocabulary Word from Column B. Write the letter of your choice on the line provided; then write the Vocabulary Word on the line preceding the definition.

COLUMN A

_____ **11.** word: _____
adj. freely given or obtained; unearned; uncalled for; without justification or cause

_____ **12.** word: _____
n. the source and development of a word; the study of word sources and development

_____ **13.** word: _____
v. to regard with deep respect, honor, or esteem; to revere

_____ **14.** word: _____
n. a statement the truth of which is obvious or well known

_____ **15.** word: _____
adj. having or displaying extensive knowledge; learned; scholarly

_____ **16.** word: _____
n. a person who falsely claims to possess expert knowledge or skill; a quack; an impostor

_____ **17.** word: _____
v. to praise highly

_____ **18.** word: _____
v. to mention for the first time; to introduce a subject; to start a discussion of

_____ **19.** word: _____
v. to create or possess a tendency or preference in advance; to make susceptible

_____ **20.** word: _____
adj. never changing; unchangeable; unalterable

COLUMN B

(A) Within fifty years of the Romans' departure in A.D. 410, the Teutonic invasions of Britain began. Dr. Hobson said that it is a **truism,** a certainty, that these invasions changed the course of Britain's history.

(B) The different Teutonic groups—the Saxons, Jutes, and Angles—seemed **predisposed** to fighting. They favored a warlike way of life to a peaceful one.

(C) These conquerors and settlers from northern Europe did not **venerate** the same gods that the Romans honored.

(D) With **gratuitous** military action, the Teutons invaded Britain and needlessly destroyed Roman architecture and influence.

(E) The thought of such wanton destruction depressed me. Seeing my reaction, Dr. Hobson opened a new topic and **broached** the subject of the origin of the name *England.*

(F) She reminded me that the **etymology** of English words includes English history. Each group that invaded England brought new words into the language and caused it to evolve.

(G) The name *England* is a form of the word *Angle*—in Old English, *Engle.* The alteration in spelling shows that language is not **immutable,** or permanent.

(H) The **erudite** Dr. Hobson informed me that *England* comes from the word *English,* and not the other way around. I was impressed by how much she knew about the subject.

(I) The English language that developed after the invasions is far different from the English my grandparents now **extol,** or acclaim.

(J) I hope my grandparents do not consider me a **charlatan** when I show them how well informed I have become about the English language—my sources are well respected, and I am definitely not a fraud.

EXERCISE 3 Sentence Completion

Directions. For each of the following items, circle the letter of the choice that best completes the meaning of the sentence or sentences.

21. Dr. Hobson, the _____ scholar, then showed me some of the letters that were in the Old English alphabet but that are not used now.
(A) immutable
(B) abject
(C) etymological
(D) truistic
(E) gratuitous

22. It is a(n) _____ that Old English, the form of English used from A.D. 450 to 1150, is a dead language; it's obvious that no one uses it anymore.
(A) charlatan
(B) truism
(C) etymology
(D) extollment
(E) veneration

23. It would be _____ to say that studying a language that no longer exists is a waste of time. Still, many people do make such unfounded statements.
(A) erudite
(B) immutable
(C) omniscient
(D) gratuitous
(E) phlegmatic

24. Dr. Hobson said no language is _____; all languages evolve as new words are created and adopted.
(A) immutable
(B) venerated
(C) gratuitous
(D) sanguine
(E) erudite

25. Therefore, it is useless to _____ a language, expecting that the features one appreciates the most will remain the same forever.
(A) broach
(B) exhort
(C) predispose
(D) proffer
(E) venerate

26. Old English seemed especially _____ to change, and many changes were _____, in the sense that they developed freely.
(A) venerated . . . immutable
(B) predisposed . . . gratuitous
(C) extolled . . . erudite
(D) broached . . . facile
(E) exhorted . . . predisposed

27. Dr. Hobson then _____, or opened, the subject of the Normans from Northern France who invaded England in 1066.
(A) predisposed
(B) extolled
(C) broached
(D) venerated
(E) gratuitous

28. The Norman Conquest was not _____, or commended, by all of England's inhabitants. It did not take an _____ person to understand that life would never be the same.
(A) broached . . . immutable
(B) predisposed . . . erudite
(C) lampooned . . . abject
(D) extolled . . . erudite
(E) predisposed . . . amorphous

29. I suggested, or _____, the subject of the Normans. Evidently, even though many Anglo-Saxons became serfs under the French-speaking Normans, they retained their language.
(A) extolled
(B) proffered
(C) broached
(D) exhorted
(E) venerated

30. Today we still use many French words, such as _____, which means "an impostor." English has never been _____ in England or America, but continues to change.
(A) gratuitous . . . erudite
(B) charlatan . . . immutable
(C) extollment . . . bellicose
(D) truism . . . gratuitous
(E) veneration . . . nondescript

30 LESSON 7

MAKING NEW WORDS YOUR OWN

Lesson 8 | CONTEXT: Literary Figures
Rudyard Kipling: At Home on Four Continents

Rudyard Kipling (1865–1936) is my favorite author. Kipling lived an interesting and varied life. He lived in India, England, the United States, and South Africa, and he wrote about all of those places. My whole family likes his writing. My father says that he tries to live up to the advice in Kipling's poem "If," and my mother is still delighted by the *Jungle Books*, which are classics of children's literature. To me, the appeal of Kipling's writing is that there's something for readers of every age.

In the following exercises, you will have the opportunity to expand your vocabulary by reading about Rudyard Kipling's life and writing. These ten Vocabulary Words will be used.

absolve	antipodes	infringe	ostensible	specious
antipathy	indigent	nettle	retroactive	subjugate

EXERCISE 1 | *Wordbusting* 🖎

Directions. Follow these instructions for this word and the nine words on the next page.
- Figure out the word's meaning by looking at its **context,** its **structure,** and its **sound.** Fill in at least one of the three **CSS** boxes. Alternate which boxes you complete.
- Then, look up the word in a dictionary, read all of its meanings, and write the meaning of the word as it is used in the sentence.
- Follow this same process for each of the Vocabulary Words on the next page. You will need to draw your own map for each word. Use a separate sheet of paper.

1.

(absolve) ➔ I vowed that before I graduated from high school I would read all of Kipling's works. However, I did not realize how much he had written, so I have had to **absolve** myself from the promise and set a new and more realistic deadline.

Context:	Structure:	Sound:

Dictionary:

2.

antipathy → Some of my friends have an **antipathy** for reading, but I love it. Maybe if they read something exciting, like Kipling's *Captains Courageous* or *Kim*, they would develop a liking for books.

3.

antipodes → Kipling was born in India but later lived in Vermont. Those points on the globe are in different hemispheres, but they are not true **antipodes**. They are far away, but not directly opposite from each other.

4.

indigent → Kipling's parents lived in India, where his father was the principal of an art school. The family was not **indigent**. In fact, they had enough money to send Kipling to England for schooling when he was five.

5.
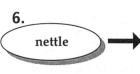
infringe → Kipling was miserable in England because the couple with whom he lived neglected and mistreated him. His parents did not realize that the couple had **infringed** on the agreement to provide proper child care.

6.

nettle → Although the abusive situation **nettled** Kipling, he had to live with the irritation until he was twelve. At that time he was sent to United Services College, where he performed in plays and began writing poetry.

7.

ostensible → When he was seventeen, Kipling returned to India, **ostensibly** to edit a newspaper. In reality he spent much of his time writing stories for it.

8.
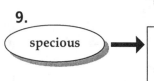
retroactive → Kipling's stories and poems were published in India and became popular with travelers, some of whom brought them to England. When he returned to England in 1889, it must have seemed to Kipling that his fame was **retroactive**: He had become famous in England months before he arrived there.

9.

specious → In England, Kipling listened to music in pubs, barracks rooms, and music halls. He thought many of the lyrics were **specious;** they sounded good on the surface but lacked meaning and truth. He wrote new lyrics for some of these songs and published them as *Barracks Room Ballads* in 1892.

10.
subjugate → Kipling loved to travel and was never able to **subjugate** his wanderlust, even after he married and supposedly submitted to a more settled life in Vermont.

EXERCISE 2   *Context Clues* 👈

Directions. Scan the definitions in Column A. Then, think about how the boldface words are used in the sentences in Column B. To complete the exercise, match each definition in Column A with the correct Vocabulary Word from Column B. Write the letter of your choice on the line provided; then write the Vocabulary Word on the line preceding the definition.

COLUMN A	COLUMN B

COLUMN A

_____ **11.** word: _____
v. to violate or disregard a law or an agreement; to trespass; to break in on

_____ **12.** word: _____
adj. seemingly desirable, reasonable, or true but not really so; having a deceptively good appearance

_____ **13.** word: _____
adj. outwardly professed; apparent; seeming

_____ **14.** word: _____
v. to declare free from guilt and blame; to set free from a promise or an obligation

_____ **15.** word: _____
v. to subdue; to conquer; to force to submit

_____ **16.** word: _____
n. any two places at directly opposite points on the earth; two opposite things

_____ **17.** word: _____
adj. applying to events that are past

_____ **18.** word: _____
n. a strong dislike; an aversion

_____ **19.** word: _____
n. a stinging plant; *v.* to sting with, or as if with, a nettle; to cause sharp annoyance; to irritate

_____ **20.** word: _____
adj. poor; needy

COLUMN B

(A) Kipling viewed Eastern and Western philosophies and lifestyles as totally different. He commented on the **antipodes** of Asian and European cultures in "The Ballad of East and West."

(B) Kipling did not consider it **specious** to say, "Oh, East is East, and West is West, and never the twain shall meet. . . ." To him, the statement made sense and was utterly true.

(C) Kipling's interest in children's stories was not **retroactive,** stemming from unfinished business in his own childhood; it grew from his desire to make up stories for his own children.

(D) In the story "The Elephant's Child," a young elephant is constantly punished for asking questions. He asks the Kolokolo Bird, who is sitting in a sharp **nettle,** to help him. The Kolokolo Bird looks down at him from its perch in the spiny plant.

(E) The Kolokolo Bird appears to help the little elephant, but his **ostensibly** friendly advice really places the elephant child in danger.

(F) The other animals have failed to **subjugate** the little elephant's curiosity, which seems to have no end. They don't know how to stop such inquisitiveness.

(G) They think that his never-ending questions **infringe** on their right to live in peace and quiet.

(H) All the animals have an **antipathy** for the Elephant Child's curiosity, but he finds ways to get even for their hostility and mistreatment of him.

(I) Eventually, the little elephant comes home with something all of his relatives want, and they **absolve** him, forgiving him for his curiosity.

(J) The popularity of this story and others in *Just So Stories* brought Kipling a good income, so he was never **indigent**.

EXERCISE 3 · Sentence Completion ✍

Directions. For each of the following items, circle the letter of the choice that best completes the meaning of the sentence or sentences.

21. Kipling held political views that were popular with many other British people at the time. For example, he did not think imperialism _____ on native people's rights, intruding upon their freedoms.
(A) nettled
(B) subjugated
(C) absolved
(D) admonished
(E) infringed

22. Kipling felt that the benefits Europeans brought to the people they defeated compensated for the _____ of their cultures.
(A) speciousness
(B) subjugation
(C) antipathy
(D) absolvement
(E) retroactivity

23. Many imperialists at the time felt that it was natural for Europeans to be affluent and for native peoples to be _____.
(A) indigent
(B) antipodal
(C) ostensible
(D) specious
(E) retroactive

24. Kipling had more than an _____ interest in native cultures; his interest was real and evident.
(A) indigent
(B) antipodal
(C) antipathetic
(D) ostensible
(E) absolvent

25. He spent time in Rhodesia each summer for eight years and seemed to have no _____ for colonial policies there. He apparently saw nothing to loathe.
(A) retroactivity
(B) infringement
(C) antipathy
(D) antipode
(E) subjugation

26. The cruel deeds of the past can't be undone _____; we can't change the past.
(A) antipathetically
(B) retroactively
(C) indigently
(D) speciously
(E) ostensibly

27. Some people see Kipling's poem "The White Man's Burden" as _____ the colonial powers of guilt for _____, or intruding, on native people's rights.
(A) subjugating . . . absolving
(B) infringing . . . subjugating
(C) absolving . . . infringing
(D) nettling . . . absolving
(E) subjugating . . . nettling

28. Even though some of Kipling's views may _____ people now (and their irritation is understandable), there is no reason to develop a(n) _____ for all of his work.
(A) subjugate . . . absolvent
(B) absolve . . . retroactivity
(C) infringe . . . speciousness
(D) absolve . . . infringement
(E) nettle . . . antipathy

29. Kipling thought the East and West were _____, or contrary, in nature, yet his stories and poems have lessened the _____ people sometimes feel for different cultures.
(A) indigent . . . retroactivity
(B) antipathetic . . . subjugation
(C) antipodal . . . antipathy
(D) specious . . . infringement
(E) retroactive . . . speciosity

30. Kipling's writings are not _____, but are of genuine value. He was awarded the Nobel Prize in literature in 1907, which is more than an _____ honor: it is a very real one.
(A) subjugated . . . absolvent
(B) retroactive . . . antipathetic
(C) specious . . . ostensible
(D) indigent . . . antipodal
(E) nettlesome . . . indigent

MAKING NEW WORDS YOUR OWN

Lesson 9 | CONTEXT: Literary Figures
Should Women Write?

Pearl S. Buck (1892–1973), Alice Walker (b. 1944), Jane Austen (1775–1817)—the list of great women writers of the past and present could go on and on. In today's literary world there certainly is no debate about women's capability to be writers. However, there was such a debate in the eighteenth century. English writer Maria Edgeworth, who herself would become a famous and respected novelist, presented both sides of the debate in *Letters to Literary Ladies* (1795).

In the following exercises, you will have the opportunity to expand your vocabulary by reading about Maria Edgeworth and the debate over "literary ladies." These ten Vocabulary Words will be used.

| abnegation | eulogy | extraneous | poignant | sonorous |
| copious | euphony | mundane | progeny | tenure |

EXERCISE 1 *Wordbusting*

Directions. Follow these instructions for this word and the nine words on the next page.
- Figure out the word's meaning by looking at its **context,** its **structure,** and its **sound.** Fill in at least one of the three **CSS** boxes. Alternate which boxes you complete.
- Then, look up the word in a dictionary, read all of its meanings, and write the meaning of the word as it is used in the sentence.
- Follow this same process for each of the Vocabulary Words on the next page. You will need to draw your own map for each word. Use a separate sheet of paper.

1.

(abnegation) → In *Letters to Literary Ladies,* a liberal and a conservative debate the subject of women authors. The conservative—if he recognized women's rights to write at all—would favor an **abnegation** of those rights, urging women to give them up.

| Context: | Structure: | Sound: |

| Dictionary: |

2.

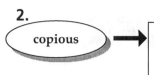

The liberal, modeled after Edgeworth's own father, provides **copious** reasons why women should be respected as authors. Among the extensive evidence he cites is the fact that women have produced significant works on natural history, education, and other subjects.

3.

One gathers that the conservative, on the other hand, thinks women should not lift their pens even to write a **eulogy** honoring a deceased friend or relative.

4.

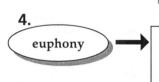

Edgeworth certainly was capable of using words in pleasant-sounding combinations. Don't you like the **euphony** of her title *Letters to Literary Ladies*?

5.

From what I've read so far, the two men in *Letters to Literary Ladies* keep to the topic—whether women should be writers—and avoid **extraneous** subjects.

6.

The conservative implies that women should confine their interests to the **mundane** pursuits of domestic life. When women venture away from these ordinary activities, he says, they may harm themselves and others.

7.

The liberal has several **poignant** comments. Particularly moving is his argument that women should be given the same educational and cultural advantages as men.

8.

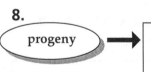

Both men agree that women are meant to be wives and mothers and to care for their **progeny,** but the liberal thinks women are capable of much more than simply rearing children.

9.

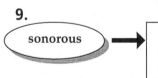

One can imagine the conservative telling women his theories in a deep, rich, **sonorous** voice: ". . . We [men] usually consider a certain degree of weakness, both of mind and body, as friendly to female grace."

10.

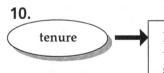

If the conservative were alive today and working as a supervisor, his **tenure** probably would not last very long. He would likely be replaced with someone whose views more closely mirror the liberal's.

EXERCISE 2 *Context Clues* ✍

Directions. Scan the definitions in Column A. Then, think about how the boldface words are used in the sentences in Column B. To complete the exercise, match each definition in Column A with the correct Vocabulary Word from Column B. Write the letter of your choice on the line provided; then write the Vocabulary Word on the line preceding the definition.

COLUMN A

_____ **11.** word: _____
adj. ordinary; commonplace; of this world (rather than the world beyond)

_____ **12.** word: _____
n. a speech or piece of writing in praise of a person or thing, especially to honor one who has recently died; a tribute; praise

_____ **13.** word: _____
n. children; offspring; descendants

_____ **14.** word: _____
adj. abundant; plentiful; full of information; wordy

_____ **15.** word: _____
n. the holding of an office; the length of time for which a position is held; the permanence of position granted to teachers, civil service employees, and others

_____ **16.** word: _____
n. agreeableness of sound; pleasant combination of sounds in spoken words

_____ **17.** word: _____
adj. giving out, capable of producing, or having a deep, rich sound

_____ **18.** word: _____
n. self-denial; a giving up or a renunciation of rights

_____ **19.** word: _____
adj. painfully felt; emotionally touching; pointed; sharp

_____ **20.** word: _____
adj. coming from outside; foreign; not necessary; irrelevant

COLUMN B

(A) The story of Maria Edgeworth's life would make a **poignant** novel. I am always moved by true success stories.

(B) Edgeworth's father was an inventor and educator who had twenty-one **progeny**. Maria was the second child.

(C) Maria's childhood was not **mundane;** in fact, it was quite unusual. Most children do not have the opportunity to grow up on an estate and be taught by their fathers.

(D) Richard Edgeworth's lessons to his daughter were **copious**. She quickly absorbed a huge amount of information.

(E) I imagine that a **sonorous** bell rang at the start of the Edgeworth children's lessons, its vibrant sound filling the estate.

(F) Richard Edgeworth apparently believed in the expansion rather than the **abnegation** of individual rights.

(G) He exposed Maria to essential ideas as well as **extraneous** ones, so that her education was broad.

(H) Although Richard Edgeworth was not a professor with **tenure,** his lack of a professional position did not diminish the fact that he was an excellent teacher.

(I) Don't you think his name has a nice ring to it? I really like the **euphony** of Richard Lovell Edgeworth.

(J) I wonder if Maria wrote a **eulogy** about her father after his death. Even if she didn't, her career itself was a homage to him.

Name _____ Date _____ Class _____

Sentence Completion ✍

Directions. For each of the following items, circle the letter of the choice that best completes the meaning of the sentence or sentences.

21. Our English teacher, Ms. Carbone, gave us _____ information about Maria Edgeworth's life and works. I'd never taken so many notes!
    (A) sonorous
    (B) mundane
    (C) extraneous
    (D) copious
    (E) eulogistic

22. Most of the information was necessary and relevant, although some may have been _____.
    (A) euphonious
    (B) extraneous
    (C) sonorous
    (D) eulogistic
    (E) copious

23. I didn't question her judgment, however. Our teacher's _____ here has lasted for thirty years; she must do her job very well in order to have kept it for so long.
    (A) eulogy
    (B) progeny
    (C) tenure
    (D) abnegation
    (E) euphony

24. Ms. Carbone told us about the _____, everyday lives of the Irish people portrayed in Edgeworth's novel *Castle Rackrent* (1800).
    (A) copious
    (B) sonorous
    (C) tenured
    (D) extraneous
    (E) mundane

25. Rackrent is a great name for a castle, I think, because the sound is so _____. Others may not agree, but I think it is pleasing.
    (A) euphonious
    (B) copious
    (C) poignant
    (D) mundane
    (E) extraneous

26. Personally, I can't imagine having twenty-one _____. I hope there was _____ food to feed so many children!
    (A) tenures . . . poignant
    (B) eulogies . . . mundane
    (C) euphonies . . . sonorous
    (D) progeny . . . copious
    (E) abnegations . . . extraneous

27. Edgeworth did not have any _____ of her own. She wrote _____, however, and her many books could be called her offspring.
    (A) tenure . . . eulogistically
    (B) eulogies . . . sonorously
    (C) abnegations . . . poignantly
    (D) progeny . . . copiously
    (E) euphonies . . . euphoniously

28. I was moved by Edgeworth's _____ comments about her father, who had taught her to defend her rights as a woman rather than to accept any _____ of them.
    (A) sonorous . . . tenure
    (B) extraneous . . . eulogy
    (C) mundane . . . progeny
    (D) sonorous . . . euphony
    (E) poignant . . . abnegation

29. Any _____ following Edgeworth's death should have mentioned her work during the Irish potato famine of 1847. The _____ story of the Irish people's suffering moved me deeply.
    (A) euphony . . . copious
    (B) abnegation . . . sonorous
    (C) eulogy . . . poignant
    (D) progeny . . . extraneous
    (E) tenure . . . mundane

30. The school bell, its tone flat rather than deep and _____, undid my note taking.
    (A) copious
    (B) sonorous
    (C) poignant
    (D) mundane
    (E) extraneous

38 LESSON 9

MAKING NEW WORDS YOUR OWN

Lesson 10 | CONTEXT: Literary Figures

Jane Austen: Laughing at Herself and Others

Jane Austen (1775–1817), whom some scholars consider the world's greatest woman writer, once said she could not write a serious romance. She explained that she needed to be able to "relax into laughing at myself" and others. In the six novels for which she is famous, including *Sense and Sensibility* (1811) and *Pride and Prejudice* (1813), Austen wittily and comically describes the lives of upper-middle-class girls in England at the end of the eighteenth century. She laughs especially at husband-hunting young ladies, their scheming mothers, self-important clergymen, and arrogant aristocrats.

In the following exercises, you will have the opportunity to expand your vocabulary by reading about the life and writings of Jane Austen. These ten Vocabulary Words will be used.

ascribe	engender	homily	idiosyncrasy	introvert
elegy	hackneyed	humdrum	inconsequential	paragon

EXERCISE 1 | *Wordbusting*

Directions. Follow these instructions for this word and the nine words on the next page.
- Figure out the word's meaning by looking at its **context,** its **structure,** and its **sound.** Fill in at least one of the three **CSS** boxes. Alternate which boxes you complete.
- Then, look up the word in a dictionary, read all of its meanings, and write the meaning of the word as it is used in the sentence.
- Follow this same process for each of the Vocabulary Words on the next page. You will need to draw your own map for each word. Use a separate sheet of paper.

1.

(ascribe) → What motive for writing should one **ascribe** to Jane Austen? Pure enjoyment probably would be an accurate motive to attribute to her. She seems genuinely to have loved writing stories about people from her social class.

Context:	Structure:	Sound:

Dictionary:

2.
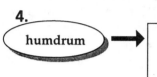 elegy → A narrator's lively, bright tone shines in each of Austen's novels. She obviously delighted in clever conversations and amusing characters. You won't find any **elegies**—sad and mournful lyrics—among Austen's writings!

3.
engender → Austen's young protagonists are always hoping that their looks and social graces will **engender** successful marriages. Sometimes the desired effects are produced, and the happy young women become engaged.

4.
 humdrum → Don't get the idea that Austen's plots are **humdrum** just because they mainly revolve around young ladies trying to find suitable husbands. In Austen's novels, such events are not commonplace and trivial: They are shrewd, calculated hunts with plenty of humor, excitement, and variety.

5.
 introvert → Obviously, the sociable, outgoing young ladies within Austen's fictional world have the best chance of attracting suitable husbands, while the **introverts** are often ignored because of their shy, retiring ways.

6.
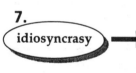 homily → While Austen has many comments about the people of her social class, she did not use **homilies**. You won't have to struggle through long, moralizing passages in Austen's novels; instead, you'll find sharp, revealing dialogue.

7.
idiosyncrasy → Austen is especially gifted in bringing out her characters' **idiosyncrasies**. She cleverly satirizes their personal quirks.

8.
hackneyed → The character descriptions in Austen's novels are fresh and pointed, not **hackneyed**. In *Pride and Prejudice,* Mrs. Bennet is described as "a woman of mean understanding, little information, and uncertain temper."

9.
paragon → Darcy, a main character in *Pride and Prejudice,* is regarded as a **paragon** by the men, but he is not viewed as a model of perfection by the women, who dislike his apparent pride.

10.
inconsequential → While reading Austen's novels, one never knows what seemingly **inconsequential** social information may become extremely important. A supposedly minor detail can turn out to be the key to marriage and fortune.

EXERCISE 2 *Context Clues* ✍

Directions. Scan the definitions in Column A. Then, think about how the boldface words are used in the sentences in Column B. To complete the exercise, match each definition in Column A with the correct Vocabulary Word from Column B. Write the letter of your choice on the line provided; then write the Vocabulary Word on the line preceding the definition.

COLUMN A	COLUMN B

COLUMN A

_____ **11.** word: _____

adj. used too often; stale from overuse; trite; clichéd

_____ **12.** word: _____

n. a model of excellence or perfection; a perfect example of something

_____ **13.** word: _____

v. to assign (as to a cause); to attribute; to think of as coming from or belonging to someone

_____ **14.** word: _____

adj. unimportant; petty; trivial

_____ **15.** word: _____

adj. without variety or excitement; monotonous; commonplace

_____ **16.** word: _____

v. to bring into being; to produce; to cause

_____ **17.** word: _____

n. a personal peculiarity that is an identifying trait; a quirk

_____ **18.** word: _____

n. a sad or mournful poem or song, often about someone who is dead

_____ **19.** word: _____

n. a person who looks inward; a shy, quiet person

_____ **20.** word: _____

n. a sermon, especially on something in the Bible; a long, often dull, moralizing talk or writing

COLUMN B

(A) Austen's novels **engendered,** or led to, much interest in Austen herself, but she avoided literary circles and publicity.

(B) Although a private person, Austen apparently was not an **introvert;** she was lively and outgoing among family and friends.

(C) The family may have regarded Austen's habit of writing in the sitting room as out of the ordinary, but they tolerated this **idiosyncrasy.**

(D) What some people would regard as **humdrum** domestic duties occupied much of Austen's time. I wonder whether she found them as dull as my friends and I would.

(E) Austen received much of her education from her father, a teacher and minister. I imagine that he was a serious, learned man who wrote scholarly **homilies** on religious topics.

(F) We might not **ascribe** an interest in acting to Austen, but such an interest was very much a part of her character.

(G) She performed in home theatrical shows. Do you think this experience was significant or **inconsequential** to Austen as a novelist?

(H) No one could complain that Austen was writing **hackneyed** stories; her work was never trite or unoriginal.

(I) Austen considered her older sister Cassandra to be a **paragon** of talent. She especially admired Cassandra's comic work.

(J) Cassandra wrote lovingly, even poetically, of her sister. Do you know if a family member wrote an **elegy** to mourn Jane's death in 1817?

Name _____ Date _____ Class _____

EXERCISE 3 *Sentence Completion* ✍

Directions. For each of the following items, circle the letter of the choice that best completes the meaning of the sentence or sentences.

21. I _____ my interest in Jane Austen to an English teacher who attributed his own initial interest to a seemingly _____ fact: His last name, too, was Austen.
  (A) engender . . . hackneyed
  (B) ascribe . . . elegiac
  (C) nettle . . . humdrum
  (D) ascribe . . . inconsequential
  (E) extol . . . introverted

22. Reading Austen's novels _____, or created, my interest in researching _____ among supposedly shy authors who write forceful and sometimes controversial books.
  (A) engendered . . . paragon
  (B) ascribed . . . elegy
  (C) broached . . . homily
  (D) venerated . . . idiosyncrasy
  (E) engendered . . . introversion

23. What I like about Austen is that she can make _____, or immaterial, conversations sound fascinating and not at all _____.
  (A) elegaic . . . humdrum
  (B) homiletic . . . inconsequential
  (C) ascribable . . . idiosyncratic
  (D) inconsequential . . . humdrum
  (E) introverted . . . hackneyed

24. Only such a(n) _____ of writing talent, could communicate people's personal oddities, or _____, so well.
  (A) paragon . . . idiosyncrasies
  (B) introvert . . . elegies
  (C) elegy . . . homilies
  (D) idiosyncrasy . . . paragons
  (E) paragon . . . elegies

25. Don't make the mistake of considering Austen's earlier writings to be totally _____; there is much in them that has value and substance.
  (A) ascribable
  (B) introverted
  (C) inconsequential
  (D) elegiac
  (E) idiosyncratic

26. Austen's early work *Love and Freindship* (her spelling) contains a few clichéd, overused ideas, but the work as a whole is not _____.
  (A) elegiac
  (B) omniscient
  (C) farcical
  (D) introverted
  (E) hackneyed

27. Austen lets readers know her ideas about moral values without writing _____ that might bore them. She knows how to make her point without preaching.
  (A) paragons
  (B) homilies
  (C) hackneys
  (D) idiosyncrasies
  (E) elegies

28. Because I consider Austen to be a(n) _____ of an accomplished author, she is the ideal for my own writing career.
  (A) elegy
  (B) homily
  (C) introvert
  (D) paragon
  (E) idiosyncrasy

29. Some people cannot decide whether Austen was an extrovert or a(n) _____, or whether Austen thought her life was _____ or exciting.
  (A) homily . . . hackneyed
  (B) paragon . . . idiosyncratic
  (C) introvert . . . humdrum
  (D) elegy . . . ascribable
  (E) introversion . . . hackneyed

30. I don't think that Austen would have wanted a(n) _____ written about her. If anything, I think she would want to be memorialized in a comic poem or story.
  (A) elegy
  (B) paragon
  (C) idiosyncrasy
  (D) introvert
  (E) inconsequentiality

42 Lesson 10

Name _____ Date _____ Class _____

MAKING NEW WORDS YOUR OWN

*L*esson 11   CONTEXT: History and Society
The First British Artists

The history of art in Great Britain began long before the first paintings were hung in London's Tate Gallery. Some fifteen thousand years ago, artists of the Old Stone Age made bone engravings. In the New Stone Age, or Neolithic period, which began around 2000 B.C., artists carved great stone tombs. Stonehenge could be considered the greatest artistic monument of the Neolithic and Early Bronze ages. Neolithic artists also made pots, jewelry, and woodcarvings. The Celts, who invaded Britain in the fifth century B.C., used bronze and gold for works of art such as mirrors, helmets, and necklaces.

In the following exercises, you will have the opportunity to expand your vocabulary by reading about prehistoric art in Great Britain. Below are ten Vocabulary Words that will be used in these exercises.

aberration	candor	dearth	herculean	retrospect
adjudge	corroborate	diurnal	ludicrous	salient

EXERCISE 1   *Wordbusting* ✍

Directions.   Follow these instructions for this word and the nine words on the next page.
- Figure out the word's meaning by looking at its **context,** its **structure,** and its **sound.** Fill in at least one of the three **CSS** boxes. Alternate which boxes you complete.
- Then, look up the word in a dictionary, **read all of its meanings,** and write the meaning of the word as it is used in the sentence.
- Follow this same process for each of the Vocabulary Words on the next page. You will need to draw your own map for each word. Use a separate sheet of paper.

1.

(aberration) → My parents say that my decision to become an art historian is an **aberration;** there have been five generations of medical doctors in my family. I am departing from that tradition to study prehistoric British art.

Context:

Structure:

Sound:

Dictionary:

Copyright © by Holt, Rinehart and Winston. All rights reserved.

MAKING NEW WORDS YOUR OWN   **43**

2.
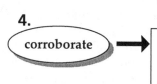
adjudge

If the law had any jurisdiction over my career, I think my parents would take my decision to court and let the court **adjudge** what I should do. Mom and Dad aren't too impressed with Irish tomb carvings!

3.
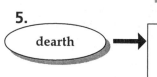
candor

"If I may speak frankly," I told them, "I much prefer examining the gold shields of Celtic warriors or even the bronze masks of their horses to examining patients." I don't think my parents appreciated my **candor**.

4.
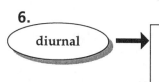
corroborate

"You see, I'm really good in art history, and I am lousy in science," I said. To **corroborate** the truth of this, I reminded them of my poor grades in biology and my excellent ones in art history.

5.
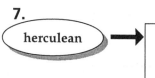
dearth

I had thought about studying Old Stone Age art in Britain, but there really is a **dearth** of artifacts from that time period. It would not be very interesting to study just a few bone engravings.

6.

diurnal

"I have been a doctor for forty years, and I'm still interested in my **diurnal** rounds at the hospital," Dad said. I replied that if I had to do the same thing every day, I would rather it be a walk through a museum!

7.

herculean

I want to study the tomb carvings at New Grange, Ireland. It must have been a demanding, **herculean** task to move the massive and heavy stones that form the tombs.

8.

ludicrous

"The image of you hiking all over Ireland and peering at old tombs is **ludicrous**," Mom said, laughing to herself over the picture in her mind.

9.
retrospect

In **retrospect,** I know that I should not have told both my parents at once about my career decision. Looking back on the scene, I realize that I should have handled it differently.

10.
salient

Most people can comment on the **salient** features of a piece of ancient art. I am fascinated, however, by features that aren't so noticeable, for they may help unlock the secrets of prehistoric cultures.

EXERCISE 2   *Context Clues* 🖎

Directions. Scan the definitions in Column A. Then, think about how the boldface words are used in the sentences in Column B. To complete the exercise, match each definition in Column A with the correct Vocabulary Word from Column B. Write the letter of your choice on the line provided; then write the Vocabulary Word on the line preceding the definition.

COLUMN A	COLUMN B

COLUMN A

_____ **11.** word: _____
v. to support or strengthen an idea or a statement; to attest to the truth of; to confirm

_____ **12.** word: _____
n. a departure from the usual course; a deviation; an abnormal development

_____ **13.** word: _____
adj. extremely demanding or difficult; requiring or having great courage or strength, like that possessed by Hercules

_____ **14.** word: _____
n. a contemplation or survey of things that happened in the past

_____ **15.** word: _____
n. a scarcity, as of food; a lack; too small a supply of something

_____ **16.** word: _____
adj. standing out; easily seen or noticed; conspicuous; noticeable; prominent

_____ **17.** word: _____
v. to decree or decide by law; to pass sentence

_____ **18.** word: _____
adj. occurring every day; daily; occurring during the daytime

_____ **19.** word: _____
n. openness; saying what one really thinks; frankness; impartiality

_____ **20.** word: _____
adj. amusingly absurd; ridiculous

COLUMN B

(A) I once had a weird dream that a jury was deciding whether I was worthy of being sent to England to study Stonehenge. In the dream, the court **adjudged** that I was indeed qualified to research ancient British art.

(B) In **retrospect,** I realize that I decided to study prehistoric British art because of that dream.

(C) I actually ended up going to Stonehenge the summer after I graduated from high school. Stonehenge is a gigantic **aberration,** an extraordinary grouping of stones on the Salisbury Plain that is totally different from anything else around it.

(D) Can you imagine the **herculean** effort required to drag the fifty-ton sandstone blocks into place?

(E) There are many theories about the meaning and purpose of Stonehenge, and some physical evidence **corroborates,** or backs up, these theories.

(F) Stonehenge may have been a temple to which some Neolithic people made **diurnal** visits, perhaps to watch the sun rise.

(G) There is a **dearth** of artistic markings on the stones, but a few still remain—carvings of a dagger and depictions of bronze axe heads, for example.

(H) These markings are difficult to see; they are not among Stonehenge's most **salient** features.

(I) Do you think it is **ludicrous** that people come from all over the world to see a group of standing stones? I certainly do not—there is nothing strange about admiring a place as powerful as Stonehenge.

(J) As an art historian, what is my true opinion of Stonehenge? With complete **candor** I can say that it is magnificent.

EXERCISE 3 Sentence Completion ✍

Directions. For each of the following items, circle the letter of the choice that best completes the meaning of the sentence or sentences.

21. The Neolithic potter noticed that his village had a _____ of bowls and drinking mugs. This shortage concerned him.
    (A) candor
    (B) salience
    (C) retrospect
    (D) dearth
    (E) corroboration

22. As he made his pots, he thought about the previous years. He realized in _____ that he had enjoyed learning from the old potters.
    (A) aberration
    (B) dearth
    (C) retrospect
    (D) salience
    (E) corroboration

23. "Some people say it is _____ to decorate the cups so carefully, but I don't think it is preposterous," the potter thought to himself.
    (A) diurnal
    (B) herculean
    (C) salient
    (D) aberrational
    (E) ludicrous

24. The potter liked his work to have _____ characteristics: markings that would make it possible for people to tell it was his work.
    (A) salient
    (B) ludicrous
    (C) herculean
    (D) diurnal
    (E) retrospective

25. The potter toiled _____, from dawn to dusk. He exhibited almost superhuman abilities, working with _____ diligence.
    (A) diurnally . . . retrospective
    (B) ludicrously . . . diurnal
    (C) saliently . . . aberrational
    (D) ludicrously . . . corroborative
    (E) diurnally . . . herculean

26. For him, a vacation would have been a(n) _____. Some thought it was _____ to be so serious about a schedule.
    (A) retrospect . . . salient
    (B) candor . . . diurnal
    (C) dearth . . . ludicrous
    (D) corroboration . . . salient
    (E) aberration . . . ludicrous

27. Digging the clay sometimes took a superhuman, _____, effort. Also, sometimes there was a lack, or _____, of good clay.
    (A) diurnal . . . retrospect
    (B) salient . . . candor
    (C) retrospective . . . aberration
    (D) herculean . . . dearth
    (E) ludicrous . . . candor

28. His son _____, or supported, his father's claim that digging clay is hard work. The boy was glad the chore was only weekly.
    (A) capitulated
    (B) adjudged
    (C) corroborated
    (D) nettled
    (E) adjudged

29. The potter and his son were frank and open with each other. This _____, the son would realize one day in _____, benefited their relationship.
    (A) retrospect . . . candor
    (B) candor . . . retrospect
    (C) dearth . . . aberration
    (D) aberration . . . dearth
    (E) retrospect . . . dearth

30. The potter knew that if he ever had to stand before the village lawmakers and defend himself, he would be _____ a good and useful member of the community.
    (A) capitulated
    (B) adjudged
    (C) emanated
    (D) corroborated
    (E) engendered

MAKING NEW WORDS YOUR OWN

Lesson 12 | CONTEXT: History and Society

England: Welcome to the Roman Empire

At its height, the Roman Empire included North Africa, Asia Minor, much of the Mediterranean, and a large portion of Europe—including Britain. The Romans began building in England in the middle of the first century A.D. Roman occupation of England continued for almost four hundred years. During that time, Roman customs and styles combined with native Celtic traditions. Roman civilization transformed England in many ways, especially in the areas of architecture and art, and fortunately, some examples of Roman-influenced art and architecture survive.

In the following exercises, you will have the opportunity to expand your vocabulary by reading about the Roman occupation of England. These ten Vocabulary Words will be used.

artifice	captivate	configuration	extant	refute
augury	chicanery	deduce	proponent	scrupulous

EXERCISE 1 | Wordbusting

Directions. Follow these instructions for this word and the nine words on the next page.
- Figure out the word's meaning by looking at its **context**, its **structure**, and its **sound**. Fill in at least one of the three **CSS** boxes. Alternate which boxes you complete.
- Then, look up the word in a dictionary, read all of its meanings, and write the meaning of the word as it is used in the sentence.
- Follow this same process for each of the Vocabulary Words on the next page. You will need to draw your own map for each word. Use a separate sheet of paper.

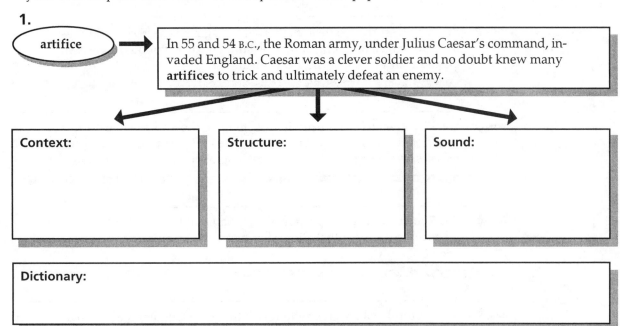

1.

artifice → In 55 and 54 B.C., the Roman army, under Julius Caesar's command, invaded England. Caesar was a clever soldier and no doubt knew many **artifices** to trick and ultimately defeat an enemy.

Context:

Structure:

Sound:

Dictionary:

2.

augury

Caesar did not conquer all of Britain; he ran out of time and money. Some Britons may have practiced **augury,** pointing to various omens that they believed predicted that other Romans would finish what Caesar had begun.

3.

captivate

Roman builders and artists probably **captivated** the Britons who, used to simple wooden huts, would have been fascinated by the stone and brick buildings erected by the Romans.

4.
chicanery

The Romans may have used some **chicanery** in gathering the Britons' support for their projects, such as the building of forts. Although the Britons may have been tricked by cleverly worded deceptions, it is certain that the Britons enabled their invaders to accomplish a great deal.

5.
configuration

Modern scholars and historians can tell the general **configurations** of Roman villas in England; the remains of foundations suggest the outlines of these buildings and the manner in which they were arranged.

6.

deduce

By studying these foundations, scholars can **deduce** what the villas looked like and how tall they were. By examining surviving fragments of artwork, scholars can also infer how the villas were decorated.

7.

extant

You may be surprised to learn that some fragments of fresco paintings from Roman villas in England are **extant**. The most famous of those still in existence are at Fishbourne, near Chichester.

8.
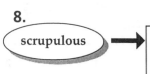
scrupulous

Wealthy Romans—and Britons who imitated the Roman style—covered their floors with mosaics. Artists had to be very **scrupulous** when creating mosaics, as placing small stones in cement to form designs is exacting work.

9.

proponent

The Romans were great **proponents** of road building. They advocated the construction of roads that allowed armies to move quickly from one fort to another.

10.

refute

It is doubtful that anyone could **refute** the statement that the Romans transformed the Britons' society. There certainly is proof that significant towns in England formed along the roads built by the Romans.

EXERCISE 2 *Context Clues* 👉

Directions. Scan the definitions in Column A. Then, think about how the boldface words are used in the sentences in Column B. To complete the exercise, match each definition in Column A with the correct Vocabulary Word from Column B. Write the letter of your choice on the line provided; then write the Vocabulary Word on the line preceding the definition.

COLUMN A	COLUMN B

COLUMN A

_____ **11.** word: _____
n. a skill; a clever device; a sly or artful trick; trickery

_____ **12.** word: _____
n. the position of parts or elements of something; a shape; an outline

_____ **13.** word: _____
adj. giving strict attention to what is right or proper; exact and careful

_____ **14.** word: _____
v. to infer by reasoning; to conclude from known facts and principles

_____ **15.** word: _____
v. to prove that someone or something is false or incorrect; to disprove

_____ **16.** word: _____
v. to catch the attention of, by beauty or excellence; to enchant; to charm; to attract

_____ **17.** word: _____
n. a person who supports a cause or idea; someone who makes a proposition; an advocate

_____ **18.** word: _____
adj. still in existence; not extinct, lost, or destroyed

_____ **19.** word: _____
n. the use of clever talk or trickery to deceive or evade

_____ **20.** word: _____
n. the practice of foretelling the future from signs and omens; an omen or a sign

COLUMN B

(A) I marvel at the **artifices** used by the talented Roman artists who created life-size bronze busts.

(B) A bronze head of the emperor Claudius shows **scrupulous** attention to proper proportions. The three-dimensional portrait is so precisely made, in fact, that it almost seems like a real face.

(C) Unlike many other Roman rulers, who were known for using shrewd talk to mislead their subjects, Claudius is not known for **chicanery**.

(D) From looking at the bronze head of Claudius, a viewer can **deduce** that Roman art was realistic. He or she might also decide that the Romans appreciated simplicity and directness.

(E) It would be difficult to **refute,** or show to be un-true, the evidence that early English sculptors were influenced by Roman artists.

(F) The stone relief of the hideous monster Medusa, carved at Bath by an early English artist, still **captivates** visitors. The image is unforgettable.

(G) The arrangement of the locks of hair tangled with snakes around Medusa's face is an especially in-teresting **configuration**.

(H) We are fortunate that the stone relief is still **extant** and that it was not demolished after the Romans withdrew from Britain.

(I) Some people may be opposed to spending money to uncover Roman artifacts in England, but I am a strong **proponent** of such efforts.

(J) If I were a believer in such things, I would look for prophecies and use **augury** to predict what won-derful discoveries may be found in the future!

EXERCISE 3 *Sentence Completion* ✍

Directions. For each of the following items, circle the letter of the choice that best completes the meaning of the sentence or sentences.

21. My friend Adam, who likes to look for omens, said that all the _____ indicated that this was the year he should go to England to study the Roman ruins.
(A) artifices
(B) chicaneries
(C) configurations
(D) proponents
(E) auguries

22. Adam is a person of many _____, and he used all of his cunning to earn money for the trip.
(A) deductions
(B) configurations
(C) artifices
(D) auguries
(E) proponents

23. Still, Adam ended up borrowing some money from relatives, asking them frankly and honestly rather than using any _____.
(A) augury
(B) proponents
(C) deduction
(D) chicanery
(E) configuration

24. Once Adam arrived in England, he was entranced by the small villages and was totally _____ by the town of Bath.
(A) deduced
(B) captivated
(C) configured
(D) refuted
(E) inundated

25. He was surprised by the _____ of the Roman baths there and carefully noted the arrangement of the rooms, imagining what it would have looked like centuries before.
(A) configuration
(B) proponent
(C) augury
(D) chicanery
(E) scrupulosity

26. From the layout, or _____, of the baths, Adam was able to _____ the Romans' bathing procedures and make other inferences about their social practices.
(A) chicanery . . . deduce
(B) configuration . . . captivate
(C) proponent . . . refute
(D) configuration . . . deduce
(E) artifice . . . captivate

27. "It's amazing that the baths are _____," he wrote us. "What's more, they are in excellent condition."
(A) scrupulous
(B) configurational
(C) extant
(D) refutable
(E) deducible

28. In the museum at Bath, Adam saw the precise, painstaking work of the _____ Roman artists and studied other _____ artifacts that had survived from Roman times.
(A) refutable . . . artificial
(B) extant . . . scrupulous
(C) scrupulous . . . deducible
(D) extant . . . refutable
(E) scrupulous . . . extant

29. "These sculptures _____ your belief that Roman art in England is second rate," Adam wrote. "Admit that you were wrong. Besides, you would be just as _____ and fascinated as I am if you were here."
(A) captivate . . . deducible
(B) refute . . . captivated
(C) deduce . . . refutable
(D) refute . . . scrupulous
(E) captivate . . . extant

30. "I am a(n) _____ of firsthand observation," he wrote. "You really must see the Roman temple area at Bath."
(A) chicanery
(B) augury
(C) configuration
(D) proponent
(E) artifice

MAKING NEW WORDS YOUR OWN

Lesson 13 | CONTEXT: History and Society

Lexicography: The Passion of Samuel Johnson

One of the major figures in the history of lexicography, the compilation of dictionaries, is Samuel Johnson (1709–1784). At the age of thirty-six, Johnson began an enormous task—writing the first major English dictionary. During the next nine years, Johnson wrote definitions for more than 40,000 words and selected 114,000 quotations from the finest English writing on various academic subjects. His *Dictionary of the English Language* was a monumental achievement. It was the model for all English dictionaries to come for more than a century.

In the following exercises, you will have the opportunity to expand your vocabulary by reading about the personality and work of English lexicographer and writer Samuel Johnson. Below are ten Vocabulary Words that will be used in these exercises.

civility	exhilaration	germane	obsequious	precocious
connoisseur	foible	gregarious	patrimony	punctilious

EXERCISE 1   *Wordbusting*

Directions. Follow these instructions for this word and the nine words on the next page.
- Figure out the word's meaning by looking at its **context,** its **structure,** and its **sound.** Fill in at least one of the three **CSS** boxes. Alternate which boxes you complete.
- Then, look up the word in a dictionary, read all of its meanings, and write the meaning of the word as it is used in the sentence.
- Follow this same process for each of the Vocabulary Words on the next page. You will need to draw your own map for each word. Use a separate sheet of paper.

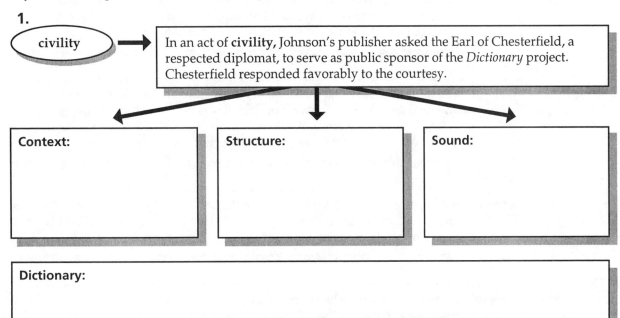

1.

civility → In an act of **civility,** Johnson's publisher asked the Earl of Chesterfield, a respected diplomat, to serve as public sponsor of the *Dictionary* project. Chesterfield responded favorably to the courtesy.

Context:

Structure:

Sound:

Dictionary:

2.

(connoisseur) ➤ Johnson became a **connoisseur** of words as he compiled the *Dictionary*. He became an expert on word meanings, usage, history, and fine shades of meaning.

3.

(exhilaration) ➤ As work on the *Dictionary* began, the **exhilaration** must have been great in Johnson's "dictionary workshop," located in the attic of his house. One reason for Johnson's high spirits was the hope that the *Dictionary* would establish his reputation.

4.

(foible) ➤ Johnson's strengths as well as his faults have been well documented in various biographies. One **foible** that he had to overcome while working on the *Dictionary* was impatience.

5.

(punctilious) ➤ Johnson was extremely **punctilious** about facts. When people later quizzed him about the details of compiling the *Dictionary*, Johnson provided precise information on the procedures he had followed.

6.

(gregarious) ➤ Johnson was **gregarious,** and his sociable manner brought him many friends. He had a great circle of admirers who loved to hear his pronouncements.

7.

(obsequious) ➤ The six assistants whom Johnson employed for the *Dictionary* project were very poor when they were hired. Despite Johnson's generosity toward these men, they probably were not **obsequious**. Johnson would have discouraged any flattering, fawning behavior toward himself.

8.

(germane) ➤ The fact that France, Italy, and Spain had already produced great dictionaries was **germane** to Johnson's project. It was pertinent because Johnson acted partly in the interest of national pride: He wanted England's dictionary to equal or surpass those of the other countries.

9.

(precocious) ➤ It is impressive that Johnson worked on the *Dictionary* during the prime of his life, not at the close of his literary career. Who knows: If Johnson had been a **precocious** child, he might have begun the dictionary at the age of ten!

10.

(patrimony) ➤ Johnson left Noah Webster and other later lexicographers an impressive **patrimony**. We know that Webster accepted the legacy because he borrowed thousands of definitions from Johnson's *Dictionary*.

EXERCISE 2   *Context Clues*

Directions. Scan the definitions in Column A. Then, think about how the boldface words are used in the sentences in Column B. To complete the exercise, match each definition in Column A with the correct Vocabulary Word from Column B. Write the letter of your choice on the line provided; then write the Vocabulary Word on the line preceding the definition.

COLUMN A	COLUMN B

COLUMN A

_____ **11.** word: _____
adj. outgoing; sociable

_____ **12.** word: _____
n. high spirits; invigoration; excitement

_____ **13.** word: _____
n. an inheritance from one's father or ancestors; any heritage or legacy

_____ **14.** word: _____
adj. too ready to please, praise, or obey; servile; fawning

_____ **15.** word: _____
n. politeness; courtesy; a polite action

_____ **16.** word: _____
adj. pertinent; to the point; truly relevant

_____ **17.** word: _____
adj. paying attention to the fine details of etiquette; meticulous; scrupulous; very exact

_____ **18.** word: _____
n. a minor weakness or fault; a minor but persistent personal failing; a shortcoming

_____ **19.** word: _____
n. someone who is an expert in some field, especially in art or in matters of taste

_____ **20.** word: _____
adj. showing unusually early development; mature or advanced for one's age

COLUMN B

(A) A greatly appreciated **patrimony** left by my father's great-grandfather is a copy of Johnson's two-volume *Dictionary of the English Language.*

(B) My father, who is very knowledgeable about lexicography as well as a **connoisseur** of rare books, keeps the dictionary in a safe.

(C) He is **punctilious** about caring for these rare leather-bound books. He even wears gloves to handle them.

(D) My father was a **precocious** child and recalls memorizing definitions from the dictionary at the age of four.

(E) I know more stories about my father's childhood, but they are not about lexicography and therefore would not be **germane** to this topic.

(F) My mother says that my father's only **foible** is talking about words too much. I don't think this is a serious deficiency at all!

(G) His **exhilaration** about the subject, especially about Johnson's achievements, adds to my enthusiasm about dictionaries.

(H) He is very **gregarious,** and in groups his tendencies are evident—he will talk to complete strangers about dictionaries and literature.

(I) Always aware of his manners, he does not want to bore anyone and goes into detail only if his listeners seem interested. They obviously appreciate his **civility**.

(J) Some people are a little **obsequious;** they may seem a little too eager to be nice to him because they feel intimidated.

EXERCISE 3 *Sentence Completion* ✍

Directions. For each of the following items, circle the letter of the choice that best completes the meaning of the sentence or sentences.

21. "I'd like to know more about Johnson," Gwen said. "Was he always ____, or was he friendly only as he got older?"
    (A) obsequious
    (B) germane
    (C) punctilious
    (D) precocious
    (E) gregarious

22. "In his later years he became a(n) ____ of conversation," Mrs. Baker said. "He considered conversation an art form, and he was a specialist at it."
    (A) civility
    (B) patrimony
    (C) connoisseur
    (D) exhilaration
    (E) foible

23. "He apparently found ____ in conversations with other literary figures. Such talks lifted his spirits."
    (A) foible
    (B) exhilaration
    (C) patrimony
    (D) connoisseur
    (E) civility

24. "What kind of ____ did Johnson leave his children?" Jesse asked. "Was it a large estate?"
    (A) civility
    (B) foible
    (C) exhilaration
    (D) patrimony
    (E) connoisseur

25. "He didn't have any children," Mrs. Baker replied with ____. She always tried to answer questions respectfully.
    (A) civility
    (B) patrimony
    (C) connoisseur
    (D) precociousness
    (E) exhilaration

26. "This question may be too far off the subject and not ____," Gwen said, "but was Johnson's biographer James Boswell as ____ as the sociable Johnson?"
    (A) gregarious . . . germane
    (B) punctilious . . . obsequious
    (C) germane . . . gregarious
    (D) obsequious . . . punctilious
    (E) precocious . . . germane

27. "Boswell behaved ____ toward Johnson," she said. "He found Johnson the most ____ companion possible. Johnson didn't seem to mind Boswell's servile manner toward him."
    (A) punctiliously . . . civil
    (B) obsequiously . . . exhilarating
    (C) precociously . . . obsequious
    (D) gregariously . . . germane
    (E) obsequiously . . . punctilious

28. "However, let's stay on the subject for now," Mrs. Baker said ____. She was a very precise person. "Let's talk about Johnson as an authority, or ____, of words."
    (A) gregariously . . . foible
    (B) precociously . . . civility
    (C) obsequiously . . . patrimony
    (D) precociously . . . exhilaration
    (E) punctiliously . . . connoisseur

29. Jesse said, "I've read that one of Johnson's ____ was impatience, but how could he have had such an imperfection and yet have been so ____, so scrupulous, about the *Dictionary*?"
    (A) patrimonies . . . precocious
    (B) civilities . . . germane
    (C) connoisseurs . . . gregarious
    (D) foibles . . . punctilious
    (E) patrimonies . . . civil

30. "I'm just sure Johnson was ____ as a child," Gwen said, "because he was such a genius as an adult. We shouldn't criticize him for his minor flaws, or ____."
    (A) precocious . . . foibles
    (B) germane . . . civilities
    (C) punctilious . . . foibles
    (D) obsequious . . . patrimonies
    (E) germane . . . connoisseurs

54 LESSON 13

MAKING NEW WORDS YOUR OWN

Lesson 14 | CONTEXT: History and Society

William Wilberforce: Britain's Antislavery Crusader

Last Tuesday during Quiz Bowl practice, our coach asked if we could name the greatest British activist for the abolition of slavery in the 1800s. Although no one on the team knew that it was William Wilberforce, the question launched a discussion about the abolition of slavery. Mr. Tucker, our coach and history teacher, told us that the British abolished slavery almost thirty years before the American Civil War even began. He told us about William Wilberforce.

In the following exercises, you will have the opportunity to expand your vocabulary by reading about Wilberforce and his fight against slavery. These ten Vocabulary Words will be used.

| affront | effusion | incarcerate | magnanimous | propitious |
| capitulate | guffaw | indulgent | munificent | querulous |

EXERCISE 1   *Wordbusting*

Directions. Follow these instructions for this word and the nine words on the next page.
- Figure out the word's meaning by looking at its **context,** its **structure,** and its **sound.** Fill in at least one of the three **CSS** boxes. Alternate which boxes you complete.
- Then, look up the word in a dictionary, read all of its meanings, and write the meaning of the word as it is used in the sentence.
- Follow this same process for each of the Vocabulary Words on the next page. You will need to draw your own map for each word. Use a separate sheet of paper.

1.

affront ⟶ "Wilberforce's opposition to buying and selling kidnapped people was an **affront** to those who were making money from it," Mr. Tucker pointed out.

| Context: | Structure: | Sound: |

| Dictionary: |

2.

(capitulate) ➔ "He was a member of Parliament and one of the leaders of a social reform group that forced Parliament in 1807 to **capitulate,** or give in, to their demand for the abolition of the slave trade."

3.

(effusion) ➔ "I didn't know Britain abolished slavery that early," said Kay. Mr. Tucker answered, and in the **effusion,** or pouring forth, of discussion, I heard him say that while slave trade was abolished in the British colonies, people who were already in slavery were not freed.

4.

(guffaw) ➔ In the meantime, Charlie was clowning around with some of the other team members. I could hear them **guffawing** at something. The coach ignored their loud laughter.

5.

(incarcerate) ➔ "The distinction I was making," Mr. Tucker, continued, "for those who did not hear me, is that slaves who were purchased before 1807 remained as **incarcerated** workers. They were not set free."

6.

(indulgent) ➔ "Slaveholders at that time thought that they were being **indulgent** if they treated enslaved people well. They were not eager to give these people their freedom."

7.

(magnanimous) ➔ "Wilberforce was a **magnanimous** man; his efforts were noble and unselfish. He worked with fierce dedication to abolish slavery," continued Mr. Tucker.

8.

(munificent) ➔ "Wilberforce's **munificent** attitude came from the teachings of evangelical Christianity, which preached generosity and love toward all. He began his abolition work soon after his conversion to evangelism."

9.

(propitious) ➔ "Many people at the time did not think that abolishing slavery was **propitious,**" Mr. Tucker continued. "But despite the fact that influential people did not look favorably on his beliefs, Wilberforce worked tirelessly for his cause."

10.

(querulous) ➔ "So the slaveholders did not practice Christianity?" asked Mike, **querulous** as always. Mike can never resist taking issue with people's arguments.

EXERCISE 2 *Context Clues* 🖎

Directions. Scan the definitions in Column A. Then, think about how the boldface words are used in the sentences in Column B. To complete the exercise, match each definition in Column A with the correct Vocabulary Word from Column B. Write the letter of your choice on the line provided; then write the Vocabulary Word on the line preceding the definition.

COLUMN A	COLUMN B
____ **11.** word: _____ *n.* a pouring forth; an unrestrained expression of feeling in talking or writing	(A) Mike's question about slaveholders began another **effusion** of comments, and soon everyone was bursting with ideas and questions.
____ **12.** word: _____ *adj.* complaining; faultfinding; peevish	(B) Mr. Tucker asserted that slavery is never a **propitious** condition. It is always wrong to keep people in a state of bondage.
____ **13.** word: _____ *adj.* very lenient; not strict enough; making allowances	(C) Joy, whose ancestors were slaves, said that the slaves' masters were far from **indulgent**. In fact, they were usually very demanding.
____ **14.** word: _____ *n.* an open, intentional insult; *v.* to insult openly; to offend	(D) "I take it as an **affront** when people assume that slavery had any positive aspects. I know they don't mean to be insulting, but it's very thoughtless."
____ **15.** word: _____ *adj.* favorable; favorably inclined	(E) "Usually, I'm **magnanimous** enough to let these comments pass," Joy continued.
____ **16.** word: _____ *adj.* extremely generous; very liberal and lavish in giving	(F) "I try not to be **querulous,** but it's hard to not get annoyed sometimes," she added.
____ **17.** word: _____ *n.* a loud or coarse burst of laughter; a horselaugh; *v.* to laugh loudly or coarsely	(G) "So what finally happened to Wilber Horse?" asked Charlie, with a **guffaw,** never missing a chance to clown and try to make us laugh.
____ **18.** word: _____ *v.* to surrender on certain terms; to give up; to stop resisting	(H) "He retired from Parliament in 1825 but continued to denounce the slave trade and the **incarceration** it involved," Mr. Tucker replied.
____ **19.** word: _____ *v.* to imprison; to confine	(I) "He died a month before Parliament **capitulated** completely, yielding to his demands and abolishing the slave trade," Mr. Tucker added.
____ **20.** word: _____ *adj.* noble in spirit; generous in forgiving; unselfish; rising above petty, mean concerns	(J) "Wilberforce was truly **munificent,** giving so much time and energy to the cause," said Joy. "I wonder why we had never heard of him."

EXERCISE 3 *Sentence Completion* ✍

Directions. For each of the following items, circle the letter of the choice that best completes the meaning of the sentence or sentences.

21. "Wilberforce's _____ paid off in the end," said Mr. Tucker. "His charity to the cause of abolition was not wasted."
    (A) affront
    (B) munificence
    (C) effusion
    (D) guffaw
    (E) incarceration

22. "Yeah, he died," said Charlie, breaking the tension with his customary _____. "What a great payoff!" Other team members also started to laugh.
    (A) effusive
    (B) indulgent
    (C) munificent
    (D) guffawing
    (E) magnanimous

23. "His dedication to the abolition of slavery was obvious in his _____ letters and speeches. His torrent of writing and speechmaking spread to other countries," said Mr. Tucker.
    (A) indulgent
    (B) querulous
    (C) effusive
    (D) magnanimous
    (E) propitious

24. "Social attitudes began to change, and more people began to view his work as _____. They developed a more approving opinion of abolition," Mr. Tucker continued.
    (A) querulous
    (B) effusive
    (C) irrevocable
    (D) munificent
    (E) propitious

25. "Britain's _____ to Wilberforce's demands influenced slavery elsewhere. It set a precedent for other governments to give in to abolitionists' demands."
    (A) incarceration
    (B) effusion
    (C) capitulation
    (D) querulousness
    (E) affrontery

26. "Venezuela and Mexico gave in to the abolitionists in 1810, soon after Britain outlawed the slave trade," said Mr. Tucker. "They then worked with _____, or high-mindedness, to stop this _____ of human beings and make all peoples free."
    (A) magnanimity . . . incarceration
    (B) munificence . . . incarceration
    (C) capitulation . . . indulgence
    (D) effusiveness . . . capitulation
    (E) querulousness . . . indulgence

27. "In 1817, Spain took a(n) _____ step and outlawed slavery. This encouraging action was weakened, however, by the government's _____ in making allowances for those who continued to buy and sell slaves."
    (A) indulgent . . . buffoonery
    (B) querulous . . . munificence
    (C) munificent . . . affront
    (D) propitious . . . indulgence
    (E) effusive . . . guffaw

28. Charlie spoke seriously for once. "They should have punished people who wouldn't give in or _____ to the new law."
    (A) guffaw
    (B) effuse
    (C) capitulate
    (D) propitiate
    (E) affront

29. "Resisting such an obviously important change is an _____ to humanity," he continued.
    (A) affront
    (B) indulgence
    (C) capitulation
    (D) effusion
    (E) incarceration

30. "I haven't been _____, have I?" asked Joy. "I actually enjoyed the discussion. I think it's great that we became so excited and _____ about this subject. "
    (A) incarcerated . . . indulgent
    (B) propitious . . . munificent
    (C) magnanimous . . . effusive
    (D) indulgent . . . magnanimous
    (E) querulous . . . effusive

58 LESSON 14

MAKING NEW WORDS YOUR OWN

Lesson 15 **CONTEXT: History and Society**

Advancing the Flags

In the late nineteenth century, people in Great Britain, Germany, Italy, and other European countries were excited by the phrase "advance of the flag." The phrase stood for a country's pride in expanding its powers beyond its own borders. Such expansion is known as imperialism. For reasons of national pride, prestige, and economic gain, European countries sought colonies and power bases in other parts of the world. Africa was a prime target of European imperialism—and an example of imperialism at its most aggressive.

In the following exercises, you will have the opportunity to expand your vocabulary by reading about European imperialism before World War I. These ten Vocabulary Words will be used.

abeyance	homogeneous	inscrutable	perfidious	primordial
discrepancy	illicit	inundate	pervade	sumptuous

EXERCISE 1 *Wordbusting* ✍

Directions. Follow these instructions for this word and the nine words on the next page.
- Figure out the word's meaning by looking at its **context**, its **structure**, and its **sound**. Fill in at least one of the three **CSS** boxes. Alternate which boxes you complete.
- Then, look up the word in a dictionary, read all of its meanings, and write the meaning of the word as it is used in the sentence.
- Follow this same process for each of the Vocabulary Words on the next page. You will need to draw your own map for each word. Use a separate sheet of paper.

1.

(abeyance) → Once European imperialism was put into motion in Africa south of the Sahara, an **abeyance** of the practice became difficult. Some people, however, wanted to temporarily suspend imperialistic activities to determine their impact.

Context:	Structure:	Sound:

Dictionary:

2.
discrepancy →

Governments led citizens to believe that imperialism was good for under-developed countries, but often a **discrepancy** existed between propaganda and the facts. The public, however, was unaware of any such inconsistency.

3.
sumptuous →

Many imperialists were not at all interested in the welfare of African soci-eties. They sought only the profits from raw materials, investments, and markets needed to maintain their own **sumptuous**, luxurious life styles.

4.
illicit →

Although many of the imperialistic practices were unfair and inhumane, they may not actually have been **illicit**, because formal laws often did not exist or apply in the new colonies.

5.
inscrutable →

The motives for European expansion should not be **inscrutable** to students who are aware of current events. They should not find it hard to under-stand that many countries practice imperialism today for exactly the same reasons countries did in the nineteenth century: greed.

6.
perfidious →

Imperialistic countries used all kinds of methods, including military force. The European military forces were mostly loyal to their leaders, but some were considered **perfidious** because of their sympathy with the people they were conquering. This attitude bordered on treachery in the minds of some commanders.

7.
inundate →

European countries seeking more wealth, land, and power **inundated** Africa after 1870. The Africans were completely overwhelmed, and Euro-peans had Africa divided within twenty-five years.

8.
homogeneous →

Africa was an enormous region inhabited by many distinct peoples. These groups did not have uniform governments or customs and therefore were not **homogeneous**. It was easy for them to be divided into colonies.

9.
primordial →

Some of the invaded regions had very ancient and rich traditions dating so far into the past that they seemed **primordial**.

10.
pervade →

When we consider these old civilizations, the widespread idea of European superiority that **pervaded** the imperialist countries seems absurd.

EXERCISE 2 *Context Clues* ✍

Directions. Scan the definitions in Column A. Then, think about how the boldface words are used in the sentences in Column B. To complete the exercise, match each definition in Column A with the correct Vocabulary Word from Column B. Write the letter of your choice on the line provided; then write the Vocabulary Word on the line preceding the definition.

COLUMN A

_____ **11.** word: _____
adj. deliberately faithless; treacherous

_____ **12.** word: _____
adj. forbidden by law; improper; unauthorized

_____ **13.** word: _____
n. an inconsistency; a contradiction; a difference

_____ **14.** word: _____
v. to cover by overflowing; to flood; to overwhelm (as if by a flood)

_____ **15.** word: _____
adj. costly; magnificent; luxurious; lavish

_____ **16.** word: _____
adj. mysterious or obscure; hard to grasp; not easily understood

_____ **17.** word: _____
n. a temporary suspension of an activity; a state of being put aside for future action

_____ **18.** word: _____
adj. from earliest times; primitive; fundamental; original

_____ **19.** word: _____
adj. of the same kind or nature; composed of similar or identical parts or elements; uniform

_____ **20.** word: _____
v. to extend all over; to spread or be diffused throughout

COLUMN B

(A) David Livingstone (1813–1873), an **inscrutable** Scottish missionary and physician, explored the interior of Africa. His original reason for going to South Africa in 1840 was to be a medical missionary, but his goals were sometimes hard to understand.

(B) Livingstone must have been fascinated by the **primordial** landscape of Africa. It seemed to have been unchanged for thousands of years.

(C) He explored many lakes and rivers, as well as areas that were sometimes **inundated** after heavy rains.

(D) Livingstone saw that the groups he visited were not always **homogeneous.** They had quite different characteristics.

(E) While exploring Africa, Livingstone did not stay in **sumptuous** houses. The tents and huts he lived in were quite simple.

(F) Livingstone became distressed by the African slave trade. Slave trading, he discovered, was **illicit** in some countries but legal in others.

(G) He called, not for a mere **abeyance** of the slave trade, but for a permanent stop to it.

(H) Some articles contain **discrepancies** in facts about Livingstone, and these variances can be confusing.

(I) All contact with Livingstone was lost for several years. Fellow explorer Henry Stanley, sent to find Livingstone in 1869, finally succeeded in 1871. Stanley proved himself to be a loyal, not **perfidious,** friend by carrying on Livingstone's work after the Scottish explorer's death.

(J) The African explorations of Stanley and Livingstone helped make possible the imperialism that eventually **pervaded** Africa. One wonders what the two men would have thought of the consequences of their explorations.

Sentence Completion 👉

Directions. For each of the following items, circle the letter of the choice that best completes the meaning of the sentence or sentences.

21. Can you even begin to understand the enormous greed of King Leopold II of Belgium (1835–1909)? I find his greed____, as difficult to grasp as a puzzle without a solution.
 (A) homogeneous
 (B) primordial
 (C) inscrutable
 (D) perfidious
 (E) illicit

22. Leopold's greed evidently expanded throughout Belgium and also eventually ____ his so-called "Congo Free State."
 (A) homogenized
 (B) reviled
 (C) corroborated
 (D) vindicated
 (E) pervaded

23. Although Leopold's activities were often unsuitable, they were not ____ because the major powers in 1885 legally recognized the Congo Free State as being under his rule.
 (A) primordial
 (B) illicit
 (C) homogeneous
 (D) sumptuous
 (E) perfidious

24. There was nothing to keep Leopold's exploitation of the Congo in ____, much less permanently put an end to it.
 (A) pervasion
 (B) sumptuousness
 (C) discrepancy
 (D) abeyance
 (E) inundation

25. Leopold employed agents whose goals were ____, identical to his own. Like Leopold, these agents did not hesitate to force Africans to work for them.
 (A) homogeneous
 (B) illicit
 (C) primordial
 (D) sumptuous
 (E) inscrutable

26. Since ____ times, before history began, the Africans had never known such cruelty as now ____ their land.
 (A) perfidious . . . pervaded
 (B) homogeneous . . . inundated
 (C) primordial . . . pervaded
 (D) illicit . . . homogenized
 (E) sumptuous . . . inundated

27. Leopold would have done anything, whether lawful or ____, for personal gain. Few of his subjects dared any deceitful, or ____, acts against him.
 (A) sumptuous . . . inscrutable
 (B) homogeneous . . . primordial
 (C) illicit . . . perfidious
 (D) inscrutable . . . illicit
 (E) perfidious . . . homogeneous

28. Leopold's motives may not be ____ if you understand the commercial importance of the Congo's rubber trees. He was able to make millions by ____, or glutting, the export market with rubber.
 (A) homogeneous . . . pervading
 (B) primordial . . . homogenizing
 (C) sumptuous . . . inundating
 (D) primordial . . . pervading
 (E) inscrutable . . . inundating

29. Europeans who became rich from the rubber trade adopted ____ lifestyles. Their wealth ____ every aspect of their lives.
 (A) primordial . . . reviled
 (B) sumptuous . . . pervaded
 (C) perfidious . . . inundated
 (D) sumptuous . . . homogenized
 (E) pervasive . . . inundated

30. Between two books I have consulted there was a(n)____ about the Congo's exact size. The contradictory figures suspended my research: I put my studies in ____ until I could verify which book was correct.
 (A) abeyance . . . discrepancy
 (B) sumptuousness . . . inscrutability
 (C) perfidy . . . discrepancy
 (D) discrepancy . . . abeyance
 (E) inundation . . . pervasion

MAKING NEW WORDS YOUR OWN

Lesson 16 CONTEXT: History and Society
St. Joan and Bernard Shaw

What does Joan of Arc (1412–1431), the young French woman who led an army to victory over the English at Orléans and who was later burned at the stake for witchcraft, have in common with Bernard Shaw (1856–1950), one of Ireland's most famous dramatists? Shaw wrote a play based on Joan's life, titled *Saint Joan*, that was first produced three years after her canonization as a saint. The discussion about Shaw's life, the play, and St. Joan's life is about to begin in my English class. Please sit in.

In the following exercises, you will have the opportunity to expand your vocabulary by reading about St. Joan and Bernard Shaw. Below are ten Vocabulary Words that will be used in these exercises.

chastise	deplore	emanate	intercede	obnoxious
demagogue	detriment	harbinger	irrevocable	prevaricate

EXERCISE 1 Wordbusting ✍

Directions. Follow these instructions for this word and the nine words on the next page.
- Figure out the word's meaning by looking at its **context,** its **structure,** and its **sound.** Fill in at least one of the three **CSS** boxes. Alternate which boxes you complete.
- Then, look up the word in a dictionary, read all of its meanings, and write the meaning of the word as it is used in the sentence.
- Follow this same process for each of the Vocabulary Words on the next page. You will need to draw your own map for each word. Use a separate sheet of paper.

1.

(chastise) ⟶ "How many of you have finished reading *Saint Joan*?" Mr. Durand asked. "I won't **chastise** you today if you haven't, but I may scold you if you haven't finished it by tomorrow."

Context:	Structure:	Sound:

Dictionary:

2.
(demagogue) →
"I don't mean to be a **demagogue**—isn't that what you said a rabble-rouser is called?—but I read the play in the time you gave us, and I don't think it's fair to give others more time," said Alan, our unofficial class upstart.

3.
(deplore) →
"How many others **deplore** my decision?" Mr. Durand asked. "Or do you approve of it and agree that we can use the time today to talk generally about Shaw and *Saint Joan*?"

4.
(detriment) →
"I'm sure there is no **detriment,** or harm, done to those studious few who have read the entire play and its fascinating preface."

5.
(emanate) →
"We may wonder how so many great plays issued from just one man, but just think of all the plays that **emanated** from the mind of Shakespeare."

6.
(harbinger) →
"Didn't Shaw's plays **harbinger** a change in modern drama?" Janell asked. "His were the first plays to indicate that 'the action is in the language . . . not in the unrolling of plot.'"

7.
(intercede) →
Alan, true to form, started arguing with Janell about her question, and Mr. Durand had to step in and settle the dispute. He **interceded** by saying, "Shaw didn't develop that type of drama, but he certainly did his share to popularize it."

8.
(irrevocable) →
"Mr. Durand, do you think Joan of Arc's story appealed to Shaw because her fate was so **irrevocable**?" Ima asked. "I mean, being burned at the stake is pretty final."

9.
(obnoxious) →
"That's an **obnoxious** idea," Micah said, obviously offended. "It wasn't Saint Joan's death but her life that interested and inspired Shaw—and that led to her being named a saint."

10.
(prevaricate) →
One thing we all admired about Joan was that when asked to renounce her visions, she refused. She could have **prevaricated** rather than being so direct.

EXERCISE 2 Context Clues 👈

Directions. Scan the definitions in Column A. Then, think about how the boldface words are used in the sentences in Column B. To complete the exercise, match each definition in Column A with the correct Vocabulary Word from Column B. Write the letter of your choice on the line provided; then write the Vocabulary Word on the line preceding the definition.

COLUMN A	COLUMN B

COLUMN A

_____ **11.** word: _____

v. to announce; to indicate what will follow; *n.* a forerunner; a herald

_____ **12.** word: _____

v. to issue from; to originate from

_____ **13.** word: _____

n. a leader who stirs up people by appealing to their emotions; a rabble-rouser

_____ **14.** word: _____

v. to evade the truth

_____ **15.** word: _____

n. damage; harm; injury; anything that causes damage or injury

_____ **16.** word: _____

adj. very disagreeable; highly offensive; hateful

_____ **17.** word: _____

v. to punish; to criticize severely; to scold

_____ **18.** word: _____

adj. not capable of being retracted, recalled, or withdrawn; unalterable

_____ **19.** word: _____

v. to feel very sorry about; to regret deeply; to lament; to disapprove of

_____ **20.** word: _____

v. to plead, or petition, on another's behalf; to act as a mediator in a dispute

COLUMN B

(A) "Mr. Durand, since Joan was a leader who inflamed people by playing on their emotions, wasn't she really a **demagogue**?" Alan asked smugly.

(B) "I don't know about that. But she certainly was a **harbinger** for a new day for France," Mr. Durand replied. "Dressed in armor, she was an imposing agent of change."

(C) "It seems that courage just poured out of her. She was like a solitary light **emanating** from an otherwise dark house," remarked Ima.

(D) "In his play, does Shaw make you **deplore** Joan's death?" Mr. Durand asked. "If so, how does he lead you to lament her fate?"

(E) "People should not have killed her just because they found her claims **obnoxious** and objected to her actions," Micah said. "Personally, I think her enemies overreacted."

(F) "It is more complicated than that," Mr. Durand said. "She was a **detriment** to the English, who were afraid she would cause even greater problems for them in the future."

(G) "The English could have simply **chastised** her," Janell said. "But I guess a severe reprimand would never have stopped Joan!"

(H) "During the play's trial scene, I kept wishing someone would **intercede** and negotiate on Joan's behalf," Ima said.

(I) "When she was questioned, she should have **prevaricated** to save herself," Micah said. "She might not have had to tell a direct lie."

(J) "What happened is history," Alan said, "and it can't be changed. The past is **irrevocable**."

EXERCISE 3 *Sentence Completion* ☞

Directions. For each of the following items, circle the letter of the choice that best completes the meaning of the sentence or sentences.

21. "What I find amazing about Shaw," Mr. Durand said, "is the number of ideas _____ from his mind."
(A) chastising
(B) harbingering
(C) prevaricating
(D) interceding
(E) emanating

22. "If he had been a political leader, George Bernard Shaw most certainly would have been a rabble-rousing _____, inciting people to action. I like to think that if he had been present at Joan's trial, he would have drummed up popular support for her."
(A) demagogue
(B) harbinger
(C) prevaricator
(D) detriment
(E) chastiser

23. "People were captivated by Shaw's wit and unusual ideas. Some saw him as a messenger, or _____, of social change."
(A) demagogue
(B) harbinger
(C) deplorer
(D) detriment
(E) chastisement

24. "Did he identify with Saint Joan?" asked a voice _____ from the back of the room.
(A) chastising
(B) prevaricating
(C) interceding
(D) emanating
(E) deploring

25. "That's a good question, Janell," Mr. Durand said. Abruptly, he changed the subject and _____ Alan for not paying attention. Alan blushed at the criticism.
(A) pervaded
(B) interceded
(C) chastised
(D) emanated
(E) prevaricated

26. "Playwrights are just _____ because they write fictional stories," Alan said. "I think Shaw sounds very disagreeable, almost _____."
(A) demagogues . . . irrevocable
(B) harbingers . . . obnoxious
(C) detriments . . . demagogic
(D) chastisers . . . irrevocable
(E) prevaricators . . . obnoxious

27. "Your views are a _____ to yourself, Alan, not an injury to anyone else," Mr. Durand said.
(A) harbinger
(B) demagogue
(C) prevarication
(D) deplorer
(E) detriment

28. "I deeply regret, even _____ your inability to see that both Shaw and Saint Joan believed strongly in certain values and ideas for which they sometimes were severely _____."
(A) prevaricate . . . deplored
(B) deplore . . . prevaricated
(C) intercede . . . emanated
(D) deplore . . . chastised
(E) emanate . . . interceded

29. "Please remember, Mr. Durand, that Alan enjoys his image as a(n) _____; he thinks it's his role to agitate the class," Micah said.
(A) detriment
(B) emanation
(C) demagogue
(D) harbinger
(E) prevaricator

30. Mr. Durand replied, "Your role is not _____, Alan; it can be changed!"
(A) obnoxious
(B) irrevocable
(C) emanative
(D) demagogic
(E) detrimental

MAKING NEW WORDS YOUR OWN

Lesson 17 | **CONTEXT:** History and Society
India: The Jewel of the British Empire

Last summer, my history club went to London. We visited several museums and saw photographs and documents from India. One museum guide explained that India was a British colony from the late 1700s until 1947. He also told us that India was once called the "jewel of the British empire" because of its size and resources. Unlike many of Britain's other colonies, India retained very little independence during the years of British control.

In the following exercises, you will have the opportunity to expand your vocabulary by reading about India under British rule. Below are ten Vocabulary Words that will be used in these exercises.

anarchy	commodious	extricate	menial	pestilence
cajole	ethnology	impair	nadir	rampant

EXERCISE 1 *Wordbusting*

Directions. Follow these instructions for this word and the nine words on the next page.
- Figure out the word's meaning by looking at its **context,** its **structure,** and its **sound.** Fill in at least one of the three **CSS** boxes. Alternate which boxes you complete.
- Then, look up the word in a dictionary, read all of its meanings, and write the meaning of the word as it is used in the sentence.
- Follow this same process for each of the Vocabulary Words on the next page. You will need to draw your own map for each word. Use a separate sheet of paper.

1.

(anarchy) ➞ "India remained in a state of **anarchy,** or political disorder, after independence from Britian was achieved," the guide said. "There had been rebellions for years, and Mohandas K. Gandhi, a Hindu reformer, had led a number of peaceful demonstrations for independence."

Context:

Structure:

Sound:

Dictionary:

2.

cajole

He continued: "Gandhi was a great leader and was sent to prison many times. The British government did not want to be **cajoled** into giving up India. Britain resisted the idea of being coaxed into action by the Indians."

3.

commodious

"Did the British treat the Indians badly?" asked James. "Well," answered the guide, "there was serious inequality. While the British lived in **commodious** houses, the great majority of Indians did not have spacious homes and, in fact, lived in great poverty."

4.

ethnology

"If you would like to know more about India," said the guide, "research in the field of **ethnology,** the branch of anthropology that deals with various races of people and their origins, distribution, characteristics, and cultures."

5.

extricate

We eventually had to **extricate** ourselves from the museum. Yet the information was so interesting that I hated to tear myself away.

6.

impair

In the bus we continued to talk. Anthony said that fighting between different religious groups and kingdoms had weakened India and **impaired** its ability to resist British colonialism.

7.

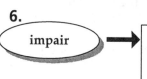
menial

"My great-grandparents worked as **menials** for the British," said Kamul. "People can learn a lot about their conquerors by being their domestic servants."

8.

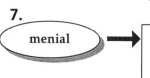
nadir

"At least India didn't represent the **nadir** of colonialism," said Amy. "The Belgians' actions in the Congo may have been the lowest point."

9.

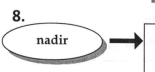
pestilence

"So do you think the British were a blessing or a **pestilence**?" asked Katie. "Were they a positive or a destructive influence in India? Was it better to have states fighting one another or to have one unified but oppressive government?"

10.

rampant

"Those are hard questions," said Anthony, "but remember the American Revolution—people want to rule themselves, and the desire to fight for independence becomes **rampant**; it spreads quickly and widely."

Name _____ Date _____ Class _____

EXERCISE 2 *Context Clues*

Directions. Scan the definitions in Column A. Then, think about how the boldface words are used in the sentences in Column B. To complete the exercise, match each definition in Column A with the correct Vocabulary Word from Column B. Write the letter of your choice on the line provided; then write the Vocabulary Word on the line preceding the definition.

COLUMN A

_____ **11.** word: _____
v. to release from an entanglement or a difficulty; to set free

_____ **12.** word: _____
adj. of or suited to a servant; servile; *n.* a domestic servant; a servile person

_____ **13.** word: _____
adj. growing without check or restraint; flourishing; widespread

_____ **14.** word: _____
v. to persuade by pleasant words; to coax with flattery and insincere talk; to wheedle

_____ **15.** word: _____
n. a contagious and often fatal disease that spreads rapidly; an illness of epidemic proportions; a destructive or evil influence or factor

_____ **16.** word: _____
n. the absence of government or law; political disorder

_____ **17.** word: _____
n. the point in the celestial sphere directly below the observer and opposite the zenith; the lowest possible point

_____ **18.** word: _____
n. the branch of anthropology that deals with recent societies or language groups, their distribution, characteristics, and cultures

_____ **19.** word: _____
v. to make worse; to damage or weaken

_____ **20.** word: _____
adj. roomy; spacious

COLUMN B

(A) A few days after my return from London, I went to the **commodious** public library and settled myself in the expansive interior to do my research on India.

(B) From one book I learned that Britain took control of India during the **rampant,** uncontrolled fighting of the Seven Years' War.

(C) In 1773, the East India Company **cajoled,** or convinced, the British Parliament to put it in control of India.

(D) The company acted as an unofficial government agency and prevented **anarchy** by providing order throughout India.

(E) Like other colonialists, the British in India had all their **menial** tasks such as housework done by the local people.

(F) An attitude of European superiority can spread like a **pestilence,** and, like a dangerous disease, have disastrous effects.

(G) Being conquered can **impair** a people's sense of themselves and undermine their confidence.

(H) Some Indians managed to **extricate,** or liberate themselves, from feelings of inferiority.

(I) According to the field of **ethnology,** which deals with customs and cultures, colonialism has far-reaching effects on both the conquered and the conquerors.

(J) Many Indians came to view British rule as the **nadir** of their history.

EXERCISE 3 · Sentence Completion 👈

Directions. For each of the following items, circle the letter of the choice that best completes the meaning of the sentence or sentences.

21. Many educated Indians began to _____ other Indians to fight against the British. In time, they enticed many others to join their cause.
    (A) extricate
    (B) impair
    (C) cajole
    (D) affront
    (E) chastise

22. In 1885, Indians formed the Hindu National Congress in an attempt to _____, or remove, themselves from British rule.
    (A) extricate
    (B) cajole
    (C) guffaw
    (D) impair
    (E) pervade

23. The educated Indians believed that if they worked hard, they, too, should have _____, or large, homes.
    (A) rampant
    (B) menial
    (C) impaired
    (D) commodious
    (E) extricable

24. They wanted Indians to stop acting as _____, or servants, to the British.
    (A) ethnologies
    (B) menials
    (C) anarchies
    (D) impairments
    (E) pestilences

25. These views, however, were not as _____ as some had hoped they would be. It would take time for the independence movement to spread through the whole country.
    (A) commodious
    (B) extricable
    (C) menial
    (D) pestilent
    (E) rampant

26. The British were not just a(n) _____, or a destructive influence, however. They also did some important work in India.
    (A) anarchic
    (B) cajoling
    (C) pestilent
    (D) ethnological
    (E) nadir

27. One _____ who wrote a book on Indian culture said the British saved India from a state of near _____, or chaos.
    (A) anarchy . . . impairment
    (B) cajolement . . . pestilence
    (C) rampancy . . . extrication
    (D) ethnologist . . . anarchy
    (E) ethnologist . . . commodiousness

28. He said that by _____ India from civil war, the British freed India from the lowest point, or _____, of its history.
    (A) cajoling . . . anarchy
    (B) extricating . . . nadir
    (C) impairing . . . pestilence
    (D) extricating . . . cajolement
    (E) impairing . . . ethnology

29. "Speaking _____, or with regard to culture and race, the most _____, harmful characteristic of British rule was their attitude of superiority toward the Indians."
    (A) ethnologically . . . pestilent
    (B) anarchically . . . commodious
    (C) menially . . . impaired
    (D) pestilently . . . rampant
    (E) cajolingly . . . commodious

30. The British _____ their own success by refusing to give up the _____ belief that they were superior. This far-reaching attitude weakened their ability to rule educated Indians.
    (A) cajoled . . . commodious
    (B) impaired . . . menial
    (C) extricated . . . rampant
    (D) cajoled . . . pestilent
    (E) impaired . . . rampant

MAKING NEW WORDS YOUR OWN

Lesson 18 | CONTEXT: History and Society

Nothing to Fear: The British in World War II

Last summer when my family took a trip to Arizona, we stopped in Phoenix to stay with my great-uncle Derek. One night, after my parents had gone to bed, Derek took out his old scrapbooks and told me stories about his years in the British army. When he was nineteen, he fell in love with and married a young British woman, and the couple settled in England. Shortly after their marriage, World War II began, and Derek left his new home to join the army.

In the following exercises, you will have the opportunity to expand your vocabulary by reading about the British in World War II. Below are ten Vocabulary Words that will be used in these exercises.

cadaverous	elocution	maim	promulgate	subversion
consign	incorrigible	profuse	strident	virulent

EXERCISE 1 *Wordbusting*

Directions. Follow these instructions for this word and the nine words on the next page.
- Figure out the word's meaning by looking at its **context,** its **structure,** and its **sound.** Fill in at least one of the three **CSS** boxes. Alternate which boxes you complete.
- Then, look up the word in a dictionary, read all of its meanings, and write the meaning of the word as it is used in the sentence.
- Follow this same process for each of the Vocabulary Words on the next page. You will need to draw your own map for each word. Use a separate sheet of paper.

1.

cadaverous → Uncle Derek showed me pictures of himself during the war. He looked so **cadaverous** in the pictures that I barely recognized the gaunt, pale man as my great-uncle. "We had to learn to do without a lot of things," he told me.

Context:	Structure:	Sound:

Dictionary:

2.

consign ➤ "I was **consigned** to a base near the English Channel," he said. "When France fell to Germany in 1940, Britain was left exposed to attack. I often wished that I had not been sent to such a dangerous place."

3.

elocution ➤ "Luckily," he continued, "Winston Churchill became Britain's prime minister just after France fell to Germany. His inspiring **elocution** kept our morale up. His style of public speaking helped convince us that we could defeat the Nazis."

4.

incorrigible ➤ "Unlike the previous prime minister, Neville Chamberlain, Churchill realized that Hitler was **incorrigible**: Churchill knew that Hitler was driven by ruthless ambition and would not honor treaties."

5.

maim ➤ "At first," he said, "most of the British were against the war. Millions of people had been **maimed** or killed in World War I, and the images of wounded soldiers were still fresh in the minds of many British citizens."

6.

profuse ➤ "The British had fresh and **profuse** memories from the previous war, but when Hitler invaded Poland and then Belgium, the Netherlands, Luxembourg, and France, they realized it would be necessary to fight again.

7.

promulgate ➤ "Even people who were initially sympathetic to the Germans for having to pay heavy compensation to the rest of the world after World War I now **promulgated** the idea that Hitler had to be stopped," he said. "Most people supported the ending of Hitler's regime."

8.

strident ➤ "I still remember the **strident** voice of my commander, harshly calling out orders. Our forces along the English Channel were assigned to eliminate the French navy to keep it from falling into German hands."

9.

subversion ➤ "Anyone convicted of **subversion** was severely punished. The British government was wary of Nazi sympathizers attempting to undermine its plans."

10.

virulent ➤ Uncle Derek pulled out a letter from a friend who had been accused of treason. "As you can imagine, Joe was extremely upset by the **virulent** accusation," said Uncle Derek. "It was a bitter and spiteful attack on his character."

EXERCISE 2   *Context Clues* ✍

Directions. Scan the definitions in Column A. Then, think about how the boldface words are used in the sentences in Column B. To complete the exercise, match each definition in Column A with the correct Vocabulary Word from Column B. Write the letter of your choice on the line provided; then write the Vocabulary Word on the line preceding the definition.

COLUMN A	COLUMN B

COLUMN A

_____ **11.** word: _____
adj. giving freely, extravagant; plentiful

_____ **12.** word: _____
adj. very poisonous or harmful; deadly; intensely bitter or spiteful

_____ **13.** word: _____
adj. having or making a harsh sound; shrill

_____ **14.** word: _____
v. to deliver; to deliver as goods to be sold; to send; to hand over; to assign to an undesirable position or place

_____ **15.** word: _____
n. the art of public speaking; a style or manner of public speaking or reading

_____ **16.** word: _____
n. the overthrowing or undermining of something established, such as a government

_____ **17.** word: _____
adj. corpselike; pale and ghastly; thin and gaunt; haggard

_____ **18.** word: _____
n. a person who will not be reformed; *adj.* incapable of being corrected or reformed; persistently bad

_____ **19.** word: _____
v. to make known to the public, declare; to make widespread

_____ **20.** word: _____
v. to wound or injure seriously; to disable in some way; to mutilate; to cripple

COLUMN B

(A) "This is Joe," said Uncle Derek, pointing to a picture of a man who was so sickly that he seemed hardly alive. His **cadaverous** face seemed to stare at me from the old photograph.

(B) "Joe was **maimed** during an attack, and the wound left him permanently disabled," Uncle Derek said.

(C) "Joe then devoted himself to **elocution**. Following the example of Churchill, he inspired us with his speeches."

(D) "I am sure the officers regretted their vicious attacks on his character," said Uncle Derek. "There had been no cause for their **virulent** words."

(E) "Some of them were **profuse** in their apologies, though it was now too late to take their words back."

(F) "During the bombing of London, Joe was in charge of **consigning**, or giving out, goods to the soldiers," Uncle Derek continued.

(G) "Hitler hoped the bombing would cause a **subversion** of our defense, but our plans were not altered."

(H) "The British saw Hitler as an **incorrigible**," said Uncle Derek. "They began to see that he was incapable of being changed."

(I) "For many British, the **strident** sounds of air-raid sirens became a piercing reminder of their determination to win the war."

(J) "People rallied together. The **promulgation** of hope for a peaceful future was the only compensation for the deaths of those they loved," he said.

EXERCISE 3 *Sentence Completion* ✍

Directions. For each of the following items, circle the letter of the choice that best completes the meaning of the sentence or sentences.

21. "The United States soon began conveying goods to the British army," said Uncle Derek. "These _____ helped Britain resist Hitler's aggression."
   (A) virulences
   (B) subversions
   (C) consignments
   (D) elocutions
   (E) incorrigibles

22. "Still, these goods and Churchill's skill as a(n) _____ were not enough. Supplies and speeches were important, but Britain needed a strong military."
   (A) consignment
   (B) incorrigible
   (C) virulence
   (D) elocutionist
   (E) cadaver

23. "Britain was able to _____ some German plans with its superior intelligence operation," he said.
   (A) maim
   (B) consign
   (C) capitulate
   (D) subvert
   (E) extricate

24. "But the Germans damaged and disabled many British ships and aircraft through frequent and _____ bombing. And, of course, countless soldiers were _____ in these extensive attacks."
   (A) incorrigible . . . consigned
   (B) profuse . . . maimed
   (C) strident . . . subverted
   (D) virulent . . . guffawed
   (E) profuse . . . cajoled

25. "Soon," he said, "the _____ sounds of air raids were less frequent, and fewer people were killed or _____ by bombs."
   (A) strident . . . maimed
   (B) incorrigible . . . consigned
   (C) promulgated . . . cajoled
   (D) elocutionary . . . maimed
   (E) cadaverous . . . subverted

26. "Churchill began using his _____ skills to make moving speeches about post-war plans," said Uncle Derek. "He _____ the sense that the British would prevail."
   (A) profuse . . . maimed
   (B) subversive . . . consigned
   (C) elocutionary . . . promulgated
   (D) consignable . . . capitulated
   (E) virulent . . . promulgated

27. "Churchill's speeches moved the British, lifted their morale, and united them in the fight against the _____ Hitler and his persistent evil," continued Uncle Derek.
   (A) strident
   (B) subversive
   (C) virulent
   (D) incorrigible
   (E) profuse

28. "There could never be sufficient compensation for the grief of losing loved ones, but Hitler's defeat provided some relief from the _____ of difficult memories," Uncle Derek said.
   (A) elocution
   (B) cajole
   (C) subversive
   (D) profusion
   (E) virulence

29. We knew that we were going to look gaunt and _____ from staying up all night.
   (A) consignable
   (B) cadaverous
   (C) strident
   (D) virulent
   (E) incorrigible

30. Although tired from not having slept, we went for a morning walk in the desert. Uncle Derek pointed out several poisonous snakes whose _____ bites could be deadly.
   (A) virulent
   (B) subversive
   (C) elocutionary
   (D) cadaverous
   (E) strident

MAKING NEW WORDS YOUR OWN

Lesson 19 | CONTEXT: History and Society

Mary Astell's Serious Proposal

"Happy retreat!" writes Mary Astell (1668–1731) in her book *A Serious Proposal to Ladies*. Just what kind of retreat did Astell have in mind? She proposed the creation of a special place where single women could withdraw from society and become educated. Astell recognized that English society at the time did not value the education of women and actually barred women from educational advantages. Believing strongly that "women are [as] capable of learning as men are," Astell proposed a retreat in which women could acquire "useful knowledge" and "right ideas."

In the following exercises, you will have the opportunity to expand your vocabulary by reading about Mary Astell and *A Serious Proposal to Ladies*. These ten Vocabulary Words will be used.

calumny	impassive	mollify	recant	retaliate
contingency	litigation	propensity	repudiate	sedentary

EXERCISE 1 *Wordbusting* ✍

Directions. Follow these instructions for this word and the nine words on the next page.
- Figure out the word's meaning by looking at its **context,** its **structure,** and its **sound.** Fill in at least one of the three **CSS** boxes. Alternate which boxes you complete.
- Then, look up the word in a dictionary, read all of its meanings, and write the meaning of the word as it is used in the sentence.
- Follow this same process for each of the Vocabulary Words on the next page. You will need to draw your own map for each word. Use a separate sheet of paper.

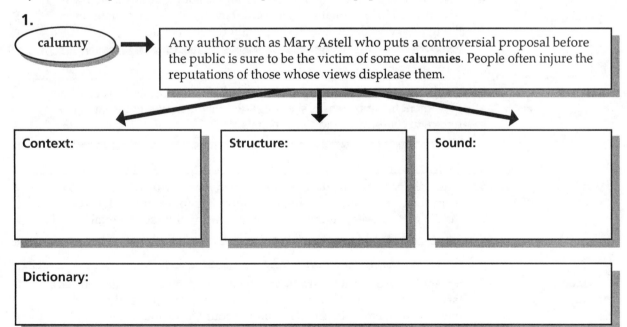

1.

calumny →

Any author such as Mary Astell who puts a controversial proposal before the public is sure to be the victim of some **calumnies**. People often injure the reputations of those whose views displease them.

Context:

Structure:

Sound:

Dictionary:

2.
contingency →

Astell probably did not imagine that her retreat could prepare women for every **contingency** in society. Even the most thorough education could not prepare students for absolutely anything that might happen in their lives.

3.
impassive →

Astell did not expect women to lead **impassive,** or emotionless, lives, but she did want women to be able to control their emotions and to accomplish worthy goals that went beyond "trifles and gaieties and secular affairs."

4.
litigation →

Astell tried to correct society's discrimination against women. At that time, complaints of discrimination against women could not be settled with **litigation** because there were no laws protecting women's rights.

5.
mollify →

Astell made no attempt to **mollify,** or pacify, readers who might be angered by her belief that women's minds should be filled "with a stock of solid and useful knowledge."

6.
propensity →

Astell felt that women had the same **propensity** for learning as men. It was a matter of cultivating this inclination with education.

7.
recant →

Astell had definite, strong opinions about the abilities of women. I would be surprised to learn that she ever **recanted** any of those opinions, even though some readers thought she should retract them.

8.
repudiate →

Astell **repudiated** society's established beliefs concerning the capabilities of women. In her proposal, she suggested that men would resent her refusal to conform to traditional beliefs.

9.
retaliate →

Astell did not want to **retaliate** against men for denying advantages to women. She was more interested in improving opportunities for women than in getting even with men for denying women these advantages.

10.
sedentary →

She spoke out against the traditional belief that women should lead **sedentary** lives. She felt that most women did not enjoy merely sitting all the time, reading, embroidering, or talking about "froth and trifles."

EXERCISE 2 — Context Clues ✍

Directions. Scan the definitions in Column A. Then, think about how the boldface words are used in the sentences in Column B. To complete the exercise, match each definition in Column A with the correct Vocabulary Word from Column B. Write the letter of your choice on the line provided; then write the Vocabulary Word on the line preceding the definition.

COLUMN A	COLUMN B
_____ **11.** word: _____ *n.* a natural tendency or ability	(A) Jay's mother, an attorney, cited an excerpt from Mary Astell's book in a **litigation** she filed for a client.
_____ **12.** word: _____ *v.* to take back formally or publicly; to withdraw or retract an opinion expressed in the past	(B) The case involved a woman who was upset by the **calumny** she swore was uttered against her by her employer. She sued him for his wrongful statement.
_____ **13.** word: _____ *n.* a possible happening; a chance event; something that depends on chance or uncertain conditions	(C) Since the employer would not openly admit to being wrong and would not **recant** his slanderous comments, the woman had to go to court.
_____ **14.** word: _____ *n.* the carrying on of a lawsuit; a lawsuit	(D) The employer said the woman was just trying to pay him back for reducing her work hours. But it was not her intention to **retaliate**.
_____ **15.** word: _____ *v.* to return an injury for an injury; to get even	(E) The woman did not have a **propensity** for litigation. It was not her inclination to confront, and she would have preferred to work out the matter without going to court.
_____ **16.** word: _____ *n.* a false statement made to injure someone's reputation; slander	(F) "My client does not agree with her employer's attitude toward women," Jay's mother wrote. "In fact, she strongly **repudiates** it."
_____ **17.** word: _____ *adj.* used to sitting much of the time; moving little and rarely; staying in one place	(G) "She will not be **mollified** by pleasing but empty words. As Mary Astell said, women have 'the faculty of thinking.'"
_____ **18.** word: _____ *adj.* not feeling or showing emotion	(H) According to Jay's mother, cases of alleged slander are never presented **impassively;** they always involve strong feelings.
_____ **19.** word: _____ *v.* to completely reject; to disown; to refuse to accept	(I) She was rarely **sedentary** as she researched and prepared the case. She was always on the go.
_____ **20.** word: _____ *v.* to soothe the temper of; to appease; to pacify	(J) She tried to prepare for every **contingency** because she didn't know exactly what might occur during the trial.

EXERCISE 3   *Sentence Completion* ✍

Directions. For each of the following items, circle the letter of the choice that best completes the meaning of the sentence or sentences.

21. The class discussion about Astell's proposal was lengthy. Some students were tired of being _____ for so long and fidgeted in their seats.
    (A) repudiated
    (B) calumnious
    (C) sedentary
    (D) contingent
    (E) retaliative

22. Most students agreed with Astell, but Yvonne _____ her ideas. She made her disagreement very plain.
    (A) mollified
    (B) consigned
    (C) retaliated
    (D) recanted
    (E) repudiated

23. Yvonne said she had a _____ for being old-fashioned. For one thing, she enjoyed reading romance novels and, for another, "froth and trifles" might have some importance.
    (A) retaliation
    (B) propensity
    (C) impassiveness
    (D) litigation
    (E) contingency

24. "You're from the Stone Age!" Greg yelled angrily, but an indifferent Yvonne sat _____.
    (A) impassively
    (B) contingently
    (C) calumniously
    (D) clandestinely
    (E) solicitously

25. "I'm not paying attention to any _____ from you because I know you delight in making me look bad," Yvonne said.
    (A) contingency
    (B) retaliation
    (C) litigation
    (D) calumny
    (E) impassiveness

26. However, Yvonne tried to _____ by insulting Greg. Her attack surprised Mr. Hansen, but he put on a bland, _____ expression.
    (A) repudiate . . . sedentary
    (B) recant . . . calumnious
    (C) mollify . . . saline
    (D) repudiate . . . retaliatory
    (E) retaliate . . . impassive

27. "Class, I thought I had prepared my lesson for every _____, but I didn't expect a fight," Mr. Hansen said. "You don't have to remain _____, but don't quarrel."
    (A) calumny . . . contingent
    (B) propensity . . . sedentary
    (C) contingency . . . impassive
    (D) retaliation . . . mollified
    (E) litigation . . . impassive

28. "Yvonne, you don't have to _____ your views. But some people may disagree with you and react very strongly."
    (A) mollify
    (B) recant
    (C) retaliate
    (D) litigate
    (E) contingent

29. The discussion jumped to current _____ about women's rights. "Would Astell have _____ or approved the motives behind these lawsuits?" Mr. Hansen asked.
    (A) contingencies . . . retaliated
    (B) propensities . . . recanted
    (C) litigation . . . repudiated
    (D) calumnies . . . mollified
    (E) propensities . . . retaliated

30. "Astell would not be _____, or satisfied, as long as society imposed a 'cloud of ignorance' over women," Amy said. "Her willingness to _____, or renounce, those ideas should inspire women today."
    (A) mollified . . . repudiate
    (B) impassive . . . mollify
    (C) retaliated . . . recant
    (D) recanted . . . retaliate
    (E) retaliated . . . repudiate

MAKING NEW WORDS YOUR OWN

Lesson 20 | CONTEXT: History and Society
The Letters of Lady Mary Wortley Montagu

As a letter writer, Lady Mary Wortley Montagu (1689–1762) should be an inspiration to all of us. Lady Montagu, a socially prominent, learned English author, lived when people corresponded extensively through personal letters. Almost nine hundred of her letters are in print. In amusing and lively correspondence with her husband, daughter, and sister, Lady Montagu recorded nearly all the major events of her life. Many of her letters describe adventures in Turkey during the two years her husband was England's ambassador to Constantinople.

In the following exercises, you will have the opportunity to expand your vocabulary by reading about Lady Mary Wortley Montagu. Below are ten Vocabulary Words that will be used in these exercises.

auspices	fervid	hiatus	solicitous	vestige
clandestine	foment	reticent	temerity	vindicate

EXERCISE 1 *Wordbusting*

Directions. Follow these instructions for this word and the nine words on the next page.
- Figure out the word's meaning by looking at its **context,** its **structure,** and its **sound.** Fill in at least one of the three **CSS** boxes. Alternate which boxes you complete.
- Then, look up the word in a dictionary, read all of its meanings, and write the meaning of the word as it is used in the sentence.
- Follow this same process for each of the Vocabulary Words on the next page. You will need to draw your own map for each word. Use a separate sheet of paper.

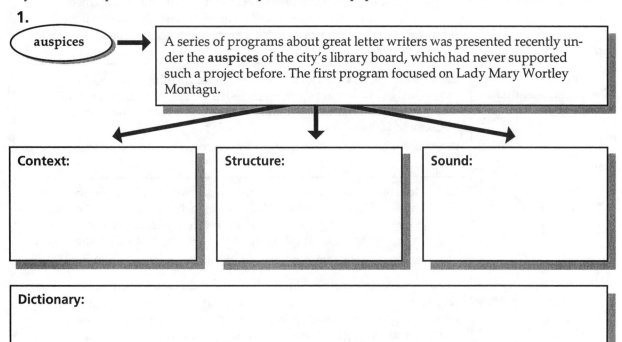

1.

auspices → A series of programs about great letter writers was presented recently under the **auspices** of the city's library board, which had never supported such a project before. The first program focused on Lady Mary Wortley Montagu.

Context:

Structure:

Sound:

Dictionary:

2.

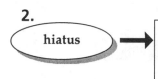

The instructor read aloud one of Lady Montagu's letters. I would have preferred to hear the entire letter without interruption, but there were several **hiatuses** in the instructor's presentation while the instructor gave us background information.

3.

The instructor was **solicitous** of our interests, though, and agreed to focus on Lady Montagu's activities at the center of a London literary circle.

4.

Lady Montagu was a colorful character who enjoyed the benefits and privileges of being a wealthy and prominent aristocrat. Her father disapproved of her courtship with Edward Wortley Montagu. The couple eloped after a number of equally **clandestine** meetings.

5.

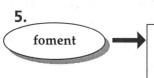

Lady Montagu did not **foment** national rebellions, but she did stir up a lot of controversy. She was educated and outspoken in a time when women were supposed to be neither.

6.

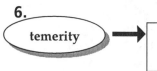

Some people of her time criticized what they considered Lady Montagu's **temerity,** or boldness, in publicly displaying her education.

7.

Lady Montagu wrote that "there is hardly a character in the world more despicable, or more liable to universal ridicule, than that of a learned woman." Do you detect a **vestige,** or trace, of sarcasm in her comment?

8.

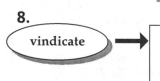

Lady Montagu, who had an innate passion for learning, often had to **vindicate** her interest in acquiring knowledge. To justify an interest in reading, she stated, "No entertainment is so cheap as reading, nor any pleasure so lasting."

9.

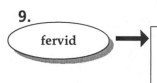

Lady Montagu is known for her quarrels with two prominent English writers, Alexander Pope and Harvey Walpole. In fact, Walpole described her as heartless and greedy, but recent studies have determined that she was a highly intelligent woman **fervidly,** or eagerly, struggling for emancipation.

10.

No one could label Lady Montagu as **reticent**. She is remembered not only for her outspokenness and for her letters, but, for introducing a method of using inoculation against smallpox, later perfected by Edward Jenner.

EXERCISE 2 *Context Clues* ✍

Directions. Scan the definitions in Column A. Then, think about how the boldface words are used in the sentences in Column B. To complete the exercise, match each definition in Column A with the correct Vocabulary Word from Column B. Write the letter of your choice on the line provided; then write the Vocabulary Word on the line preceding the definition.

COLUMN A

_____ **11.** word: _____
v. to clear of suspicion or blame; to justify or support

_____ **12.** word: _____
adj. reserved; reluctant, discreet

_____ **13.** word: _____
n. reckless boldness; rashness; foolhardiness

_____ **14.** word: _____
adj. giving off intense heat; impassioned, enthusiastic

_____ **15.** word: _____
v. to foster trouble, rebellion, or strife; to stir up; to incite

_____ **16.** word: _____
adj. showing concern or worry; anxiously concerned; eager

_____ **17.** word: _____
n. approval and support; patronage

_____ **18.** word: _____
n. a space where something is missing; any break in continuity

_____ **19.** word: _____
adj. concealed, usually for a forbidden purpose; secret; covert

_____ **20.** word: _____
n. a slight remnant; a trace of something that no longer exists; a minute quality

COLUMN B

(A) There was a twenty-minute intermission during the library program. We were told that the discussion about Lady Montagu would resume after the **hiatus**.

(B) The heat that day was **fervid,** and I wanted to stay inside where it was cooler, so I looked around for my friend Leslie.

(C) I wanted to talk to her in private. While no one was noticing us, we went upstairs for a **clandestine** meeting.

(D) I had heard that Leslie had been **fomenting** agitation and getting the library board angry.

(E) I wanted to give her a chance to **vindicate** herself if she was not in the wrong.

(F) I was afraid that Leslie would be **reticent** in speaking of the problem with me, but she showed no hesitation.

(G) Leslie explained, "I want future series to be held under the **auspices** of the Literary Guild, which is eager to support programs like this and willing to double our funding."

(H) "I'm concerned about the **vestige,** or hint, of hostility that exists between the library board and the Literary Guild," she said.

(I) I felt loyal to the library board and couldn't believe my own **temerity** in speaking to Leslie, but my assertiveness didn't seem to upset her.

(J) Leslie was unexpectedly **solicitous** toward me, upset that I had been uneasy about her talks with the board.

EXERCISE 3 *Sentence Completion* ✍

Directions. For each of the following items, circle the letter of the choice that best completes the meaning of the sentence or sentences.

21. When we resumed the meeting, the instructor discussed Lady Montagu's _____ and said some people accused her of recklessness.
    (A) temerity
    (B) hiatus
    (C) auspices
    (D) vestige
    (E) reticence

22. She read a rather strange letter in which Lady Montagu was _____ about her granddaughter, seemingly worried about the girl's future.
    (A) clandestine
    (B) solicitous
    (C) temerarious
    (D) fervid
    (E) hiatal

23. Lady Montagu apparently did not have even a slight bit, or _____, of hope that her granddaughter would ever get married.
    (A) hiatus
    (B) reticence
    (C) auspice
    (D) temerity
    (E) vestige

24. "I hope Lady Montagu felt some _____ about expressing this to her granddaughter," Dorothy said. "There are ways to get across the point discreetly."
    (A) solicitousness
    (B) vindication
    (C) fervidness
    (D) reticence
    (E) temerity

25. In the letter, Lady Montagu tries to _____, or justify, her claim that learning will make the girl content and happy.
    (A) foment
    (B) dissent
    (C) vindicate
    (D) impair
    (E) recant

26. Perhaps the girl and her mother went off in secret for _____ meetings to discuss Lady Montagu's letter.
    (A) reticent
    (B) hiatal
    (C) clandestine
    (D) solicitous
    (E) fervid

27. "Was Lady Montagu trying to _____ trouble between her daughter and granddaughter?" Dorothy asked.
    (A) impair
    (B) vindicate
    (C) recant
    (D) dissent
    (E) foment

28. "The granddaughter surely would have thrived under Lady Montagu's _____," Leslie said. "Do you find any _____ or even lukewarm expressions of love in the letter?"
    (A) reticence . . . solicitous
    (B) auspices . . . fervid
    (C) vestiges . . . clandestine
    (D) hiatuses . . . fervid
    (E) foment . . . solicitous

29. "Some people suspect that the granddaughter had a severe attitude that scared away suitors. But perhaps I'm only trying to _____ Lady Montagu," the instructor said.
    (A) vindicate
    (B) foment
    (C) recant
    (D) dissent
    (E) impair

30. "There may have been a(n) _____ of some years since Lady Montagu last saw her granddaughter. The lapse of time may have clouded her judgment," I said.
    (A) vestige
    (B) temerity
    (C) hiatus
    (D) reticence
    (E) auspice

MAKING NEW WORDS YOUR OWN

Lesson 21 | **CONTEXT:** Science and Technology

From Alchemy to Chemistry: The Development of Science in England

Science as we know it today is a fairly recent development. Modern British chemistry, for example, dates only from about the seventeenth century. Chemistry has its roots in alchemy, an early form of chemistry practiced during the Middle Ages. The primary aims of alchemy were to change base metals into gold and to find a substance that would cure all ailments and prolong life. Because the different branches of science were not distinct until the 1600s, the term chemist is used here to refer to someone who studies both chemistry and related disciplines.

In the following exercises, you will have the opportunity to expand your vocabulary by reading about the development of science in England. Below are ten Vocabulary Words that will be used in these exercises.

| differentiate | empirical | officious | renounce | testimonial |
| disparity | facetious | quiescent | scathing | treatise |

EXERCISE 1 *Wordbusting*

Directions. Follow these instructions for this word and the nine words on the next page.
- Figure out the word's meaning by looking at its **context,** its **structure,** and its **sound.** Fill in at least one of the three **CSS** boxes. Alternate which boxes you complete.
- Then, look up the word in a dictionary, read all of its meanings, and write the meaning of the word as it is used in the sentence.
- Follow this same process for each of the Vocabulary Words on the next page. You will need to draw your own map for each word. Use a separate sheet of paper.

1.

(differentiate) → Paracelsus (1493–1541), a Swiss scholar, helped to **differentiate,** or distinguish, chemistry from alchemy. Instead of using the alchemist's traditional approach, he identified chemical reactions that could cure diseases.

| Context: | Structure: | Sound: |

| Dictionary: |

2.

disparity ➤ A great **disparity,** or inequality, exists between the recognition given to Mary Boyle (c. 1626–1678), a little-known scientist, and her brother, the famous chemist Robert Boyle (1627–1691).

3.

scathing ➤ Robert Boyle had to defend his first important work against **scathing** criticism. It is remarkable that he persisted in his efforts when faced with such harsh judgment.

4.

empirical ➤ The English physician William Harvey (1578–1657), by performing various experiments, **empirically** demonstrated that blood circulation begins in the heart.

5.

renounce ➤ Seventeenth-century scientists, such as Harvey and Boyle, pursued scientific inquiry for its own sake. Some scientists today, concerned with the practical application of their work, have **renounced,** or turned their backs on, this approach to research.

6.

facetious ➤ Satirist Jonathan Swift's witty depiction of the Academy of Projectors in *Gulliver's Travels* is **facetious,** showing misguided scientists attempting to extract sunshine from cucumbers.

7.

officious ➤ The Italian author and chemist Primo Levi (1919–1987) satirized British chemists through his comic portrayal of the character Caselli, a meddlesome, **officious** servant to an English professor of chemistry.

8.

testimonial ➤ Two men received the Nobel Prize for their roles in the discovery of the structure of the DNA molecule. But a woman, Rosalind Franklin (1920–1958), received little **testimonial,** or tribute, for her contribution to the discovery.

9.

treatise ➤ A. Sayre's **treatise** *Rosalind Franklin and DNA: A Vivid View of What It Is Like to be a Gifted Woman in an Especially Male Profession* (1975) is an extensive discussion of Rosalind Franklin's case. It's in our library's collection.

10.

quiescent ➤ Chemists today cannot remain **quiescent,** or inactive, in the face of industrial pollution; their contributions are necessary to help solve such environmental problems.

EXERCISE 2 *Context Clues* ✍

Directions. Scan the definitions in Column A. Then, think about how the boldface words are used in the sentences in Column B. To complete the exercise, match each definition in Column A with the correct Vocabulary Word from Column B. Write the letter of your choice on the line provided; then write the Vocabulary Word on the line preceding the definition.

COLUMN A	COLUMN B

COLUMN A

____ **11.** word: _____

n. inequality; difference; unlikeness

____ **12.** word: _____

v. to give up; to abandon; to cast off something; to disown; to repudiate

____ **13.** word: _____

adj. too ready to please, praise, or obey; meddlesome; offering unwanted or unneeded advice or comments

____ **14.** word: _____

adj. harsh or caustic; extremely severe or bitter

____ **15.** word: _____

adj. joking; said in fun; meant to be amusing

____ **16.** word: _____

adj. based on experiment and observation; based entirely on practical experience rather than theory

____ **17.** word: _____

v. to make or become different; to tell the difference between; to note differences

____ **18.** word: _____

n. a formal, written discussion of a subject

____ **19.** word: _____

n. inactivity; quietness; stillness

____ **20.** word: _____

n. a recommendation of a person or product; a tribute to a person's accomplishments

COLUMN B

(A) Chemistry became possible when scientists, starting in about the sixteenth century, **renounced** their alchemical practices, turning their backs on the futile quest to turn base metals into gold.

(B) Robert Boyle's **treatise** *The Skeptical Chemist* (1661), widely read in its day, paved the way for the science of modern chemistry.

(C) In a **scathing** criticism of Robert Boyle's atomic theory, science historian Stephen F. Mason claims that Boyle failed to give a complete and accurate description of known chemical properties.

(D) When chemists submit their articles to scholarly journals, they must expect that at least one **officious** critic will make trivial or worthless comments.

(E) The English chemist and physicist John Dalton (1766–1844) developed theories from **empirical** evidence gathered through years of meticulous real-world research.

(F) The statue of John Dalton in Manchester, England, is a **testimonial** to his scientific contributions.

(G) Nonetheless, Princeton professor Charles Coulson Gillispie, seeing the humor in his subject, writes in a **facetious** tone about John Dalton's inexact chemical methods.

(H) The Victorian era was not a time of **quiescence** in the field of chemistry. On the contrary, there was great activity, and the number of recognized chemical elements increased steadily throughout the period.

(I) Only recently has the **disparity** between women's scientific achievements and the actual recognition of these achievements been acknowledged.

(J) We can **differentiate** chemical engineering from chemistry in the following way: chemical engineering applies the principles of chemistry to industrial uses.

Name _____ Date _____ Class _____

Sentence Completion ✍

Directions. In each of the following items, circle the letter of the choice that best completes the meaning of the sentence or sentences.

21. Paracelsus (1493–1541) made the harshly humorous, _____ comment that his shoe-buckles knew more than his colleagues.
(A) scathing
(B) disparate
(C) officious
(D) empirical
(E) quiescent

22. Robert Boyle's appreciation for _____ observation helped establish the use of the experimental method.
(A) officious
(B) empirical
(C) quiescent
(D) scathing
(E) facetious

23. Author Trevor Levere is being _____ when he remarks jokingly that British chemist Humphrey Davy's (1778–1829) high opinion of himself was rivaled only by his achievements.
(A) disparate
(B) facetious
(C) officious
(D) empirical
(E) quiescent

24. You can _____ the discoveries of Ernest Rutherford and Henry G. J. Moseley by remembering that Rutherford found that each atom has a nucleus, while Moseley discovered that the atoms of each element have a unique number of protons.
(A) recant
(B) prevaricate
(C) renounce
(D) differentiate
(E) deplore

25. Henry Moseley's experiments in physical chemistry helped scientists _____, or distinguish, the atoms of the various elements.
(A) renounce
(B) vindicate
(C) mollify
(D) differentiate
(E) foment

26. The in-depth _____ that would later be published as the *Handbook of Chemical Engineering* was first published by its author, George E. Davis in 1901.
(A) testimonial
(B) treatise
(C) chicanery
(D) proponent
(E) disparity

27. Hazel P. Gump's (1912–1992) professional progress was hampered by the interference of her _____, meddlesome assistant. Perhaps this explains why no memorials have been erected as _____ to Gump's contributions.
(A) officious . . . testimonials
(B) quiescent . . . treatises
(C) scathing . . . disparities
(D) facetious . . . treatises
(E) empirical . . . testimonials

28. Chemist Dorothy Hodgkin (1910–1994) discovered a _____ between her salary and the higher salaries of her male colleagues.
(A) disparity
(B) treatise
(C) testimonial
(D) quiescence
(E) residual

29. Since England _____ its colonization of India, giving up its claim to that country in 1947, Indian scientists have been able to clearly _____ their achievements from those of British scientists.
(A) differentiated . . . renounce
(B) renounced . . . vindicate
(C) renounced . . . differentiate
(D) differentiated . . . cajole
(E) differentiated . . . prevaricate

30. Faced with the observable, _____ evidence of industrial pollution, chemists could no longer be _____, or immovable.
(A) quiescent . . . facetious
(B) disparate . . . empirical
(C) empirical . . . quiescent
(D) officious . . . empirical
(E) empirical . . . disparate

86 LESSON 21

MAKING NEW WORDS YOUR OWN

Lesson 22 | CONTEXT: Science and Technology
Imperialism: Technology's Child

Advances in shipbuilding and the refinement of the factory system during the Industrial Revolution helped Britain to establish and maintain control of one of its greatest colonies: India. At the time of colonization by Britain, Indians wore garments made inexpensively from Indian-grown cotton that was hand-spun and hand-woven into cloth, but this changed with the technological advances of the British textile industry. The British government required the export of inexpensive cotton from India to England, where cloth was manufactured by British workers. Under British rule, Indians no longer wove their own cloth but had to buy it from the British. Mohandas K. Gandhi (1869–1948) perceived the unfairness of this system. His solution was to boycott British manufacturers and encourage Indians to spin and weave their own cloth. This rejection of Western technology helped India regain its independence.

In the exercises below, you will have the opportunity to expand your vocabulary by reading about the role of technology in India's struggle for independence. These ten Vocabulary Words will be used.

| chauvinism | devoid | inexorable | regimen | sagacity |
| cosmopolitan | epitome | moot | repository | tenuous |

EXERCISE 1   *Wordbusting*

Directions. Follow these instructions for this word and the nine words on the next page.
- Figure out the word's meaning by looking at its **context**, its **structure**, and its **sound**. Fill in at least one of the three **CSS** boxes. Alternate which boxes you complete.
- Then, look up the word in a dictionary, read all of its meanings, and write the meaning of the word as it is used in the sentence.
- Follow this same process for each of the Vocabulary Words on the next page. You will need to draw your own map for each word. Use a separate sheet of paper.

1.

$\boxed{\text{chauvinism}}$ ⟶ In retrospect, the fierce patriotism of the colonial powers seems **chauvinistic** because it is based on a biased belief in Western superiority.

| Context: | Structure: | Sound: |

Dictionary:

2.

cosmopolitan → Colonization brought people of diverse cultures together, resulting in the evolution of new, more **cosmopolitan** societies.

3.

repository → The inventions and improved manufacturing techniques of the Industrial Revolution made Britain a **repository** of advanced technology; it was a storehouse for the most up-to-date technological information.

4.

devoid → English leaders who financed early expeditions were so concerned with profit that they seemed **devoid** of conscience. Their primary consideration was capital gain, not the good of the people.

5.

epitome → The **epitome** of British imperialism was the East India Company. This representative example of the colonial power's business interests was able to establish trading posts all along the coast of India through gifts and bribes.

6.

inexorable → When internal disorder broke out in India, the British turned their trading posts into forts. This, combined with the military power of the English, made the British domination of India seem **inexorable** and unstoppable.

7.

regimen → Warren Hastings, Lord Charles Cornwallis, and Richard Wellesley continued the **regimen** of British imperialism. By the beginning of the nineteenth century, the system that had been put in place enabled London to control India.

8.

tenuous → The British were often overconfident, and it was in the places where the British considered their rule to be strongest that the Indian resistance proved British rule **tenuous**. The British were shaken to discover that their hold on India was far less substantial than they had assumed.

9.

sagacity → Mohandas "Mahatma" Gandhi is renowned for his **sagacity** as a leader. Gandhi's wisdom and sound judgment enabled him to lead successful campaigns of nonviolent resistance in India and South Africa.

10.

moot → What would be the condition of the Indian economy today if colonization had never taken place? A **moot,** or debatable, question like this can never be conclusively answered.

EXERCISE 2 *Context Clues* ✍

Directions. Scan the definitions in Column A. Then, think about how the words are used in the sentences in Column B. To complete the exercise, match each definition in Column A with the correct Vocabulary Word from Column B. Write the letter of your choice on the line provided; then write the Vocabulary Word on the line preceding the definition.

COLUMN A	COLUMN B

COLUMN A

_____ **11.** word: _____
n. fanatical patriotism; biased belief in the superiority of one's own group, sex, or nation

_____ **12.** word: _____
n. a person or thing typical of an entire class; an ideal example; a summary

_____ **13.** word: _____
adj. unalterable; relentless

_____ **14.** word: _____
adj. international; beyond national boundaries; having great worldly experience; sophisticated; at home anywhere

_____ **15.** word: _____
adj. entirely without; empty; totally lacking

_____ **16.** word: _____
n. a center for storage; a place where things are put for safekeeping; a person to whom something is confided or entrusted

_____ **17.** word: _____
n. a particular form of government; a systematic procedure; a regulated system for improving health

_____ **18.** word: _____
n. keen, sound judgment; mental acuteness; shrewdness

_____ **19.** word: _____
adj. thin; not substantial; flimsy

_____ **20.** word: _____
adj. debatable; resolved and not worth further discussion or consideration

COLUMN B

(A) The British East India Company was the **epitome** of the workings of British imperialism; it embodied all the qualities that made colonial power so relentless and all-encompassing.

(B) British **chauvinism** was demonstrated in the belief that Britain was better fit to rule India than India itself was.

(C) Mohandas "Mahatma" Gandhi challenged the seemingly **inexorable** power of British imperialism in India by condemning the nonstop mechanization of industry.

(D) Gandhi prescribed a **regimen** for the Indian people that included the wearing of only hand-spun and hand-woven cloth. This prescribed procedure was just one of the methods the Indians used to protest British rule.

(E) Gandhi's humble demeanor and the loincloth he usually wore made it easy to forget his **cosmopolitan** background. His experiences in other countries made him more knowledgeable than his appearance suggested.

(F) Gandhi's argument for a single, unified India was not **moot;** it was disputed by people all over the world.

(G) Gandhi's **sagacity** eventually convinced many British people of India's right to govern itself, for they recognized that Gandhi was an astute leader.

(H) After Gandhi popularized the concept of Indian independence, the British hold on India became increasingly weak and **tenuous.**

(I) The British port at Surat was once a **repository** of goods that were being kept for shipment to Europe.

(J) Although the British called the fort at Surat a factory, there was nothing in the fort to suggest that it was devoted to manufacturing; the fort was, in fact, **devoid** of industrial equipment.

EXERCISE 3 — Sentence Completion ☞

Directions. For each of the following items, circle the letter of the choice that best completes the meaning of the sentence or sentences.

21. The British were able to maintain control of India for nearly one hundred years. Some see that as a testament to the _____, or cleverness, of British administrators.
(A) repository
(B) austerity
(C) tenuousness
(D) sagacity
(E) epitome

22. The British _____ in India was often accused of being _____ of concern for the Indian people—completely lacking in consideration.
(A) regimen . . . devoid
(B) regimen . . . inexorable
(C) repository . . . moot
(D) repository . . . devoid
(E) sagacity . . . devoid

23. The _____, or representative example, of British _____ can be found in the attitudes of British colonials. They believed absolutely in the superiority of Britain.
(A) chauvinism . . . epitome
(B) repository . . . sagacity
(C) epitome . . . chauvinism
(D) repository . . . regimen
(E) regimen . . . sagacity

24. Many consider Gandhi a supreme example of a world leader, the _____ of a wise and just statesman whose _____ served his people well.
(A) repository . . . regimen
(B) repository . . . tenuousness
(C) repository . . . chauvinism
(D) epitome . . . sagacity
(E) regimen . . . sagacity

25. Gandhi had a(n) _____ education and experience, gained through university study in London, work in South Africa, and extensive travel throughout India.
(A) inexorable
(B) tenuous
(C) moot
(D) chauvinistic
(E) cosmopolitan

26. Gandhi's treatise *Hind Swaraj* is the _____ of many of his central ideas, functioning as a collection of his most important thoughts.
(A) subversion
(B) regimen
(C) repository
(D) sagacity
(E) chauvinism

27. Critics accused Gandhi of having a _____ grasp of reality. They felt that because he was anti-industrial, his practical sense must be weak and frail.
(A) cosmopolitan
(B) devoid
(C) inexorable
(D) moot
(E) tenuous

28. Popular opposition to the British salt tax was made irrelevant by the Irwin-Gandhi agreement, which permitted the making of salt for personal use. Further argument or debate on the issue became _____.
(A) tenuous
(B) moot
(C) inexorable
(D) chauvinistic
(E) cosmopolitan

29. The seemingly _____ and relentless domination of India by the British became _____ when India finally achieved independence.
(A) inexorable . . . moot
(B) cosmopolitan . . . inexorable
(C) moot . . . tenuous
(D) inexorable . . . devoid
(E) cosmopolitan . . . moot

30. Some people may have only a _____, vague understanding of the cultural diversity and _____ nature of India's cities, which include people from all parts of the world.
(A) cosmopolitan . . . tenuous
(B) inexorable . . . cosmopolitan
(C) cosmopolitan . . . inexorable
(D) tenuous . . . cosmopolitan
(E) tenuous . . . sagacious

MAKING NEW WORDS YOUR OWN

Lesson 23 | CONTEXT: Science and Technology
Of Chimneys and Chimney Sweeps

Both "good guys"—Santa Claus—and "bad guys"—the Big Bad Wolf—use chimneys. Some of us still heat our homes with wood and depend on chimneys to draw the smoke from the fireplace, stove, or furnace. I learned a lot about chimneys from talking to Tom, our chimney sweep, while he was cleaning our chimney.

In the following exercises, you will have the opportunity to expand your vocabulary by reading about chimneys and chimney sweeps. Below are ten Vocabulary Words that will be used in these exercises.

bode	coerce	gauntlet	misnomer	terra firma
burnish	esoteric	mete	mottled	vantage point

EXERCISE 1   *Wordbusting* 👈

Directions. Follow these instructions for this word and the nine words on the next page.
- Figure out the word's meaning by looking at its **context,** its **structure,** and its **sound.** Fill in at least one of the three **CSS** boxes. Alternate which boxes you complete.
- Then, look up the word in a dictionary, read all of its meanings, and write the meaning of the word as it is used in the sentence.
- Follow this same process for each of the Vocabulary Words on the next page. You will need to draw your own map for each word. Use a separate sheet of paper.

1.

(bode) ➝ The smell of smoke within the house **boded** chimney problems, but I was not alert to the omen. Late the next evening, however, I realized there was a serious problem when the whole house filled with smoke.

Context:

Structure:

Sound:

Dictionary:

2.

(burnish) → The exterior of the wood stove in the den looked fine. I had recently polished the bronze decorations on the stove's door and legs, and the **burnish** gave the stove a glossy, new look.

3.

(coerce) → Since the problem was with the chimney, I quickly called Tom, our local chimney sweep, and asked if I could **coerce** him to come out on a cold winter's night. "When there's a problem, you don't have to force me to get moving," Tom told me.

4.

(esoteric) → Chimney sweeping had always seemed like an **esoteric** profession to me because I did not understand exactly what it involved. Tom was born in London and learned the profession there.

5.

(gauntlet) → Tom doesn't look anything like my mental picture of a chimney sweep. I'd probably be disappointed, too, if I could see a real medieval knight because he probably wouldn't be wearing a visored helmet on his head or shiny **gauntlets** protecting his hands.

6.

(mete) → Smoke was filling the house, and I was willing to take whatever advice Tom would give me. Since I obviously had neglected the chimney, he probably would **mete** out some deserving reprimands.

7.

(misnomer) → "This chimney is a mess," Tom said after climbing up his ladder and onto the roof. "Calling this a chimney is a **misnomer;** its real name should be *smoke stopper*."

8.

(mottled) → Tom reached into the chimney and started pulling out huge, hard chunks of **mottled** soot. The dark blotches and streaks actually made an interesting design, but I was horrified at the chunks in my chimney.

9.

(terra firma) → High places make me nervous, and I felt uneasy to see Tom so far off the ground. I was glad my feet were solidly on **terra firma**.

10.

(vantage point) → Tom, however, evidently enjoyed his **vantage point** atop the house. He definitely had the best view of the neighborhood at the moment.

EXERCISE 2 *Context Clues*

Directions. Scan the definitions in Column A. Then, think about how the boldface words are used in the sentences in Column B. To complete the exercise, match each definition in Column A with the correct Vocabulary Word from column B. Write the letter of your choice on the line provided; then write the Vocabulary Word on the line preceding the definition.

COLUMN A	COLUMN B
_____ **11.** word: _____ *n.* a position that allows a clear view or understanding, an advantageous position	(A) "Your hand coverings don't look sturdy enough for that work," I told Tom. "What you need is a knight's metal **gauntlet**!"
_____ **12.** word: _____ *v.* to be a sign or omen of; to portend	(B) "These poles will do," Tom said, pointing to long instruments that he had brought with him. He must have **burnished** them because they gleamed.
_____ **13.** word: _____ *n.* a long, heavy, protective glove; a metal-plated glove, part of a knight's armor	(C) "Isn't it a **misnomer** to call you a chimney sweep?" I asked. "I mean, you don't really sweep the chimney."
_____ **14.** word: _____ *adj.* marked with spots, blotches, or streaks of different colors	(D) "Well, from my **vantage point,** acquired by experience, sweeping is cleaning, and I'm cleaning with the stiff brush on this pole," Tom replied, pausing to glance at the sky, now becoming cloudy.
_____ **15.** word: _____ *n.* a wrong name; an error in naming a person, place, or thing	(E) "I'd better hurry," he said. "Those clouds signal a change in the weather—they may **bode** more snow."
_____ **16.** word: _____ *n.* solid earth; firm ground	(F) Bits of soot covered Tom's face. His **mottled** face and tired expression looked comical in the moonlight.
_____ **17.** word: _____ *v.* to polish; to make shiny by rubbing; *n.* a glossy finish; a luster	(G) "If I could, I'd stay up on a roof all day and all night," Tom said with a sigh as he climbed down the ladder to **terra firma**.
_____ **18.** word: _____ *adj.* intended for or understood by only a few; confidential; private	(H) Tom motioned me to him as if he were going to give me some **esoteric** or secret bit of knowledge.
_____ **19.** word: _____ *v.* to give according to measure or one's judgment; to allot or distribute	(I) "I have some advice to **mete** out to you—burn your wood hotter and clean your chimney more often," Tom said.
_____ **20.** word: _____ *v.* to compel; to force; to dominate or restrain by force	(J) "I can't **coerce** you into getting your chimney cleaned regularly," he continued, "but what has happened tonight should impel you to do so."

EXERCISE 3   *Sentence Completion* ✍

Directions. For each of the following items, circle the letter of the choice that best completes the meaning of the sentence or sentences.

21. "I once started reading about how chimneys work," I told Tom, "but the information seemed _____, like it was written solely for chimney engineers."
(A) burnished
(B) mottled
(C) esoteric
(D) coerced
(E) gauntleted

22. "I always think of fireplaces as signs of comfort and security. Do you think chimneys always _____ comfort, Tom?"
(A) burnish
(B) renounce
(C) coerce
(D) malign
(E) bode

23. "If they are not stopped up," Tom said, trying to _____ his dirty poles with a polishing cloth.
(A) coerce
(B) malign
(C) mete
(D) burnish
(E) bode

24. "I may have to throw these gloves away," he said, laughing, "and maybe buy some _____!"
(A) gauntlets
(B) a misnomer
(C) a vantage point
(D) coercions
(E) terra firma

25. "My son, Little Tom (a _____ since he is six-feet tall) is a good metalworker," Tom said.
(A) vantage point
(B) misnomer
(C) terra firma
(D) burnish
(E) gauntlet

26. "He wants to be a chimney sweep, too. I'm not _____ him to follow in my footsteps, though, anymore than I am forcing him to walk on solid ground, or _____."
(A) meting . . . coercing
(B) burnishing . . . misnomer
(C) coercing . . . terra firma
(D) meting . . . gauntlet
(E) coercing . . . burnish

27. By going with me on assignments, at times, he will have a _____ from which to choose a career that others might not have.
(A) misnomer
(B) burnish
(C) gauntlet
(D) vantage point
(E) terra firma

28. I grew dizzy just looking so far above _____, which was solid beneath my feet. My last name, Skyway, is a real _____!
(A) burnish . . . terra firma
(B) gauntlet . . . vantage point
(C) terra firma . . . burnish
(D) misnomer . . . gauntlet
(E) terra firma . . . misnomer

29. Tom's clothes were _____, and I didn't know if the soot blotches would come out. I supposed he had some _____ method of cleaning soot that only chimney sweeps know.
(A) esoteric . . . mottled
(B) gauntleted . . . firmamental
(C) burnished . . . gauntleted
(D) mottled . . . esoteric
(E) mottled . . . vantage point

30. As I _____ out the last of our holiday cookies, Tom pointed out how well the evening, which first had not _____ well, had ended.
(A) meted . . . boded
(B) coerced . . . burnished
(C) boded . . . mottled
(D) meted . . . coerced
(E) mottled . . . maligned

MAKING NEW WORDS YOUR OWN

Lesson 24 · CONTEXT: Science and Technology
Clocks: Once Upon a Time

Once upon a time, there were no clocks as we know them. Sundials and water clocks were used to mark time in the ancient world. Mechanical clocks first started to appear in the thirteenth century in Europe. Town clocks with chimes that struck the hours appeared in Europe in the late fourteenth century. Household clocks and even wristwatches were used in England and the Netherlands by the sixteenth century. By this time the balance spring had been introduced, and clocks had become much more accurate. Today, we have electric clocks, quartz clocks, and clocks run by electronic chips—all of which keep time with an accuracy undreamed of when the first mechanical clocks came into use.

In the following exercises, you will have the opportunity to expand your vocabulary by reading about clocks in the Middle Ages. Below are ten Vocabulary Words that will be used in these exercises.

acrimonious	atrophy	desist	expound	precursor
anachronism	consternation	enigma	loquacious	voluminous

EXERCISE 1 · Wordbusting ✍

Directions. Follow these instructions for this word and the nine words on the next page.
- Figure out the word's meaning by looking at its **context,** its **structure,** and its **sound.** Fill in at least one of the three **CSS** boxes. Alternate which boxes you complete.
- Then, look up the word in a dictionary, read all of its meanings, and write the meaning of the word as it is used in the sentence.
- Follow this same process for each of the Vocabulary Words on the next page. You will need to draw your own map for each word. Use a separate sheet of paper.

1.

(acrimonious) → It was 1450 A.D., and Charles was **acrimoniously** discussing clocks with his old friend Thomas. "Who needs these noisy new timepieces?" Charles asked sharply.

Context:

Structure:

Sound:

Dictionary:

2.

anachronism

→ "As far as I am concerned," Charles said, "these new clocks are an **anachronism**. They should have been invented long after I am gone, so I wouldn't have to be bothered with them."

3.
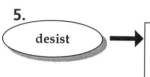
atrophy

→ "All I need to do is look at the sun in order to tell what time it is," Charles continued. "If I used a clock all the time, my mind would start to **atrophy**. It would slowly waste away from disuse."

4.

consternation

→ "I must confess, Thomas," Charles said, "that I am filled with **consternation** at the city fathers' decision to put up a clock for the whole town rather than using the funds to sink new wells. It's really dismaying."

5.
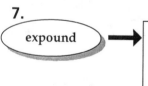
desist

→ "Please **desist**," Thomas said. "If you don't stop protesting, others will follow your example, and there will be trouble throughout the town, all because of a clock."

6.

enigma

→ "Well," Charles said, "why everyone should want to know what time it is and run their lives accordingly is a real **enigma**. I can't figure it out."

7.
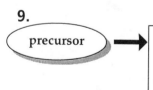
expound

→ "You should have come to the lecture Tuesday night and listened to Mayor Goodman **expound** on the history and benefits of the mechanical clock," Thomas said. "He even predicted that we would have clocks in our houses one day."

8.
loquacious

→ "I can believe that," Charles said. "I've never heard anyone else so **loquacious**; I am not surprised that he could go on and on about a topic as trivial and fleeting as clocks."

9.

precursor

→ "I say that clocks are **precursors** of bad times ahead," Charles continued. "I think they indicate that we'll have more and more mechanized tools in the future and that we'll use our brains less and less. We'll be the slaves of machines."

10.
voluminous

→ "I don't care if the mayor posts a **voluminous** report with enough pages to fill several volumes. I still wouldn't be in favor of clocks," Charles said.

EXERCISE 2 *Context Clues* ✍

Directions. Scan the definitions in Column A. Then, think about how the boldface words are used in the sentences in Column B. To complete the exercise, match each definition in Column A with the correct Vocabulary Word from Column B. Write the letter of your choice on the line provided; then write the Vocabulary Word on the line preceding the definition.

COLUMN A	COLUMN B

COLUMN A

_____ **11.** word: _____
n. a riddle or puzzle; something puzzling or unexplainable; a mystery

_____ **12.** word: _____
adj. very large; capable of filling volumes

_____ **13.** word: _____
n. great fear or shock that leaves one confused and bewildered; great dismay

_____ **14.** word: _____
adj. sharp or bitter in language or manner

_____ **15.** word: _____
n. something or someone that goes before and indicates what is to follow; a forerunner; a predecessor, as in office

_____ **16.** word: _____
v. to waste away; to wither; *n.* a wasting away, especially of a part or parts of the body

_____ **17.** word: _____
v. to interpret; to set forth or explain in detail

_____ **18.** word: _____
n. anything out of its proper historical or chronological time; the thing incorrectly placed; a person or idea considered as out of date

_____ **19.** word: _____
n. to stop doing something; to cease; to abstain

_____ **20.** word: _____
adj. fond of talking; talkative

COLUMN B

(A) "Please **expound** to me, if you can, your reasons for disliking clocks," Thomas said to Charles. "I'd like to hear the particulars."

(B) "If you must have help telling time, what is wrong with using a sundial?" Charles snapped. His **acrimonious** manner startled Thomas, who was not used to hearing such a rude tone from his friend.

(C) "It's no mystery: Sundials are not practical on cloudy days," Thomas quickly replied. "Surely you can understand that people might prefer a time-telling instrument that can be used in all times and conditions. Why is this such an **enigma** to you?"

(D) "The mayor owns **voluminous** manuscripts about clocks," Charles said, "enough to stock a library. Why doesn't he want a water clock?"

(E) "Everyone knows water clocks freeze," Thomas said in some **consternation**. He was surprised that Charles was so stubborn and single-minded on this subject.

(F) "You should **desist** from trying to think up substitutes for the mechanical clock," Thomas continued, "and go with the times."

(G) "I think you should go visit the **loquacious** Mayor Goodman. As you know, he will gladly speak with you at length about clocks—or anything else, for that matter," Thomas said.

(H) "Mayor Goodman is a **precursor** of the coming mechanized world in which machines will run our lives," Charles said. "He's the herald of a way of life that I want nothing to do with."

(I) "Just as your muscles will **atrophy** if you don't exercise them," Charles continued, "your mind will weaken if you don't use it."

(J) "I appreciate your concern, Thomas. Just consider me an **anachronism,** but I don't agree with your views and prefer to live with the old-fashioned ways."

EXERCISE 3 *Sentence Completion* ✍

Directions. For each of the following items, circle the letter of the choice that best completes the meaning of the sentence or sentences.

21. "I talked to Mayor Goodman," Charles told Thomas a few days later. "He was _____ as usual and talked nonstop."
(A) voluminous
(B) acrimonious
(C) atrophic
(D) loquacious
(E) precursory

22. "In fact, I think he could keep talking if the whole town _____ around him and became a wasteland."
(A) expounded
(B) atrophied
(C) meted
(D) consternated
(E) desisted

23. "He didn't convince me of anything," Charles said _____. "I'm still furious that the town is using funds to buy a clock instead of something we really need."
(A) anachronistically
(B) enigmatically
(C) loquaciously
(D) impeccably
(E) acrimoniously

24. "Goodman believes that the mechanical clock is the _____ of a tiny clock that people will be able to wear on their wrists with a band."
(A) atrophy
(B) enigma
(C) precursor
(D) consternation
(E) anachronism

25. "My _____ was evident when he told me that," Charles said. "I told him that I really fear for civilization's future."
(A) consternation
(B) anachronism
(C) atrophy
(D) precursor
(E) enigma

26. "I'm sure that he finds you a(n) _____," Thomas said. "You are hard to figure out."
(A) consternation
(B) precursor
(C) enigma
(D) atrophy
(E) achronistic

27. "Supporting statements for the town clock are _____; they could fill a great hall. But our town could _____ and die before you would accept the clock, Charles."
(A) acrimonious . . . desist
(B) loquacious . . . expound
(C) enigmatic . . . desist
(D) voluminous . . . atrophy
(E) anachronistic . . . expound

28. "What if I were to give you a mechanical clock?" Thomas asked. "Maybe you would enjoy using it and therefore consider its invention timely, rather than a(n) _____.
(A) consternation
(B) enigma
(C) precursor
(D) atrophy
(E) anachronism

29. "You're wrong, Thomas. I would stop you from giving me such a gift and also ask you to _____ from teasing me." I don't care if the mechanical clock is a _____ of things to come. I am just not interested."
(A) expound . . . consternation
(B) desist . . . precursor
(C) atrophy . . . enigma
(D) expound . . . precursor
(E) desist . . . atrophy

30. "I could _____ for hours on the clock's benefits, to no avail," Thomas said, his _____ evident in his confused, bewildered expression.
(A) desist . . . voluminosity
(B) atrophy . . . precursor
(C) expound . . . consternation
(D) atrophy . . . anachronism
(E) expound . . . precursor

MAKING NEW WORDS YOUR OWN

Lesson 25 | CONTEXT: Science and Technology
Electricity in England

"The day must come when electricity will be for everybody. . . ." declared French writer Émile Zola in *Travail* (1901). That day was just dawning in England, as well as throughout Europe and the United States. Scientists had been investigating electrical currents since around 1800. Since the 1880s, some major cities in England had been using electricity for street lights, in buildings and factories, and for transportation systems. At that time, electricity was still a luxury throughout England, but an electrical boom period had begun.

In the following exercises, you will have the opportunity to expand your vocabulary by reading about the development of electricity in England. These ten Vocabulary Words will be used.

assiduous	cessation	equanimity	inordinate	pecuniary
aver	denizen	iniquity	mercurial	tenable

EXERCISE 1 *Wordbusting* 🖎

Directions. Follow these instructions for this word and the nine words on the next page.
- Figure out the word's meaning by looking at its **context,** its **structure,** and its **sound.** Fill in at least one of the three **CSS** boxes. Alternate which boxes you complete.
- Then, look up the word in a dictionary, read all of its meanings, and write the meaning of the word as it is used in the sentence.
- Follow this same process for each of the Vocabulary Words on the next page. You will need to draw your own map for each word. Use a separate sheet of paper.

1.

(assiduous) ➡ An **assiduous** researcher into the development of electricity in England will note the achievements of Michael Faraday (1791–1867). Such an attentive researcher can locate details of Faraday's experiments at the Royal Institution in London.

Context:

Structure:

Sound:

Dictionary:

2.

aver

> Historians declare that Faraday's experiments with converting electrical energy into mechanical energy in 1821 were extremely important. In these experiments, they **aver,** Faraday demonstrated the principle of the electric motor.

3.

cessation

> There was no **cessation** of Faraday's work then, however. Instead of "resting on his laurels," Faraday continued with his research. He found a way to generate a continuous electric current, thus discovering the principle of the generator.

4.

equanimity

> Faraday must have carried out his experiments with considerable **equanimity;** one would certainly have to remain calm when working with an unknown force such as electricity.

5.

denizen

> By the mid-1800s, Britain's inhabitants saw practical uses of electrical experiments. For example, **denizens** of some lighthouses adjusted to electric generators producing arc lighting.

6.

iniquity

> Some people in the late 1800s and early 1900s probably viewed the development of electricity as an **iniquity,** but others, perhaps more farsighted, saw it as a blessing.

7.

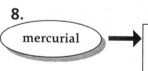
inordinate

> In the late 1800s, some investors in England had **inordinate** expectations for electricity. Their expectations were excessive because they did not take into account the effects of gas prices and legislation on the new electric industry.

8.

mercurial

> The electric industry in its early years could be described as **mercurial** because there were constant changes as new technologies were developed to meet increasing public demands.

9.

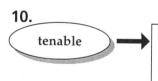
pecuniary

> Of course, **pecuniary** interests drove the new electric industry. Investors were ultimately interested in making money.

10.

tenable

> The statement that Thomas Edison's lighting exhibit at the London Exhibition of 1882 helped spark public interest in electricity is **tenable;** it can be defended with historical evidence.

EXERCISE 2 *Context Clues*

Directions. Scan the definitions in Column A. Then, think about how the boldface words are used in the sentences in Column B. To complete the exercise, match the definition in Column A with the correct Vocabulary Word from Column B. Write the letter of your choice on the line provided; then write the Vocabulary Word on the line preceding the definition.

COLUMN A

_____ **11.** word: _____
n. evenness of mind or temper; calmness; composure

_____ **12.** word: _____
adj. capable of being held or defended; defensible

_____ **13.** word: _____
adj. much too great; excessive; immoderate

_____ **14.** word: _____
v. to declare to be true; to state positively

_____ **15.** word: _____
adj. concerning money; in the form of money

_____ **16.** word: _____
n. an inhabitant; a person, a plant, or an animal at home in a particular region

_____ **17.** word: _____
adj. unpredictably changeable; quick and changeable in character

_____ **18.** word: _____
adj. careful and attentive; persevering

_____ **19.** word: _____
n. sin; wickedness; injustice

_____ **20.** word: _____
n. a temporary or final ceasing; a pause or stop

COLUMN B

(A) The **denizens** of the Thames countryside—wild animals such as birds, badgers, and hedgehogs—were affected by the construction of a huge electrical power station in southeast London.

(B) S. Z. de Ferranti was the **assiduous** engineer of the station. Through thorough planning and persistence he was able to begin construction in 1888.

(C) Ferranti's London Electric Supply Company did not take an **inordinate** amount of time to build the station; it was completed in two years.

(D) Historians **aver** that the venture was a failure, but they also maintain that it was a partial model for future electrical stations.

(E) Statements that customers were unhappy with disruptions of the electrical supply are **tenable**—company records support this.

(F) The company's failure did not mean a **cessation** of interest in electricity. On the contrary, interest grew.

(G) Electricity seemed to have won steady favor with the British people. The usually **mercurial** public was, for once, stable in its desires. As a result, power stations were common by 1903.

(H) You can imagine the **pecuniary** interests in the growing electrical industry. There was much profit to be made, which would grow with demand.

(I) Did pioneering companies in electricity proceed with **equanimity** as they expanded and consolidated? Or was their serenity disrupted by greed and the promise of profits?

(J) Some **iniquities** surely occurred in the electric companies' growth period, but my resource mentions very few instances of unfairness during the boom years.

EXERCISE 3   *Sentence Completion* ✍

Directions. For each of the following items, circle the letter of the choice that best completes the meaning of the sentence or sentences.

21. Although I usually do not make strong declarations, I _____ that my research into this subject was extremely fascinating.
   (A) bode
   (B) desist
   (C) renounce
   (D) aver
   (E) quell

22. My theories about the British Electrical Development Association (EDA), which was formed in 1919, are completely defensible. You can look in any history book to see that they are _____.
   (A) mercurial
   (B) pecuniary
   (C) tenable
   (D) assiduous
   (E) inordinate

23. The EDA, formed by several associations, definitely had _____ interests; it wanted to profit from the use of electricity.
   (A) tenable
   (B) pecuniary
   (C) mercurial
   (D) assiduous
   (E) iniquitous

24. The EDA did not spend a(n) _____ amount of time deciding upon its approach. On the contrary, it quickly decided upon its consumer target.
   (A) pecuniary
   (B) assiduous
   (C) mercurial
   (D) tenable
   (E) inordinate

25. The EDA's ads were aimed at particular _____ of the regions supplied by electricity: female housekeepers.
   (A) fissures
   (B) iniquities
   (C) denizens
   (D) cessations
   (E) firmaments

26. The EDA ad campaign was not _____. It was consistently based upon the _____, or defensible, theory that women wanted the most modern appliances.
   (A) pecuniary . . . assiduous
   (B) assiduous . . . mercurial
   (C) inordinate . . . iniquitous
   (D) mercurial . . . tenable
   (E) tenable . . . inordinate

27. The ads _____ that the most conscientious and _____ housekeepers used electric carpet cleaners, declaring this in no uncertain terms.
   (A) boded . . . tenable
   (B) averred . . . assiduous
   (C) desisted . . . assiduous
   (D) averred . . . pecuniary
   (E) averred . . . mercurial

28. The ads urged the _____ of old ways and the beginning of modern methods of housekeeping. Electricity would reduce the _____, excessive amount of time women spent cleaning house.
   (A) cessation . . . inordinate
   (B) denizen . . . assiduous
   (C) equanimity . . . tenable
   (D) iniquity . . . mercurial
   (E) tenability . . . pecuniary

29. Some ads almost seemed to _____ that electricity was the solution to a number of ills, declaring that electricity could cure all domestic and social _____—or at least the sin of bad housekeeping!
   (A) desist . . . denizens
   (B) aver . . . cessations
   (C) renounce . . . iniquities
   (D) aver . . . denizens
   (E) aver . . . iniquities

30. Did British consumers react with _____, or did they get excited?
   (A) iniquity
   (B) assiduousness
   (C) equanimity
   (D) cessation
   (E) mercurialness

MAKING NEW WORDS YOUR OWN

Lesson 26 | **CONTEXT:** Science and Technology
England and the Suez Canal

In January my debate team was assigned to select and then support an argument about which of the world's canals is the most important. While some of the members favored the Panama Canal, we finally decided to research and debate the importance of the Suez Canal. At our next meeting, I brought all the information that I could find, along with a map that showed how the canal connected the Mediterranean and Red seas.

In the following exercises, you will have the opportunity to expand your vocabulary by reading about the history of the Suez Canal. Below are ten Vocabulary Words that will be used in these exercises.

avarice	corollary	espouse	fissure	quell
conciliate	duress	extenuate	impeccable	rancor

EXERCISE 1 · *Wordbusting*

Directions. Follow these instructions for this word and the nine words on the next page.
- Figure out the word's meaning by looking at its **context,** its **structure,** and its **sound.** Fill in at least one of the three **CSS** boxes. Alternate which boxes you complete.
- Then, look up the word in a dictionary, read all of its meanings, and write the meaning of the word as it is used in the sentence.
- Follow this same process for each of the Vocabulary Words on the next page. You will need to draw your own map for each word. Use a separate sheet of paper.

1.

(**avarice**) ➔ "So, was the Suez Canal built as a result of **avarice**?" asked Faith at our meeting. "I've heard that many historical developments in trade have occurred because of greed. Perhaps it's not always a bad thing."

Context:

Structure:

Sound:

Dictionary:

2.

conciliate

"The canal was actually built by a Frenchman, Ferdinand de Lesseps," I explained. He worked hard to **conciliate** the canal's supporters and opponents."

3.

corollary

"Why would the Egyptian government have resisted building the canal?" asked Mark. "I should think that its approval would have been a **corollary,** a natural consequence, of the proposal. Wasn't there a smaller canal where the Suez is now?"

4.

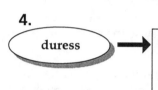
duress

"That's true," I said. "A canal connecting the Nile River and the Red Sea was built nearly 4,000 years ago and later abandoned. Many people had seen the advantages of connecting these bodies of water, so De Lesseps did not have to put the Egyptian government under **duress** to get their aid."

5.

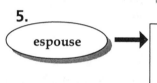
espouse

"De Lessep's private corporation, the Suez Canal Company, also persuaded many French investors to **espouse** the canal. The French were interested in providing a shorter route between Europe and Asia."

6.

extenuate

"Isn't there some way the British can be **extenuated,** or excused, for their lack of interest during the early stages of the project?" asked Faith.

7.

rancor

"Yes," I replied. "They knew that a canal would open up trade routes to their competitors. This helps to explain their reluctance, which grew for a time into **rancor**."

8.

quell

"Their objections were obviously **quelled**," Matt said. "They became major shareholders."

9.

fissure

"Asia and Africa were once a single land mass, but millions of years ago a **fissure** opened between them," I explained.

10.

impeccable

"While plans for the canal were not **impeccable,** or flawless, they took advantage of the bodies of water that had developed from that ancient fissure."

104 LESSON 26

Name _____ Date _____ Class _____

EXERCISE 2 *Context Clues*

Directions. Scan the definitions in Column A. Then, think about how the boldface words are used in the sentences in Column B. To complete the exercise, match each definition in Column A with the correct Vocabulary Word from Column B. Write the letter of your choice on the line provided; then write the Vocabulary Word on the line preceding the definition.

COLUMN A	COLUMN B

COLUMN A

____ **11.** word: _____

v. to excuse or serve as an excuse; to make the magnitude of something, such as a guilt, fault or offense, seem less

____ **12.** word: _____

n. the use of force or threats to compel someone to act in a certain manner; coercion

____ **13.** word: _____

v. to quiet; to put down or suppress by force; to put an end to something

____ **14.** word: _____

n. ongoing bitter hate or ill will

____ **15.** word: _____

v. to win over; to appease; to gain good will or favor by being friendly

____ **16.** word: _____

adj. faultless; without flaw; incapable of wrongdoing

____ **17.** word: _____

n. something that follows once something else has been proven; a deduction; a natural consequence; a result

____ **18.** word: _____

n. too great a desire for money and property; greed

____ **19.** word: _____

n. a narrow or deep split, crack, or opening; *v.* to split or break open; to break into parts

____ **20.** word: _____

v. to advocate or support a cause; to take up; to marry

COLUMN B

(A) Napoleon's enthusiasm for a canal was finally **quelled,** and the project was tabled.

(B) Napoleon had been misled by his chief engineer, Le Père, whose calculations were far from **impeccable:** He mistakenly calculated a 33-foot difference in sea level between the Red Sea and the Mediterranean.

(C) There were **extenuating** circumstances, however. Le Père did not have access to sophisticated means of measuring sea level.

(D) The **corollary** to such a difference in levels was a need for a series of locks so ships could move through the canal from one sea to the other.

(E) Later engineers **espoused** Le Père's ideas, and for years this nonexistent difference in levels was a serious obstacle.

(F) A **fissure** developed between France and Britain over plans for the canal.

(G) Relations were sometimes **rancorous** between these two countries with such a long history of conflict.

(H) The British prime minister Disraeli was **conciliatory,** however, and actually bought out Egypt's financial interest in the canal.

(I) The Egyptian government was under **duress** because of financial problems and was almost forced to sell.

(J) Those holding shares in the canal certainly had any **avarice** rewarded: The value of the shares rose enormously.

EXERCISE 3 *Sentence Completion* ✍

Directions. For each of the following items, circle the letter of the choice that best completes the meaning of the sentence or sentences.

21. "Some of Egypt's leaders fell into debt," I answered, "and as a(n) _____, a natural consequence, Britain bought Egypt's stocks in the canal in 1875."
    (A) extenuation
    (B) corollary
    (C) duress
    (D) rancor
    (E) avarice

22. By purchasing shares to the Suez Canal Company, Britain may have acted _____ in a desire to accumulate wealth.
    (A) impeccably
    (B) commiseratively
    (C) ingenuously
    (D) avariciously
    (E) evanescently

23. "Who had the original charter on the canal?" asked Matt, pointing out that my explanation was not _____ because it had some inconsistencies.
    (A) avaricious
    (B) extenuating
    (C) impeccable
    (D) quelled
    (E) conciliatory

24. "The Suez Canal Company was given a 99-year lease on the canal land and all nations were given access to the canal," I explained. "However, national _____ developed that affected canal use."
    (A) extenuations
    (B) espousals
    (C) corollaries
    (D) avarices
    (E) fissures

25. "_____ circumstances during the Arab-Israeli war in 1948 and 1949 served as a justification for Egypt to close the canal to Israel," I pointed out.
    (A) Extenuating
    (B) Impeccable
    (C) Conciliatory
    (D) Avaricious
    (E) Evanescent

26. "The nations of the Middle East were unable to _____ the fighting. Because of the failure to curb violence, another war began in 1956, and British and French troops were sent in."
    (A) espouse
    (B) extenuate
    (C) quell
    (D) rancor
    (E) fissure

27. "Did Egypt force Britain to go in under _____, by using some kind of intimidation?" asked Faith.
    (A) espousal
    (B) duress
    (C) rancor
    (D) corollary
    (E) avarice

28. "_____ again caused the canal to close," I explained. "During the Arab-Israeli War, Israel occupied the canal's east bank. The resulting standoff led Egypt to close the canal for eight years."
    (A) Quelled
    (B) Duress
    (C) Avarice
    (D) Extenuation
    (E) Rancor

29. "The canal was reopened in 1975, when Egypt was _____, or pacified," added Matt.
    (A) espoused
    (B) conciliated
    (C) quelled
    (D) fissured
    (E) extenuated

30. "I _____ the idea of the 1888 Convention of Constantinople that the canal is to be open to all nations, whether in peace or war."
    (A) conciliate
    (B) quell
    (C) fissured
    (D) espouse
    (E) extenuate

MAKING NEW WORDS YOUR OWN

Lesson 27 | **CONTEXT:** Science and Technology

Charles Dickens and Industry

Charles Dickens (1812–1870) is undoubtedly one of the most famous English writers in history. People around the world have sympathized with his characters and enjoyed his stories. But Dickens was more than simply a wonderful storyteller. He was also a social commentator who used his stories to speak out against the poverty, poor working conditions, and other social injustices of the Victorian age. One of Dickens's most fervent concerns was the changes brought by the Industrial Revolution—the machine age which Dickens viewed as retrogressive, damaging, and hardhearted.

In the following exercises, you will have the opportunity to expand your vocabulary by reading about Charles Dickens and his view of industry. These ten Vocabulary Words will be used.

burgeoning	commiserate	festoon	maudlin	remuneration
caricature	evanescent	gambol	pallor	venal

EXERCISE 1 | *Wordbusting* ✍

Directions. Follow these instructions for this word and the nine words on the next page.
- Figure out the word's meaning by looking at its **context,** its **structure,** and its **sound.** Fill in at least one of the three **CSS** boxes. Alternate which boxes you complete.
- Then, look up the word in a dictionary, read all of its meanings, and write the meaning of the word as it is used in the sentence.
- Follow this same process for each of the Vocabulary Words on the next page. You will need to draw your own map for each word. Use a separate sheet of paper.

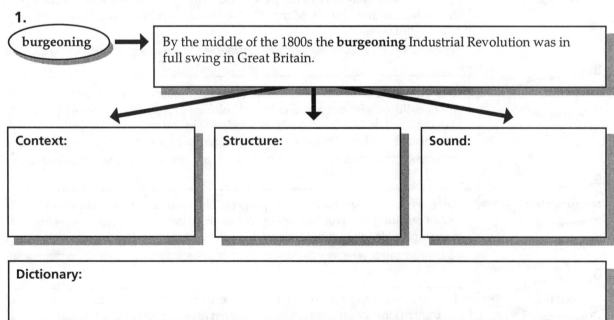

1.

burgeoning → By the middle of the 1800s the **burgeoning** Industrial Revolution was in full swing in Great Britain.

Context:

Structure:

Sound:

Dictionary:

Name _____ Date _____ Class _____

2.
caricature → Dickens's feelings toward industry are clearly reflected in the way he **caricatures** industrial innovations. In his novel *Dombey and Son* (1848), he satirizes railroads, referring to them as shrieking, rattling monsters.

3.
evanescent → Dickens's description of the construction of a railroad is equally satirical. He gives everything a sense of impermanence and confusion, describing houses that are knocked down and **evanescent** flames that vanish as soon as they appear.

4.
commiserate → Apparently many people **commiserated,** or sympathized, with Dickens's viewpoint, for his books were phenomenally successful.

5.
festoon → In Dickens's world, the urban landscape is not **festooned** with things of beauty. On the contrary, it has no adornments at all and is reduced to shabby tenements, unfinished walls, and strewn bricks.

6.
gambol → Few children **gambol** and frolic in Dickens's books, as one might expect them to do. Instead, the wilderness of progress seems to render all people—both young and old—solemn and grave.

7.
maudlin → Although critics charged that Dickens was too **maudlin,** clinging with excessive sentimentality to the past, Dickens was not alone in deploring the Industrial Revolution. Many other Victorian writers joined in his criticism of "progress."

8.
pallor → Dickens was a master of description. He created moving images of the **pallor** of children's faces, turned pale and colorless from poverty, cruelty, and exhaustion. His 1838 book *Nicholas Nickleby* told the story of "ragged schools" in northern England where children were mercilessly abused.

9.
remuneration → Dickens did not believe that the "progress" brought about by technology was a **remuneration** for the loss of compassion, beauty, and good working conditions. He felt that nothing could make up for these losses.

10.
venal → Dickens was not **venal,** so he would certainly have refused bribes offered by industrialists wanting him to tone down his criticism of industry.

EXERCISE 2 *Context Clues* ✍

Directions. Scan the definitions in Column A. Then, think about how the boldface words are used in the sentences in Column B. To complete the exercise, match each definition in Column A with the correct Vocabulary Word from Column B. Write the letter of your choice on the line provided; then write the Vocabulary Word on the line preceding the definition.

<table>
<tr><td align="center">COLUMN A</td><td align="center">COLUMN B</td></tr>
</table>

COLUMN A

_____ **11.** word: _____

n. a skipping or running about; *v.* to run and jump in play; to frolic

_____ **12.** word: _____

n. a payment for goods or services; a compensation for losses

_____ **13.** word: _____

n. a lack of color, particularly in the face

_____ **14.** word: _____

v. to develop or grow quickly; to sprout

_____ **15.** word: _____

adj. willing to sell one's services or influence for money; open to bribes; corruptible

_____ **16.** word: _____

adj. excessively sentimental

_____ **17.** word: _____

n. a picture or description of a person or thing in which certain features are exaggerated for a satirical effect; a ludicrous imitation; *v.* to create such a picture or description

_____ **18.** word: _____

n. a string of flowers, paper or the like hung as a decoration; *v.* to decorate with such an adornment

_____ **19.** word: _____

v. to sympathize with or express sympathy for; to condole

_____ **20.** word: _____

adj. tending to disappear or fade away; fleeting; vanishing

COLUMN B

(A) Dickens did not confine his **caricatures** to industry. He also overstated the positive qualities of life before the machine age.

(B) In *Martin Chuzzlewit*, Dickens describes a delightful carriage ride, complete with four horses spiritedly **gamboling**.

(C) The evening is described as "mild and bright," with the **evanescent** hum of the wheels dispersing into the pleasant air.

(D) The harness is **festooned** with bells that tinkle on bright ribbons.

(E) The man in the carriage is enjoying his ride, looking forward to the sight of trees **burgeoning** with springtime foliage and other beauties of London.

(F) Although some of the writing is rather **maudlin,** the reader feels that the overemotional episode—with its fairy-tale quality—is justified.

(G) It is easy to **commiserate** with Dickens and understand his views, when we realize that such carriages were replaced by dirty, mechanical trains.

(H) While the carriage ride is colorful and bright, the railroad journey is characterized by a sense of drabness, a **pallor** that is the legacy of industrialization.

(I) Dickens did not view the advantages brought by industry as sufficient **remuneration** for the end of simple, heartfelt pleasures like the fairy-tale beauty of the carriage ride.

(J) Unlike many of the industrialists whom he criticized in his works, Dickens was not **venal**. His convictions and values were strong and not dishonorable.

EXERCISE 3 Sentence Completion ✍

Directions. For each of the following items, circle the letter of the choice that best completes the meaning of the sentence or sentences.

21. One of Dickens's goals was for industry to _____, or reimburse, workers and urban dwellers for illness and poor living conditions.
    (A) caricature
    (B) festoon
    (C) gambol
    (D) remunerate
    (E) commiserate

22. His novel *Nicholas Nickleby* made readers of the time _____ with the difficult lives of the school boys. This pity eventually led to extensive school reforms.
    (A) commiserate
    (B) caricature
    (C) festoon
    (D) gambol
    (E) remunerate

23. Dickens's *A Christmas Carol* deals with the _____ Scrooge, who has been corrupted by the values of industrial society.
    (A) evanescent
    (B) venal
    (C) burgeoning
    (D) maudlin
    (E) commiserative

24. Dickens's descriptions of Cratchit, Scrooge's employee, are very moving. Cratchit's skin has an unnatural _____ from working long hours indoors.
    (A) venality
    (B) remuneration
    (C) gambol
    (D) pallor
    (E) festoon

25. Dickens fully intended for his writing to inspire changes in the working and living conditions brought about as the Industrial Revolution _____. The rapid growth of cities caused many of the problems.
    (A) commiserated
    (B) remunerated
    (C) burgeoned
    (D) gamboled
    (E) festooned

26. Such moving descriptions were not too sentimental or _____ to bring about better working conditions for the poor.
    (A) evanescent
    (B) commiserative
    (C) maudlin
    (D) venal
    (E) burgeoning

27. But the social conditions Dickens described were not _____; they persisted. Empathy, or _____, with the plight of working people was not enough.
    (A) maudlin . . . remuneration
    (B) burgeoning . . . caricature
    (C) venal . . . festoon
    (D) evanescent . . . gambol
    (E) evanescent . . . commiseration

28. While Dickens lived before the automobile, he realized that the days of gaily _____ carriages had passed. He knew that rapid change was inevitable in the _____ industrial world.
    (A) maudlin . . . burgeoning
    (B) festooned . . . burgeoning
    (C) gamboled . . . venal
    (D) commiserative . . . evanescent
    (E) festooned . . . maudlin

29. Dickens wanted to see _____ horses bearing ruddy-cheeked riders on their backs rather than the _____ of passengers riding trains.
    (A) gamboling . . . maudlin
    (B) festooned . . . evanescence
    (C) venal . . . remuneration
    (D) evanescent . . . caricature
    (E) gamboling . . . pallor

30. Although Dickens's characters are sometimes _____, they remind us that adjustment to change is a permanent rather than _____ fact of life.
    (A) pallors . . . a venal
    (B) evanescence . . . maudlin
    (C) caricatures . . . an evanescent
    (D) festoons . . . a remunerative
    (E) caricatures . . . a maudlin

Name _____ Date _____ Class _____

MAKING NEW WORDS YOUR OWN

Lesson 28 **CONTEXT: Science and Technology**

Artists Take on Industrial England

How's this for an art exhibition title: "Public Health and Housing in Industrial England"? As a summer intern at our local newspaper, I was asked to review the exhibition at our local Museum of Modern Art. The show was the idea of the museum director, who is from London. He gave local artists information about the unsanitary living conditions in England during the 1800s and asked the artists to interpret those conditions.

In the following exercises, you will have the opportunity to expand your vocabulary by reading about an art exhibit. Below are ten Vocabulary Words that will be used in these exercises.

abstruse	bauble	fresco	iridescent	promontory
apostasy	bullion	frugal	opulence	usury

EXERCISE 1 *Wordbusting*

Directions. Follow these instructions for this word and the nine words on the next page.
- Figure out the word's meaning by looking at its **context,** its **structure,** and its **sound.** Fill in at least one of the three **CSS** boxes. Alternate which boxes you complete.
- Then, look up the word in a dictionary, read all of its meanings, and write the meaning of the word as it is used in the sentence.
- Follow this same process for each of the Vocabulary Words on the next page. You will need to draw your own map for each word. Use a separate sheet of paper.

1.

abstruse → The background information on health and housing conditions in Victorian England was **abstruse.** Especially hard to understand was the excerpt from the 1842 *Report on the Sanitary Conditions of the Labouring Population of Great Britain.*

Context:

Structure:

Sound:

Dictionary:

2.

(apostasy) ➡️ My first impression of the exhibit was not favorable because I had always believed that art should show happy, positive views of life. However, as a result of the exhibit, I experienced an artistic **apostasy;** the works displayed made me realize that art should also show life's unhappiness.

3.

(bauble) ➡️ One of the first paintings that caught my attention shows a sick child sadly playing with some useless toy, a **bauble**. She is sitting between two houses built so close to each other that little light or air reaches her.

4.

(bullion) ➡️ Another painting shows the Parliament building made of **bullion**. The brick-shaped gold bars shine like the sun. Around the building, protesting workers carry signs bearing such slogans as "Needed: Clean Water" and "Give Us Sanitary Streets."

5.

(fresco) ➡️ I know that the **fresco** is Larry Sawyer's preferred artistic medium, but there was no way to exhibit his work with watercolors on wet plaster at the museum. Instead, he did a disturbing oil painting of hospital patients with tuberculosis.

6.

(frugal) ➡️ Sawyer was extremely **frugal** with his paint, using only thin, spare lines to suggest the patients' forms, their beds, and the walls. Black is the dominant color, as befits tuberculosis, a prominent killer during the industrial era.

7.

(iridescent) ➡️ On the wall in Sawyer's painting is a small, **iridescent** pattern. These rainbow colors, perhaps symbols of faint hope, are projected from a prism hanging in a window.

8.

(opulence) ➡️ Several paintings effectively contrast the wealth and **opulence** of the houses of royalty and upper-class citizens with the poverty and miserable living conditions of the poor and working classes.

9.

(promontory) ➡️ I particularly like the painting showing Edwin Chadwick of London, who began reforms for health and living and working conditions in the mid-nineteenth century. This painting shows Chadwick standing on a rocky **promontory** overlooking the North Sea, welcoming fresh air to English cities.

10.

(usury) ➡️ An interesting black-and-white drawing portrays moneylenders found guilty of **usury,** the practice of charging a high or unlawful rate of interest on a loan.

112 LESSON 28

Name _____ Date _____ Class _____

EXERCISE 2 *Context Clues* ☞

Directions. Scan the definitions in Column A. Then, think about how the boldface words are used in the sentences in Column B. To complete the exercise, match each definition in Column A with the correct Vocabulary Word from Column B. Write the letter of your choice on the line provided; then write the Vocabulary Word on the line preceding the definition.

<table>
<tr><td>

COLUMN A

_____ **11.** word: _____
n. a high point of land extending into a body of water; headland

_____ **12.** word: _____
n. wealth or riches; luxuriousness; abundance

_____ **13.** word: _____
adj. hard to understand

_____ **14.** word: _____
adj. avoiding waste; thrifty; economical

_____ **15.** word: _____
n. the practice of charging a very high or an unlawful rate of interest on a loan

_____ **16.** word: _____
n. a complete forsaking of what one has believed in

_____ **17.** word: _____
n. the art of painting with watercolors on wet plaster; a picture so painted

_____ **18.** word: _____
n. a showy trifle of little value; a useless toy or trinket

_____ **19.** word: _____
adj. showing the colors of the rainbow in a changing pattern

_____ **20.** word: _____
n. ingots, bars, or plates of gold or silver

</td><td>

COLUMN B

(A) An artist who signs his work Z, reportedly a former loan officer accused of **usury,** entered one of my favorite paintings in the exhibit.

(B) Biographical information about Z is vague. "I no longer care about money, and my **apostasy** shocks many," he is quoted as saying.

(C) "I consider my paintings **baubles,**" the biographical note continues, "but if anyone finds value in these trivialities, that's okay with me."

(D) Z ends his biographical note with this statement: "You'll seldom find me in a studio. Instead, you'll find me, paintbrush in hand, standing on a rocky **promontory,** looking out to sea."

(E) Z's work in the exhibit is a painting within a painting. It portrays an artist working on a **fresco** on a fresh ceiling. The **fresco** within the painting shows the same image: an artist painting on a ceiling.

(F) The connection of Z's painting to the exhibit's theme is **abstruse,** but however difficult the connection is to grasp, the painting is extremely colorful.

(G) The **iridescent** windowpanes in Z's painting are beautiful. They throw spots of the spectrum on the painter and the ceiling.

(H) I wish I could buy the painting. I would guard it as carefully as the government guards the **bullion** deposited at Fort Knox.

(I) Some art collectors aren't exactly **frugal;** they would probably pay a high price for Z's painting.

(J) The painting seems to belong in a setting of **opulence** because its impressive colors and jewel-like tones suggest prosperity.

</td></tr>
</table>

Copyright © by Holt, Rinehart and Winston. All rights reserved.

MAKING NEW WORDS YOUR OWN   **113**

EXERCISE 3   *Sentence Completion* ✍

Directions. For each of the following items, circle the letter of the choice that best completes the meaning of the sentence or sentences.

21. The museum itself is situated on a(n) _____ overlooking the river.
(A) fresco
(B) bauble
(C) promontory
(D) usury
(E) apostasy

22. The museum is richly decorated, but the _____ is not overdone.
(A) promontory
(B) bullion
(C) apostasy
(D) usury
(E) opulence

23. A stained-glass window in the entry hall throws _____ patterns on the walls. The changing colors look beautiful below the pale colors of the ceiling _____.
(A) frugal . . . promontory
(B) abstruse . . . usury
(C) frugal . . . bauble
(D) iridescent . . . fresco
(E) opulent . . . bullion

24. Many problems are depicted, from urban poverty and tuberculosis to interest rates, loans, and even the crime of _____.
(A) bauble
(B) bullion
(C) abstruseness
(D) usury
(E) iridescence

25. An interesting painting near the main entrance depicts a well-dressed man standing between two tall stacks of _____, which cast a golden glow on his face.
(A) baubles
(B) bullion
(C) promontories
(D) usuries
(E) apostasies

26. The 1800s clearly were not a time for _____ in government financing for housing and health; on the contrary, it was a time that called for massive spending.
(A) bauble
(B) apostasy
(C) promontory
(D) opulence
(E) frugality

27. An impressive painting shows a banker confessing a(n) _____: He renounces his profession and wants to help the poor.
(A) promontory
(B) bullion
(C) bauble
(D) apostasy
(E) opulence

28. The artistic media are varied, too. To artist Larry Sawyer's disappointment, there are no _____, as painted plaster walls would be almost impossible to exhibit.
(A) apostasies
(B) promontories
(C) frescoes
(D) bullion
(E) baubles

29. One child at the exhibit tried to touch a brightly colored painting as though it were a pretty _____, meant to be played with.
(A) bauble
(B) promontory
(C) apostasy
(D) fresco
(E) usury

30. Since you haven't seen the art exhibit, I hope my comments are not too _____ and that you can make sense out of them.
(A) frugal
(B) abstruse
(C) opulent
(D) iridescent
(E) biennial

MAKING NEW WORDS YOUR OWN

Lesson 29 | CONTEXT: Science and Technology

Watson, Crick, and the Double Helix

Last month, my science class did a project on genetics, a branch of biology that deals with hereditary features in plants and animals. During one of our lab periods, my teacher, Mr. Farley, explained the discovery of deoxyribonucleic acid, or DNA. He told us that the currently accepted structural model of DNA was first discovered in 1953 by American James Watson (b. 1928) and Englishman Francis Crick (b. 1916). Watson and Crick were biologists who worked together at the Cavendish Laboratory at Cambridge University in England.

In the following exercises, you will have the opportunity to expand your vocabulary by reading about the discovery of DNA. Below are ten Vocabulary Words that will be used in these exercises.

abscond	aspersion	ethereal	malign	prognosis
adjure	circumvent	ignominy	malinger	remonstrate

EXERCISE 1 | *Wordbusting* 🖎

Directions. Follow these instructions for this word and the nine words on the next page.
- Figure out the word's meaning by looking at its **context,** its **structure,** and its **sound.** Fill in at least one of the three **CSS** boxes. Alternate which boxes you complete.
- Then, look up the word in a dictionary, read all of its meanings, and write the meaning of the word as it is used in the sentence.
- Follow this same process for each of the Vocabulary Words on the next page. You will need to draw your own map for each word. Use a separate sheet of paper.

1.

(abscond) ➔ "The 1950s were a very tense time for biologists," said Mr. Farley. "Many of them were working on DNA models, and they worried that someone would **abscond** with their research. I am sure some scientists did leave a lab taking others' ideas with them."

Context:	Structure:	Sound:

Dictionary:

Name _____ Date _____ Class _____

2.

(adjure) ➔ "Watson and Crick had to **adjure** the other scientists at Cambridge not to reveal their theories," Mr. Farley continued. "They asked their colleagues to swear an oath of secrecy."

3.

(aspersion) ➔ "At the risk of spreading **aspersion,** I must tell you that Watson and Crick saw some other scientists' models before announcing their discovery. I don't want to slander them, but some people charge that they used the work of molecular biologist Rosalind Franklin."

4.

(circumvent) ➔ "I'm sure," stated Mr. Farley, "it would be tempting to try to **circumvent,** or go around, the rules during a race for the Nobel Prize. Besides Crick and Watson, many others were working on DNA models."

5.

(ethereal) ➔ "DNA is the basic substance of life, but at the same time it is almost **ethereal,** or unearthly, because of its minute size."

6.

(ignominy) ➔ "Did any of the scientists ever experience the **ignominy** of being publicly disgraced for stealing each other's work?" asked Cora. "No; such charges are difficult to prove," said Mr. Farley. "Also, it is natural that they would build somewhat on one another's work."

7.

(malign) ➔ "As I said before, I do not want to **malign** anyone. I refuse to defame scientists who made such an important contribution to humanity. Along with the splitting of the atom, the discovery of the DNA helix is seen as one of the most important findings of the twentieth century."

8.

(malinger) ➔ "By the way, while I'm thinking of it, we're going to be dissecting frogs next week, and I don't want any of you **malingering** to get out of it. We've had enough fake sicknesses already this term," said Mr. Farley.

9.

(prognosis) ➔ "Mr. Farley, does knowledge of DNA structure help a doctor make a clearer **prognosis** of a patient?" asked Ira, getting us back on the subject. "It seems that it would help doctors make more accurate predictions about a patient's chance of recovery."

10.

(remonstrate) ➔ Mr. Farley was just about to answer when Cora **remonstrated**. "I object to dissecting frogs. I believe in animal rights, and I think that using frogs for lab experiments is wrong."

116 LESSON 29

Copyright © by Holt, Rinehart and Winston. All rights reserved.

EXERCISE 2 *Context Clues* ✍

Directions. Scan the definitions in Column A. Then, think about how the boldface words are used in the sentences in Column B. To complete the exercise, match each definition in Column A with the correct Vocabulary Word from Column B. Write the letter of your choice on the line provided; then write the Vocabulary Word on the line preceding the definition.

COLUMN A	COLUMN B

COLUMN A

_____ **11.** word: _____

n. public disgrace; public dishonor; disgraceful, shameful behavior

_____ **12.** word: _____

v. to surround and trap by cleverness; to avoid or go around

_____ **13.** word: _____

v. to pretend to be sick to escape work or duty; to shirk

_____ **14.** word: _____

n. a damaging, false remark; slander; a slur; the act of slandering or defaming someone

_____ **15.** word: _____

v. to object; to protest; to argue against some action

_____ **16.** word: _____

n. a forecast; a prediction about the course of a disease and the chance of recovery

_____ **17.** word: _____

v. to command or charge someone, often under oath or penalty, to do something; to ask or to entreat earnestly

_____ **18.** word: _____

v. to run away; to leave suddenly and secretly and hide, especially to escape the law

_____ **19.** word: _____

adj. evil; malicious; *v.* to speak evil of; to defame or slander

_____ **20.** word: _____

adj. very light and airy; delicate; unearthly; celestial

COLUMN B

(A) "We should really get back to DNA," Mr. Farley **adjured,** seriously asking us to pay attention.

(B) "You certainly have the right to **remonstrate,** but it would be best to save your opposition for later so that we can continue discussing DNA structure."

(C) "In the 1950s, some scientists hypothesized that DNA might be a helix so **ethereal** and fine that it could not be seen by a microscope."

(D) "But no one was able to **circumvent** the exact structure, despite attempts to encircle and trap the solution," Mr. Farley said.

(E) "Several scientists suffered **ignominy** when they were publicly censured for drawing obviously incorrect conclusions."

(F) "Although other scientists cast **aspersions** on these errors, the theories, though incorrect, did not deserve these criticisms."

(G) "The scientists," Mr. Farley said, "should not have been **maligned**. They were, after all, able to rule out some faulty theories and come up with new ones."

(H) "The **prognosis** for DNA was good," he continued, "because the outlook in a field is always best when there is both competition and cooperation."

(I) "The scientists helped each other. They didn't just **abscond** or run off with each others' theories.

(J) "But the race was far too tight for **malingering,**" said Mr. Farley. "No one was lazy about his or her research."

EXERCISE 3 *Sentence Completion* ✍

Directions. For each of the following items, circle the letter of the choice that best completes the meaning of the sentence or sentences.

21. "Watson and Crick often thought that someone else would _____ with the Nobel Prize and experience the fame," Mr. Farley said.
(A) adjure
(B) abscond
(C) circumvent
(D) malign
(E) malinger

22. "But Watson and Crick were destined for public honor, rather than _____ and scandal."
(A) aspersion
(B) prognosis
(C) ignominy
(D) remonstration
(E) adjuration

23. "In 1953," he continued, "they published their discovery in *Nature* magazine. No one _____, or took exception to, the authenticity of their finding."
(A) absconded
(B) adjured
(C) circumvented
(D) remonstrated
(E) malingered

24. "At last, someone had made substance of the unearthly, _____ DNA," said Mr. Farley. "Crick and Watson had pinpointed it as a helical acid."
(A) ethereal
(B) maligned
(C) ignominable
(D) prognostic
(E) adjuratory

25. "Their model was unlike any previously proposed, but it did not _____ scientific evidence," he continued. "It dealt directly with the facts."
(A) adjure
(B) circumvent
(C) abscond
(D) malign
(E) remonstrate

26. "Watson and Crick were not _____; they had worked tirelessly."
(A) maligners
(B) ignominies
(C) prognoses
(D) malingerers
(E) aspersions

27. "Still," he said, "some critics cast _____ on Watson and Crick by reporting that the two had _____ ethics by shunning the usual acknowledgment rules."
(A) aspersions . . . remonstrated
(B) prognoses . . . adjured
(C) ignominies . . . maligned
(D) remonstrations . . . malingered
(E) aspersions . . . circumvented

28. "Critics _____ other scientists to enforce these rules. They especially wanted to prevent scientists from _____, or fleeing, with their colleagues' work."
(A) adjured . . . circumventing
(B) remonstrated . . . malingering
(C) adjured . . . absconding
(D) absconded . . . maligning
(E) remonstrated . . . maligning

29. "The _____ who belittle these scientists may be justified, or they may simply be casting slanderous _____," said Mr. Farley.
(A) aspersions . . . prognoses
(B) maligners . . . aspersions
(C) ignominies . . . circumvention
(D) etherealness . . . adjuration
(E) maligners . . . prognoses

30. "The discovery of DNA structure provided a positive _____ for the future of genetics."
(A) prognosis
(B) remonstration
(C) aspersion
(D) adjuration
(E) ignominy

MAKING NEW WORDS YOUR OWN

Lesson 30 | **CONTEXT: Science and Technology**

Making a Documentary

Reading the book *Framing Science—The Making of a BBC Documentary* by Roger Silverstone gave me the idea for a short story I was recently assigned. The author of the book details the production of a program for the British Broadcasting Corporation's *Horizon* science series. My idea was to write a story about a recent high school graduate, Len, who wins a prize to make a documentary of his own.

In the following exercises, you will have the opportunity to expand your vocabulary by reading excerpts from the fictional account of a young man's experiences in making a BBC documentary. Below are ten Vocabulary Words that will be used in these exercises.

biennial	elicit	equivocal	fiasco	reprisal
capricious	emaciate	extort	longevity	taciturn

EXERCISE 1 *Wordbusting*

Directions. Follow these instructions for this word and the nine words on the next page.
- Figure out the word's meaning by looking at its **context,** its **structure,** and its **sound.** Fill in at least one of the three **CSS** boxes. Alternate which boxes you complete.
- Then, look up the word in a dictionary, read all of its meanings, and write the meaning of the word as it is used in the sentence.
- Follow this same process for each of the Vocabulary Words on the next page. You will need to draw your own map for each word. Use a separate sheet of paper.

1.

biennial → "This isn't a **biennial** series, you know. We'd all have more time if it were, but a new *SciSense* season starts every year, not every two years," said Mr. Russell, the producer.

Context:

Structure:

Sound:

Dictionary:

2.

capricious →

"We need to get busy and come up with an idea for the show right now," Len said to the production crew. Then he quickly changed his mind and said, "No, let's take as much time as we need," displaying his **capricious** nature.

3.

elicit →

"Actually," he said, "you should stay because I need to **elicit** from you some ideas about the subject for our program, which we need to start filming in two weeks. Does anybody have any ideas I can draw out?"

4.

emaciate →

Mr. Berry, the scriptwriter, said, "How about a program showing what people can do to protect their cats from distemper and other diseases? Distemper can **emaciate** cats by robbing them of their appetite. You should see how gaunt and skinny they can get."

5.

equivocal →

"The last time we did a program like that," said Ms. Lofler, the program's assistant director, "the public response was **equivocal**. We weren't sure whether the public liked it or not."

6.

extort →

"Would people let us film their sick animals?" asked the camera operator. "Of course," he continued with a wicked grin, "we could always **extort** permission in some way or other."

7.

fiasco →

"You have a weird sense of humor," Len said. "Anyway, a show about sick cats could be a complete failure. I don't want a **fiasco**, so we need to get serious and think of a good science subject."

8.

longevity →

"A subject such as **longevity** would be good," Ms. Lofler said. "We could find out who the oldest people in England are, interview them and their families."

9.

reprisal →

"Another good subject is the environmental impact of war," Len said, "and the damages done when one nation starts a fight and another nation responds with **reprisals**."

10.

taciturn →

One of the show's writers, Mr. Edwards, who is known for being **taciturn**, startled everyone by speaking up: "I don't want to write about sick cats or war, so let's talk to the elderly Brits."

EXERCISE 2 *Context Clues* 👈

Directions. Scan the definitions in Column A. Then, think about how the boldface words are used in the sentences in Column B. To complete the exercise, match each definition in Column A with the correct Vocabulary Word from Column B. Write the letter of your choice on the line provided; then write the Vocabulary Word on the line preceding the definition.

COLUMN A	COLUMN B

COLUMN A

____ **11.** word: _____

v. to obtain by threats or force

____ **12.** word: _____

n. injury done for injury received, especially by one nation to another; the act of returning an injury for an injury received; retaliation

____ **13.** word: _____

v. to draw out; to bring forth; to evoke

____ **14.** word: _____

adj. not fond of speaking; quiet; reserved

____ **15.** word: _____

n. a complete or ridiculous failure

____ **16.** word: _____

adj. occurring every two years; living or lasting for two years

____ **17.** word: _____

v. to make unnaturally thin; to waste away from hunger or disease

____ **18.** word: _____

n. long life; length of life

____ **19.** word: _____

adj. tending to change quickly without apparent reason; erratic; impulsive

____ **20.** word: _____

adj. having two or more meanings; ambiguous; evasive; of uncertain value or outcome; undecided; questionable

COLUMN B

(A) I read part of *Framing Science*, Len thought, and I certainly don't recall reading about any **fiascoes** like this—not even any minor misfires.

(B) I'm still young, but at this rate my **longevity** is questionable. Do all directors burn out early?

(C) One of the writers called me **capricious**, but I think I'm a steady person.

(D) Working almost around the clock and forgetting to eat may **emaciate** me. My mother says I'm already just skin and bones.

(E) I'm really glad that my director's prize is just for one year and not a **biennial** job that I have to do every other year.

(F) The hardest part of directing is getting straight answers from people who talk out of both sides of their mouths. Some of them actually seem to enjoy being **equivocal**.

(G) On the other hand, **taciturn** people are just as difficult. Getting them to talk about their lives is a challenge.

(H) Sometimes I try too hard to **elicit** responses from people, probably because I'm still young and inexperienced.

(I) Then I start thinking of things I could do to get even with the people who ignored me, but so far any **reprisals** are just in my head.

(J) As the director, I guess I could **extort** responses from them, but intimidation usually backfires.

EXERCISE 3 *Sentence Completion* 👉

Directions. For each of the following items, circle the letter of the choice that best completes the meaning of the sentence or sentences.

21. Len worried that shooting on location at a retirement home would be a(n) _____, but the filming was a great success.
    - (A) reprisal
    - (B) longevity
    - (C) elicitation
    - (D) fiasco
    - (E) extortion

22. One woman, who was 103 years old, was especially willing to share her secrets of _____ with television audiences.
    - (A) extortion
    - (B) fiasco
    - (C) longevity
    - (D) equivocalness
    - (E) reprisal

23. "Always be gentle and nonthreatening," she said. "Don't ever _____ favors from anyone. It will always backfire on you."
    - (A) elicit
    - (B) extort
    - (C) gambol
    - (D) emaciate
    - (E) festoon

24. "It seems to be human nature to return evil for evil," she said, "but you will live longer if you avoid _____."
    - (A) longevity
    - (B) equivocalness
    - (C) bienniums
    - (D) taciturnity
    - (E) reprisals

25. Len thought that the senior citizens would be _____, but instead they were very outgoing and talkative.
    - (A) taciturn
    - (B) biennial
    - (C) equivocal
    - (D) capricious
    - (E) emaciated

26. Len hired a famous actor to _____ responses from residents. The actor skillfully extracted the secrets of the elderly residents' _____.
    - (A) elicit . . . reprisal
    - (B) emaciate . . . biennium
    - (C) elicit . . . longevity
    - (D) emaciate . . . extortion
    - (E) extort . . . fiasco

27. One _____ woman, who weighed about eighty pounds, was _____ at first, but when she finally spoke, she was the most fascinating of all the residents.
    - (A) biennial . . . taciturn
    - (B) equivocal . . . capricious
    - (C) capricious . . . biennial
    - (D) emaciated . . . taciturn
    - (E) biennial . . . capricious

28. Len _____ from one man the secret of his long life: a(n) _____ hike in the mountains. "Every other year is my limit," he said.
    - (A) emaciated . . . taciturn
    - (B) extorted . . . elicitable
    - (C) elicited . . . emaciated
    - (D) emaciated . . . capricious
    - (E) elicited . . . biennial

29. A 101-year-old woman was _____; she changed her answer fives times. Len pretended to be _____ the truth from her, and after several joking "warnings," she laughingly shouted, "Radishes!"
    - (A) emaciated . . . eliciting
    - (B) biennial . . . emaciating
    - (C) capricious . . . extorting
    - (D) extortive . . . emaciating
    - (E) elicited . . . extorting

30. The interview results may seem _____ to some viewers, but the overall impression was not at all vague. Len hoped the program would _____ favorable reviews.
    - (A) taciturn . . . extort
    - (B) equivocal . . . elicit
    - (C) biennial . . . elicit
    - (D) capricious . . . emaciate
    - (E) emaciated . . . extort

Why We Practice Analogies

Practice with analogies develops proficiency in logic. To answer analogy questions correctly, you analyze two words and identify the relationship between them; then you identify another pair of words that has the same relationship. In addition, when you study analogies, you think about the precise meanings of words and fix these definitions in your memory. Finally, studying word analogies will help you to gain higher scores on national tests that include multiple-choice analogy questions. The new Scholastic Aptitude Test-I Verbal Reasoning Test, for example, includes analogy questions.

Understanding Word Analogies

A word analogy is a comparison between two pairs of words. Here's how word analogies are written:

Example 1   FIND : LOCATE :: lose : misplace

The colon (:) stands for the phrase "is related to." Here's how to read the relationships in Example 1:

> FIND [is related to] LOCATE
> lose [is related to] misplace

The double colon [::] between the two pairs of words stands for the phrase "in the same way that." Here is how to read the complete analogy:

> FIND [is related to] LOCATE
> [in the same way that]
> lose [is related to] misplace

Here is another way:

> FIND is to LOCATE as lose is to misplace.

A properly constructed analogy, then, tells us that the relationship between the first pair of words is the same as the relationship between the second pair of words. In Example 1, *find* and *locate* are synonyms, just as *lose* and *misplace* are synonyms.

Let's look at another example:

Example 2   GIFT : JOY :: grief : tears

What's the relationship here? A *gift* causes *joy,* just as *grief* causes *tears*. A cause-and-effect relationship links the two pairs of words in Example 2. To help you identify the relationships expressed in analogies, we have designed the chart on page 124. No chart, of course, could include all possible relationships between words, but these twelve relationships are frequently presented. You should familiarize yourself with these relationships.

TYPES OF ANALOGIES		
RELATIONSHIP	**EXAMPLE**	**EXPLANATION**
Synonym	DRY : ARID :: lost : mislaid	*Dry* is similar in meaning to *arid*, just as *lost* is similar in meaning to *mislaid*.
Antonym	KIND : CRUEL :: happy : sad	*Kind* is the opposite of *cruel*, just as *happy* is the opposite of *sad*.
Part and Whole	CHAPTER : BOOK :: fender : automobile	A *chapter* is a part of a *book*, just as a *fender* is a part of an *automobile*.
	POEM : STANZAS :: play : acts	A *poem* is composed of *stanzas*, just as a *play* is composed of *acts*.
Characteristic Quality	MIRROR : SMOOTH :: sandpaper : rough	*Mirrors* are characteristically *smooth*, just as *sandpaper* is characteristically *rough*.
Classification	POLKA : DANCE :: frog : amphibian	A *polka* may be classified as a *dance*, just as a *frog* may be classified as an *amphibian*.
	BIRD : CARDINAL :: house : igloo	A *cardinal* is classified as a *bird*, just as an *igloo* is classified as a *house*.
Cause and Effect	GIFT : JOY :: rain : flood	A *gift* can cause *joy*, just as *rain* can cause a *flood*.
	TEARS : SADNESS :: smiles : joy	*Tears* are an effect of *sadness*, just as *smiles* are an effect of *joy*.
Function	KNIFE : CUT :: shovel : dig	The function of a *knife* is to *cut*, just as the function of a *shovel* is to *dig*.
Location	FISH : SEA :: moose : forest	A *fish* can be found in the *sea*, just as a *moose* can be found in a *forest*.
Degree	CHUCKLE : LAUGH :: whimper : cry	*Chuckle* and *laugh* have similar meanings, but differ in degree in the same way that *whimper* and *cry* have similar meanings but differ in degree.
Performer and Related Object	CASHIER : CASH :: plumber : pipe	A *cashier* works with *cash*, just as a *plumber* works with *pipe*.
Performer and Related Action	AUTHOR : WRITE :: chef : cook	You expect an *author* to *write*, just as you expect a *chef* to *cook*.
Action and Related Object	BOIL : EGG :: throw : ball	You *boil* an *egg*, just as you *throw* a *ball*. (In these items, the object always receives the action.)

A Process for Solving Analogies

Your job in solving multiple-choice analogy questions is to identify the relationship between the first two words and then to find the pair of words that has the most similar relationship. Here are four hints to help you:

Hint #1. Eliminate choices that represent relationships that do not match the relationship between the capitalized words.

Hint #2. Eliminate choices that have vague relationships. Remember, the original relationship will always be clear. So, too, will the answer's relationship.

Hint #3. Eliminate word pairs that express the same relationship as the capitalized pair, but appear in the opposite word order.

Hint #4. If you can not determine the relationship between two words, try reading them backward. Remember that a cause-and-effect relationship, for example, exists whether the pair is written *Cause : Effect* or *Effect : Cause*.

Here's a process that will help you with analogy questions:

> **Answering Analogy Questions: A 3-Step Method**
> 1. Identify the relationship between the capitalized pair of words.
> 2. Look for that relationship in the pairs of words in the answer choices. Eliminate those that do not have that relationship.
> 3. Choose the pair of words whose relationship and word order match those of the capitalized pair.

Let's apply this pattern to a sample question in Example 3.

Example 3 FISH : SEA ::

    (A) sun : star
    (B) hero : villain
    (C) moose : forest
    (D) spacesuit : astronaut
    (E) garage : car

1. *Identify the relationship.* It is location; a *fish* can be found in the *sea*.
2. *Eliminate choices.* Choice A has a relationship of classification; the *sun* is a *star*. Choice B has two opposites; *hero* is an antonym for *villain*. Choice D consists of a performer (*astronaut*) and a related object (*spacesuit*). None of these choices match.
3. *Choose the correct answer.* Choices C and E both have location relationships: A *moose* can be found in a *forest,* and a *car* can be found in a *garage.* But Choice E could only be correct if the words appeared in the opposite order— *car : garage.* So Choice C must be correct.

A Final Word

Analogies are easier to tackle if you approach them with flexibility. Allow yourself to discover the relationship between the first pair of words and to explore the relationships between the words in the answer choices. Keep in mind that some words can represent more than one part of speech and that most words have multiple meanings. Remember, these little verbal puzzles are a test of your ability to demonstrate flexibility as well as logic.

CONNECTING NEW WORDS AND PATTERNS

Lesson 1 ANALOGIES

Directions. For each of the following items, choose the lettered pair of words that expresses a relationship that is most similar to the relationship between the pair of capitalized words. Write the letter of your answer on the line provided before the number of the item. *(1 point each)*

_____ **1.** ADMONISH : CONDEMN ::
  (A) change : alter
  (B) acknowledge : ignore
  (C) look : glare
  (D) advise : suggest
  (E) admit : deny

_____ **2.** BANAL : COMMONPLACE ::
  (A) extraordinary : average
  (B) forbidden : acceptable
  (C) nosy : respectful
  (D) famous : familiar
  (E) strange : unusual

_____ **3.** LUGUBRIOUS : SAD ::
  (A) luxurious : shabby
  (B) dismayed : happy
  (C) awkward : silly
  (D) cluttered : tidy
  (E) jubilant : pleased

_____ **4.** NEBULOUS : FOG ::
  (A) dry : shower
  (B) hazy : mirror
  (C) soft : blanket
  (D) hoarse : whisper
  (E) cold : sun

_____ **5.** NEFARIOUS : VILLAIN ::
  (A) cowardly : hero
  (B) neat : chaos
  (C) vicious : rabbit
  (D) amusing : clown
  (E) grievous : merriment

_____ **6.** NEMESIS : PUNISH ::
  (A) savior : help
  (B) crane : hoist
  (C) stranger : avoid
  (D) masterpiece : imitate
  (E) pillow : sleep

_____ **7.** PHLEGMATIC : LOAFER ::
  (A) congested : vacuum
  (B) creative : artist
  (C) plentiful : void
  (D) cloudy : clarity
  (E) unusual : system

_____ **8.** PROSAIC : EXCEPTIONAL ::
  (A) mistaken : erased
  (B) written : composed
  (C) poetic : theatrical
  (D) promoted : elevated
  (E) fancy : plain

_____ **9.** PSEUDONYM : NAME ::
  (A) actor : performer
  (B) preface : novel
  (C) classroom : textbook
  (D) artist : musician
  (E) staff : writer

_____ **10.** PURLOIN : THIEF ::
  (A) protect : vault
  (B) rob : bank
  (C) hide : disguise
  (D) counterfeit : money
  (E) measure : surveyor

Name _____ Date _____ Class _____

CONNECTING NEW WORDS AND PATTERNS

Lesson 2 | ANALOGIES

Directions. For each of the following items, choose the lettered pair of words that expresses a relationship that is most similar to the relationship between the pair of capitalized words. Write the letter of your answer on the line provided before the number of the item. *(1 point each)*

____ 1. ASSIMILATE : FOOD ::
(A) serve : waiter
(B) water : hose
(C) build : carpenter
(D) join : organization
(E) bolt : horse

____ 2. BLAZON : KNIGHT ::
(A) helmet : safety
(B) badge : police officer
(C) professional : lawyer
(D) border : carpet
(E) musician : performance

____ 3. CHOLERIC : HOTHEAD ::
(A) brilliant : genius
(B) intolerant : baby sitter
(C) weak : gorilla
(D) aggressive : butterfly
(E) patriotic : traitor

____ 4. COLLOQUY : CHAT ::
(A) bridge : river
(B) field : grain
(C) conclusion : argument
(D) opinion : disagreement
(E) festival : gathering

____ 5. DESPOT : OPPRESSOR ::
(A) destroy : invent
(B) discover : find
(C) expect : wish
(D) erase : add
(E) ridicule : advise

____ 6. DIRGE : FUNERAL ::
(A) cousin : relative
(B) death : sorrow
(C) hymn : music
(D) scenery : play
(E) instrument : composition

____ 7. ENNUI : INACTIVITY ::
(A) route : map
(B) placement : location
(C) number : graph
(D) energy : power
(E) fatigue : labor

____ 8. FARCICAL : HILARIOUS ::
(A) sincere : charitable
(B) foolish : intense
(C) good : excellent
(D) violent : valiant
(E) foreign : familiar

____ 9. FEIGN : TRICKSTER ::
(A) operate : surgeon
(B) nourish : food
(C) falsify : document
(D) gain : loser
(E) write : proposal

____ 10. FORTUITOUS : PLANNED ::
(A) forfeited : given up
(B) punished : blamed
(C) functional : practical
(D) wealthy : prosperous
(E) unfortunate : lucky

Name _____ Date _____ Class _____

CONNECTING NEW WORDS AND PATTERNS

Lesson 3 | ANALOGIES

Directions. For each of the following items, choose the lettered pair of words that expresses a relationship that is most similar to the relationship between the pair of capitalized words. Write the letter of your answer on the line provided before the number of the item. *(1 point each)*

_____ 1. ASCETIC : SELF-DENYING ::
  (A) supporter : condemning
  (B) avenue : directionless
  (C) visitor : unwelcoming
  (D) concrete : rubbery
  (E) athlete : active

_____ 2. DOGGEREL : VERSE ::
  (A) van : motor vehicle
  (B) kennel : puppy
  (C) leash : trainer
  (D) list : item
  (E) book : literature

_____ 3. DOGMA : PREACH ::
  (A) opinion : shout
  (B) social studies : teach
  (C) memo : remind
  (D) shepherd : watch
  (E) bridle : restrain

_____ 4. EXHORT : ADVISOR ::
  (A) inspire : poem
  (B) ignore : counselor
  (C) correct : mistake
  (D) exhale : oxygen
  (E) testify : witness

_____ 5. FACILE : SINCERE ::
  (A) remorseful : regretful
  (B) guilty : innocent
  (C) fatal : fanciful
  (D) honest : frank
  (E) sorrowful : unhappy

_____ 6. INVEIGLE : DECEIVER ::
  (A) befriend : enemy
  (B) investigate : detective
  (C) follow : leader
  (D) celebrate : deputy
  (E) ring : receiver

_____ 7. PROFFER : SUBMIT ::
  (A) pleasure : gift
  (B) package : wrapping
  (C) thought : dilemma
  (D) trade : exchange
  (E) offense : defense

_____ 8. SANGUINE : OPTIMIST ::
  (A) joyful : mourner
  (B) defenseless : warrior
  (C) dissatisfied : protestor
  (D) genuine : hypocrisy
  (E) bright : shadow

_____ 9. SCURRILOUS : REFINED ::
  (A) horrible : unpleasant
  (B) favorable : fortunate
  (C) scattered : distributed
  (D) flexible : rigid
  (E) hurried : frenzied

_____ 10. SERAPHIC : ANGELIC ::
  (A) earnest : superficial
  (B) impatient : stubborn
  (C) spiritual : worldly
  (D) wicked : kindly
  (E) anxious : worried

CONNECTING NEW WORDS AND PATTERNS

Lesson 4 | ANALOGIES

Directions. For each of the following items, choose the lettered pair of words that expresses a relationship that is most similar to the relationship between the pair of capitalized words. Write the letter of your answer on the line provided before the number of the item. *(1 point each)*

_____ 1. ABSOLVE : JURY ::
   (A) lead : baton
   (B) conduct : orchestra
   (C) absorb : plastic
   (D) harmonize : choir
   (E) reach : solution

_____ 2. ANTIPATHY : AVOIDANCE ::
   (A) success : confidence
   (B) emotion : happiness
   (C) remorse : victory
   (D) felony : crime
   (E) withdrawal : embrace

_____ 3. ANTIPODES : OPPOSITES ::
   (A) circles : squares
   (B) electrons : atoms
   (C) friends : comrades
   (D) antagonists : conflicts
   (E) petals : flowers

_____ 4. CHARLATAN : DECEIVE ::
   (A) banner : advertise
   (B) chivalry : rescue
   (C) campaign : organize
   (D) pedestrian : swim
   (E) impostor : trick

_____ 5. ERUDITE : SCHOLAR ::
   (A) faithless : dog
   (B) strong : wrestler
   (C) freezing : sunshine
   (D) shy : leader
   (E) responsible : winner

_____ 6. IMMUTABLE : CHANGEABLE ::
   (A) copied : imitated
   (B) sound : solid
   (C) allowable : permissible
   (D) steadfast : fickle
   (E) magnetic : powerful

_____ 7. INDIGENT : WEALTHY ::
   (A) desperate : frantic
   (B) impoverished : poor
   (C) dignified : conservative
   (D) accurate : precise
   (E) solemn : silly

_____ 8. INFRINGE : VIOLATOR ::
   (A) predict : outcome
   (B) cooperate : partner
   (C) arrange : meeting
   (D) protect : awning
   (E) substitute : original

_____ 9. NETTLE : PLANT ::
   (A) herd : cattle
   (B) cactus : desert
   (C) quarter : coin
   (D) kettle : whistle
   (E) crystal : gold

_____ 10. OSTENSIBLE : APPARENT ::
   (A) fragile : delicate
   (B) clever : foolish
   (C) obvious : hidden
   (D) radiant : radical
   (E) sensible : sensitive

Name _____ Date _____ Class _____

CONNECTING NEW WORDS AND PATTERNS

Lesson 5   ANALOGIES

Directions. For each of the following items, choose the lettered pair of words that expresses a relationship that is most similar to the relationship between the pair of capitalized words. Write the letter of your answer on the line provided before the number of the item. *(1 point each)*

_____ **1.** ELEGY : POEM ::
(A) stanza : line
(B) preface : novel
(C) fabric : linen
(D) jet : airplane
(E) forest : fern

_____ **2.** EULOGY : PRAISE ::
(A) apology : demand
(B) cartoon : amuse
(C) fire : ignite
(D) gymnast : exercise
(E) masterpiece : create

_____ **3.** EUPHONY : PLEASANT ::
(A) lightning : bright
(B) whale : miniature
(C) thunder : silent
(D) miracle : understandable
(E) mirror : dull

_____ **4.** EXTRANEOUS : ESSENTIAL ::
(A) outrageous : enraged
(B) excessive : limitless
(C) assured : confident
(D) desirable : worthwhile
(E) cautious : careless

_____ **5.** HOMILY : MINISTER ::
(A) greenhouse : orchid
(B) tropics : parrot
(C) steeple : church
(D) examination : doctor
(E) politician : senator

_____ **6.** INTROVERT : WITHDRAW ::
(A) proposal : present
(B) destination : arrive
(C) entertainer : perform
(D) announcement : inform
(E) change : suggest

_____ **7.** MUNDANE : EXCEPTIONAL ::
(A) meaningful : kindly
(B) simple : complex
(C) acceptable : appropriate
(D) insufferable : unbearable
(E) matted : woven

_____ **8.** PARAGON : MODEL ::
(A) football : goal
(B) teenager : high school
(C) column : base
(D) narrative : story
(E) thoughtfulness : appreciation

_____ **9.** PROGENY : DESCENDANTS ::
(A) retina : eye
(B) granite : rock
(C) projector : film
(D) test : problem
(E) kin : relatives

_____ **10.** SONOROUS : CELLO ::
(A) destructive : typhoon
(B) silver : jewelry
(C) functional : decoration
(D) electrical : field
(E) public : elopement

130   CONNECTING NEW WORDS AND PATTERNS

Copyright © by Holt, Rinehart and Winston. All rights reserved.

CONNECTING NEW WORDS AND PATTERNS

Lesson 6 | ANALOGIES

Directions. For each of the following items, choose the lettered pair of words that expresses a relationship that is most similar to the relationship between the pair of capitalized words. Write the letter of your answer on the line provided before the number of the item. *(1 point each)*

_____ **1.** CANDOR : DECEITFULNESS ::
  (A) frankness : openness
  (B) growth : decline
  (C) concern : consideration
  (D) respect : honor
  (E) art : creativity

_____ **2.** CONFIGURATION : SHAPE ::
  (A) science : chemistry
  (B) alteration : change
  (C) element : formula
  (D) constellation : star
  (E) museum : collection

_____ **3.** CORROBORATE : EVIDENCE ::
  (A) confirm : fact
  (B) meet : convention
  (C) cooperate : team
  (D) assist : copilot
  (E) hold : anchor

_____ **4.** DEARTH : SCARCITY ::
  (A) planet : galaxy
  (B) pleasure : anxiety
  (C) starvation : appetite
  (D) exaggeration : overstatement
  (E) wedding : ceremony

_____ **5.** DEDUCE : THINKER ::
  (A) reduce : taxes
  (B) give : contributor
  (C) produce : evidence
  (D) sing : orator
  (E) dedicate : monument

_____ **6.** DIURNAL : NOCTURNAL ::
  (A) urban : rural
  (B) advanced : sophisticated
  (C) argumentative : quarrelsome
  (D) fragile : breakable
  (E) vocational : occupational

_____ **7.** EXTANT : EXTINCT ::
  (A) swollen : enlarged
  (B) sheltered : exposed
  (C) tolerable : bearable
  (D) delightful : divine
  (E) exact : precise

_____ **8.** HERCULEAN : DIFFICULT ::
  (A) noble : mean
  (B) debatable : agreeable
  (C) exceptional : commonplace
  (D) challenging : easy
  (E) fascinating : interesting

_____ **9.** LUDICROUS : FOOL ::
  (A) remorseful : guilt
  (B) punctual : arrival
  (C) offensive : joke
  (D) funny : comedian
  (E) cloudy : day

_____ **10.** PROPONENT : SUPPORT ::
  (A) volcano : extinct
  (B) wool : spin
  (C) expenses : report
  (D) column : rise
  (E) forerunner : precede

Name _____ Date _____ Class _____

CONNECTING NEW WORDS AND PATTERNS

Lesson 7 | ANALOGIES

Directions. For each of the following items, choose the lettered pair of words that expresses a relationship that is most similar to the relationship between the pair of capitalized words. Write the letter of your answer on the line provided before the number of the item. *(1 point each)*

_____ **1.** CAPITULATE : LOSER ::
  (A) invest : money
  (B) complete : assignment
  (C) cook : chef
  (D) tune : instrument
  (E) reason : fanatic

_____ **2.** CIVILITY : RUDENESS ::
  (A) receiver : telephone
  (B) civilization : behavior
  (C) decency : courtesy
  (D) disobedience : anger
  (E) acceptance : rejection

_____ **3.** CONNOISSEUR : APPRECIATE ::
  (A) loner : join
  (B) scholar : study
  (C) conversationalist : convert
  (D) warrant : issue
  (E) initiator : follow

_____ **4.** FOIBLE : WEAKNESS ::
  (A) step : procedure
  (B) edge : disadvantage
  (C) oil : engine
  (D) failure : discouragement
  (E) division : separation

_____ **5.** GUFFAW : JOKE ::
  (A) expression : face
  (B) drawer : bureau
  (C) giggle : laugh
  (D) error : carelessness
  (E) inch : measurement

_____ **6.** INCARCERATE : JAILER ::
  (A) control : traffic
  (B) ignite : carburetor
  (C) lose : victor
  (D) fly : pilot
  (E) circulate : news

_____ **7.** INDULGENT : LENIENT ::
  (A) melodious : mellow
  (B) legitimate : illegal
  (C) fortified : strengthened
  (D) intense : evidence
  (E) diligent : lazy

_____ **8.** MAGNANIMOUS : SELFISH ::
  (A) divided : united
  (B) despised : hated
  (C) magnetic : attractive
  (D) selected : chosen
  (E) insistent : instant

_____ **9.** OBSEQUIOUS : OBEDIENT ::
  (A) impolite : impatient
  (B) gigantic : large
  (C) inspirational : boring
  (D) sequential : disorganized
  (E) obliging : harmful

_____ **10.** PUNCTILIOUS : CAREFUL ::
  (A) valuable : worthless
  (B) hostile : unfriendly
  (C) prompt : tardy
  (D) careless : thorough
  (E) superficial : artificial

CONNECTING NEW WORDS AND PATTERNS

Lesson 8   ANALOGIES

Directions. For each of the following items, choose the lettered pair of words that expresses a relationship that is most similar to the relationship between the pair of capitalized words. Write the letter of your answer on the line provided before the number of the item. *(1 point each)*

_____ **1.** CHASTISE : DISCIPLINARIAN ::
   (A) limit : regulation
   (B) learn : student
   (C) pose : solution
   (D) enclose : wall
   (E) arise : question

_____ **2.** DEMAGOGUE : LEADER ::
   (A) democracy : equality
   (B) government : dictatorship
   (C) flavoring : vanilla
   (D) banana : fruit
   (E) vessel : ocean

_____ **3.** DETRIMENT : HARM ::
   (A) secretary : schedule
   (B) scheme : plot
   (C) garden : lettuce
   (D) retirement : relaxation
   (E) error : correction

_____ **4.** DISCREPANCY : INCONSISTENCY ::
   (A) failure : achievement
   (B) grief : jubilation
   (C) constancy : irregularity
   (D) harassment : prejudice
   (E) resolution : determination

_____ **5.** ILLICIT : BRIBERY ::
   (A) absent : presence
   (B) forgotten : remembrance
   (C) rough : silkiness
   (D) tall : skyscraper
   (E) strenuous : ease

_____ **6.** INSCRUTABLE : MYSTERIOUS ::
   (A) scholarly : learned
   (B) immeasurable : sufficient
   (C) worthless : valuable
   (D) exquisite : coarse
   (E) suitable : inappropriate

_____ **7.** INTERCEDE : PEACEMAKER ::
   (A) interfere : loner
   (B) interject : opinion
   (C) advertise : commercial
   (D) climb : ladder
   (E) oppose : antagonist

_____ **8.** OBNOXIOUS : PLEASANT ::
   (A) opinionated : inflexible
   (B) nozzle : hose
   (C) retiring : modest
   (D) ornery : agreeable
   (E) decent : respectable

_____ **9.** PERFIDIOUS : FAITHFUL ::
   (A) cordial : unfriendly
   (B) accommodating : helpful
   (C) strained : awkward
   (D) elevated : raised
   (E) stern : serious

_____ **10.** SUMPTUOUS : PALACE ::
   (A) crooked : highway
   (B) delicious : scenery
   (C) strenuous : relaxation
   (D) humble : mansion
   (E) skeptical : doubter

CONNECTING NEW WORDS AND PATTERNS

Lesson 9 ANALOGIES

Directions. For each of the following items, choose the lettered pair of words that expresses a relationship that is most similar to the relationship between the pair of capitalized words. Write the letter of your answer on the line provided before the number of the item. *(1 point each)*

_____ **1.** ANARCHY : CHAOS ::
   (A) gorge : mountain
   (B) treaty : diplomat
   (C) order : court
   (D) diploma : graduate
   (E) poverty : deprivation

_____ **2.** CAJOLE : COAX ::
   (A) hinder : encourage
   (B) advance : retreat
   (C) coach : play
   (D) start : begin
   (E) joke : insult

_____ **3.** COMMODIOUS : CRAMPED ::
   (A) melodious : harmonic
   (B) packed : concentrated
   (C) confident : assured
   (D) defensible : attached
   (E) boundless : limited

_____ **4.** ETHNOLOGY : ANTHROPOLOGY::
   (A) technology : artistry
   (B) pediatrics : medicine
   (C) obstetrician : delivery
   (D) botany : plants
   (E) talent : culture

_____ **5.** IMPAIR : DESTROY ::
   (A) group : gather
   (B) decrease : build
   (C) create : finish
   (D) nibble : devour
   (E) persuade : discourage

_____ **6.** NADIR : HIGH POINT ::
   (A) galaxy : Milky Way
   (B) ocean : sky
   (C) failure : success
   (D) nation : country
   (E) tropics : heat

_____ **7.** PESTILENCE : DESTRUCTIVE ::
   (A) misconduct : acceptable
   (B) benefactor : kind
   (C) violence : creative
   (D) complexion : pale
   (E) revolution : peaceful

_____ **8.** PROMULGATE : PROCLAIM ::
   (A) evaluation : recommendation
   (B) cowardice : intimidation
   (C) disintegration : composition
   (D) consideration : thoughtfulness
   (E) intrusion : invitation

_____ **9.** SUBVERSION : ESTABLISHMENT ::
   (A) conclusion : ending
   (B) initiation : acceptance
   (C) reduction : increase
   (D) substitution : replacement
   (E) division : subtraction

_____ **10.** VIRULENT : DEADLY ::
   (A) courageous : brave
   (B) tiny : immense
   (C) polluted : purified
   (D) healthful : alive
   (E) aggressive : meek

CONNECTING NEW WORDS AND PATTERNS

Lesson 10 | ANALOGIES

Directions. For each of the following items, choose the lettered pair of words that expresses a relationship that is most similar to the relationship between the pair of capitalized words. Write the letter of your answer on the line provided before the number of the item. *(1 point each)*

_____ 1. CALUMNY : SLANDER ::
(A) shock : ease
(B) thrill : excitement
(C) bribery : crime
(D) remorse : wrongdoing
(E) barbarity : civility

_____ 2. FERVID : HEAT ::
(A) complexity : comprehension
(B) imagination : facts
(C) contract : lease
(D) starvation : hunger
(E) constitution : law

_____ 3. FOMENT : INSTIGATOR ::
(A) torment : tournament
(B) sleep : insomniac
(C) instruct : teacher
(D) conduct : investigation
(E) invent : computer

_____ 4. IMPASSIVE : EMOTIONAL ::
(A) refined : wealthy
(B) nervous : frantic
(C) violated : abused
(D) maintained : neglected
(E) quiet : shy

_____ 5. LITIGATION : LAWYER ::
(A) negotiation : diplomat
(B) publication : president
(C) calculator : computer
(D) curriculum : course
(E) university : library

_____ 6. MOLLIFY : SOOTHE ::
(A) welcome : thank
(B) moisten : saturate
(C) glorify : degrade
(D) offend : protect
(E) scramble : mix

_____ 7. REPUDIATE : DISOWN ::
(A) forbidding : crude
(B) shallow : deep
(C) excessive : sufficient
(D) occasional : regular
(E) coarse : rough

_____ 8. RETICENT : UNRESERVED ::
(A) dashing : attractive
(B) exhausted : empty
(C) agitated : calm
(D) obstructive : obstinate
(E) devoted : incompetent

_____ 9. SEDENTARY : TYPIST ::
(A) willing : hostage
(B) passive : aggressor
(C) retiring : celebrity
(D) conceited : snob
(E) sincere : deceiver

_____ 10. TEMERITY : NERVE ::
(A) absurdity : silliness
(B) agility : awkwardness
(C) convenience : suitability
(D) timidity : braveness
(E) grace : skill

CONNECTING NEW WORDS AND PATTERNS

*L*esson 11 ┃ ANALOGIES

Directions. For each of the following items, choose the lettered pair of words that expresses a relationship that is most similar to the relationship between the pair of capitalized words. Write the letter of your answer on the line provided before the number of the item. *(1 point each)*

____ **1.** CHAUVINISM : DEVOTION ::
  (A) criticism : insecurity
  (B) foreigner : nationality
  (C) cavalry : soldier
  (D) reverence : respect
  (E) nationalism : anthem

____ **2.** FACETIOUS : SERIOUS ::
  (A) sane : reasonable
  (B) comic : ridiculous
  (C) uplifting : inspiring
  (D) ashamed : hopeful
  (E) caring : indifferent

____ **3.** INEXORABLE : UNRELENTING ::
  (A) variable : constant
  (B) intricate : complex
  (C) competitive : cooperative
  (D) delicate : robust
  (E) creative : unoriginal

____ **4.** MOOT : CONTROVERSY ::
  (A) flimsy : vault
  (B) strange : familiarity
  (C) moist : desert
  (D) gritty : velvet
  (E) illegal : crime

____ **5.** OFFICIOUS : MEDDLER ::
  (A) graceless : ballerina
  (B) urban : farmer
  (C) innocent : flatterer
  (D) inhospitable : host
  (E) photogenic : model

____ **6.** QUIESCENT : INACTIVE ::
  (A) quiet : absent
  (B) sceptical : doubting
  (C) extinguished : kindled
  (D) secretive : public
  (E) uncertain : confident

____ **7.** REGIMEN : SOLDIER ::
  (A) barracks : sailor
  (B) region : country
  (C) coast : harbor
  (D) base : military
  (E) curriculum : student

____ **8.** RENOUNCE : ADOPT ::
  (A) reinforce : strengthen
  (B) withhold : give
  (C) assume : guess
  (D) allow : permit
  (E) announce : whisper

____ **9.** REPOSITORY : CONTAIN ::
  (A) sieve : strain
  (B) method : devise
  (C) scoop : drill
  (D) dialogue : establish
  (E) paratrooper : jump

____ **10.** TREATISE : SCHOLAR ::
  (A) contract : document
  (B) lobby : hotel
  (C) treaty : peace
  (D) novel : scientist
  (E) memorandum : administrator

CONNECTING NEW WORDS AND PATTERNS

*L*esson 12 | ANALOGIES

Directions. For each of the following items, choose the lettered pair of words that expresses a relationship that is most similar to the relationship between the pair of capitalized words. Write the letter of your answer on the line provided before the number of the item. *(1 point each)*

_____ **1.** ACRIMONIOUS : BITTER ::
 (A) recognized : introduced
 (B) pale : colorful
 (C) dutiful : disobedient
 (D) shocked : enraged
 (E) perpetual : continuous

_____ **2.** ATROPHY : DETERIORATION ::
 (A) balcony : theater
 (B) onion : odor
 (C) donation : charity
 (D) production : auditorium
 (E) courage : bravery

_____ **3.** COERCE : TYRANT ::
 (A) sculpt : model
 (B) transport : freighter
 (C) grieve : mourner
 (D) solve : problem
 (E) pierce : needle

_____ **4.** CONSTERNATION : TRAGEDY ::
 (A) celebration : victory
 (B) scandal : embarrassment
 (C) miracle : amazement
 (D) academy : institution
 (E) celebrity : autograph

_____ **5.** DESIST : PERSIST ::
 (A) detach : separate
 (B) affirm : confirm
 (C) occupy : vacate
 (D) inspire : conspire
 (E) determine : decide

_____ **6.** ENIGMA : MYSTERIOUS ::
 (A) enthusiasm : deadly
 (B) satin : bumpy
 (C) neatness : tidiness
 (D) honey : sweet
 (E) elastic : rigid

_____ **7.** GAUNTLET : ARMOR ::
 (A) museum : gallery
 (B) knight : horse
 (C) infirmary : patient
 (D) bristle : brush
 (E) chivalry : death

_____ **8.** LOQUACIOUS : TALKATIVE ::
 (A) abrupt : dull
 (B) venomous : poisonous
 (C) slippery : shiny
 (D) horizontal : vertical
 (E) gratifying : frustrating

_____ **9.** MISNOMER : ERROR ::
 (A) name : passport
 (B) editor : review
 (C) word : speech
 (D) distraction : mistake
 (E) dime : coin

_____ **10.** MOTTLED : SPOTTED ::
 (A) strong : athletic
 (B) brisk : brilliant
 (C) vivid : colorful
 (D) corrupt : honest
 (E) considerate : impulsive

CONNECTING NEW WORDS AND PATTERNS

Lesson 13 | ANALOGIES

Directions. For each of the following items, choose the lettered pair of words that expresses a relationship that is most similar to the relationship between the pair of capitalized words. Write the letter of your answer on the line provided before the number of the item. *(1 point each)*

____ 1. ASSIDUOUS : CARELESS ::
   (A) meaningful : significant
   (B) prompt : tardy
   (C) important : critical
   (D) abrupt : sudden
   (E) careful : precise

____ 2. AVARICE : GREED ::
   (A) tray : waiter
   (B) monotony : variety
   (C) hill : depression
   (D) vice : fault
   (E) selfishness : solitude

____ 3. CONCILIATE : NEGOTIATOR ::
   (A) converse : conservationist
   (B) push : lever
   (C) arrive : deserter
   (D) measure : fabric
   (E) inherit : heir

____ 4. DENIZEN : INHABIT ::
   (A) ornament : decorate
   (B) batter : swing
   (C) ruler : measure
   (D) tape : rewind
   (E) rent : collect

____ 5. DURESS : FORCE ::
   (A) perfection : flawlessness
   (B) convenience : necessity
   (C) entrance : exit
   (D) communication : understanding
   (E) punishment : reward

____ 6. EQUANIMITY : EXCITABILITY ::
   (A) arrangement : schedule
   (B) oversight : accident
   (C) enforcement : obedience
   (D) order : chaos
   (E) equality : democracy

____ 7. INIQUITY : PUNISHMENT ::
   (A) monarchy : government
   (B) physician : surgery
   (C) experimentation : discovery
   (D) money : poverty
   (E) hospital : institution

____ 8. INORDINATE : EXCESSIVE ::
   (A) intellectual : physical
   (B) foolhardy : reckless
   (C) ordinary : exceptional
   (D) experimental : traditional
   (E) insubstantial : solid

____ 9. MERCURIAL : CONSTANT ::
   (A) mischievous : harmful
   (B) virtuous : evil
   (C) villainous : wicked
   (D) consistent : habitual
   (E) parched : dry

____ 10. RANCOR : MISTREATMENT ::
   (A) proofreader : check
   (B) newspaper : print
   (C) balloon : inflate
   (D) suffering : compassion
   (E) editor : calculate

CONNECTING NEW WORDS AND PATTERNS

Lesson 14 ANALOGIES

Directions. For each of the following items, choose the lettered pair of words that expresses a relationship that is most similar to the relationship between the pair of capitalized words. Write the letter of your answer on the line provided before the number of the item. *(1 point each)*

____ 1. BAUBLE : SHOWY ::
  (A) attic : underground
  (B) marionette : alive
  (C) cellar : elevated
  (D) fish : feathered
  (E) lace : delicate

____ 2. COMMISERATE : SYMPATHIZER ::
  (A) memorize : motto
  (B) investigate : investor
  (C) penalize : penalty
  (D) disagree : debater
  (E) protect : shield

____ 3. FESTOON : DECORATIVE ::
  (A) repellent : pleasant
  (B) ring : round
  (C) festival : mournful
  (D) vegetable : plastic
  (E) peacock : plain

____ 4. FRESCO : PAINTER ::
  (A) blueprint : architect
  (B) monastery : church
  (C) painting : frame
  (D) stanza : poem
  (E) bishop : cathedral

____ 5. FRUGAL : THRIFTY ::
  (A) momentary : eternal
  (B) frigid : cool
  (C) new : antique
  (D) frustrated : satisfied
  (E) evident : obvious

____ 6. MAUDLIN : SENTIMENTAL ::
  (A) modern : antique
  (B) priceless : valuable
  (C) crude : refined
  (D) indestructible : fragile
  (E) insufficient : enough

____ 7. OPULENCE : POVERTY ::
  (A) privacy : solitude
  (B) insurance : protection
  (C) simplicity : complexity
  (D) interruption : disturbance
  (E) luxury : comfort

____ 8. PALLOR : ILLNESS ::
  (A) cancer : disease
  (B) patient : medicine
  (C) tiredness : insomnia
  (D) hospital : lobby
  (E) isolation : loneliness

____ 9. PROMONTORY : SEACOAST ::
  (A) height : ladder
  (B) alligator : swamp
  (C) state : county
  (D) theater : projector
  (E) island : beach

____ 10. REMUNERATION : COMPENSATION ::
  (A) calculation : retaliation
  (B) expectation : disappointment
  (C) analysis : economics
  (D) comprehension : understanding
  (E) detonation : bomb

CONNECTING NEW WORDS AND PATTERNS

Lesson 15 | ANALOGIES

Directions. For each of the following items, choose the lettered pair of words that expresses a relationship that is most similar to the relationship between the pair of capitalized words. Write the letter of your answer on the line provided before the number of the item. *(1 point each)*

_____ **1.** ABSCOND : CRIMINAL ::
   (A) exchange : money
   (B) hoard : miser
   (C) whisper : secret
   (D) arrest : prisoner
   (E) write : report

_____ **2.** ADJURE : COMMAND ::
   (A) acquire : lose
   (B) require : suggest
   (C) acknowledge : deny
   (D) plead : beg
   (E) allow : forbid

_____ **3.** CAPRICIOUS : FICKLE ::
   (A) conditional : absolute
   (B) friendly : hostile
   (C) nonsensical : silly
   (D) sensible : sensitive
   (E) stylish : functional

_____ **4.** EMACIATE : BODY ::
   (A) carve : knife
   (B) sharpen : blade
   (C) nourish : food
   (D) build : carpenter
   (E) eat : dieter

_____ **5.** ETHEREAL : WORLDLY ::
   (A) required : optional
   (B) similar : identical
   (C) striped : marked
   (D) popular : common
   (E) elegant : luxurious

_____ **6.** FIASCO : UNSUCCESSFUL ::
   (A) scheme : unplanned
   (B) insult : kind
   (C) obligation : optional
   (D) outburst : calm
   (E) disagreement : unpleasant

_____ **7.** IGNOMINY : WRONGDOING ::
   (A) magazine : publication
   (B) manuscript : writer
   (C) persistence : success
   (D) virtue : reward
   (E) skill : training

_____ **8.** LONGEVITY : HEALTHFULNESS ::
   (A) distance : perspective
   (B) personality : humor
   (C) teaching : vocation
   (D) fitness : exercise
   (E) vandalism : destruction

_____ **9.** MALIGN : SLANDERER ::
   (A) play : umpire
   (B) govern : mayor
   (C) regulate : law
   (D) spread : rumor
   (E) designate : designer

_____ **10.** PROGNOSIS : PHYSICIAN ::
   (A) tradesman : butcher
   (B) sentencing : judge
   (C) athlete : gymnasium
   (D) education : course
   (E) vacation : camera

Why We Read Strategically

Reading is active. As you read, you step into the writer's world. When you come across a new idea, you usually look for a clue to help you determine the writer's meaning. You move ahead to see if the idea is explained, or you retrace your steps to look for any signs you missed.

You can use these same strategies to build your vocabulary. If you don't know the meaning of a word, you should look in the passage surrounding the word for hints. These hints are called context clues. The more you practice hunting for context clues, the better you can teach yourself new words, and the greater your vocabulary will grow. Strengthening your vocabulary skills also will help you to score higher on standardized vocabulary tests.

The following example shows the kinds of context clues you will find in Reading New Words in Context lessons.

Strategic Reading: An Example

The state of Oklahoma is a state of nations. Although many people are aware that large numbers of American Indians such as the Choctaw and the Chickasaw live in Oklahoma, they are not aware that the Indian nations of Oklahoma are **sovereign** peoples with their own constitutional governments. *In other words, like any other nation, they have the right to manage their own affairs.* However, because the tribes are nations within a nation, the United States government does have some **jurisdiction** over them. *For example, the federal government has the authority to govern its own activities when they take place on American Indian land.* Even in these cases, though, the federal government's authority is limited.

The ancestors of large numbers of American Indians living in Oklahoma today came to Oklahoma on the **infamous** Trail of Tears. *In the 1830s, the United States government began to remove tribes of the Southeastern United States from their homelands. The government pushed these tribes on a forced march to the west that resulted in the death of up to one half of the members of some nations.* At the time, many Americans did not seem to recognize the inhumanity of this action. Today, *however,* almost everyone **acknowledges** the tragedy of the Indian Removal. It remains a *barbaric,* **hideous,** *and shameful* blot on the pages of United States history.

In this case, the writer uses *restatement* to provide a clue to the meaning of the word **sovereign**.

Here, an *example* is used to provide a clue to the meaning of **jurisdiction**.

A *summary* of the events concerning the Trail of Tears provides a clue to the meaning of **infamous**.

Here, the writer makes the meaning of **acknowledges** clear through *contrast*.
The use of *items in a series* clarifies the meaning of **hideous**.

Many people who live in states without large American Indian populations mistakenly believe that the tribes in Oklahoma live on large federal reservations. *This* **fallacy** may result from the assumption that American Indians have been unable *either* to accommodate modern society *or* to **reconcile** ancient tribal ways with the modern world. The fact is that American Indians in Oklahoma own their own tribal lands and are not tenants on government-owned property.

Today, the Choctaw, the Chickasaw, the Creek, the Seminole, and the Cherokee—as well as the other tribes in Oklahoma—are involved in modern occupations. American Indians are employed in the fields of education, civil service, law, medicine, computer technology, and so on. But maintaining the traditional cultures remains a **priority**, *the number-one concern,* of many tribal elders.

In many cases, the younger tribal members in Oklahoma are most **reluctant** to abandon the values of their traditional culture *because they find those values important in their own lives.* Younger American Indians are also learning the old arts and crafts. A young Choctaw might learn to create the jewelry, headpieces, shawls, or leggings that *are* the traditional **garb** of the tribe. Others concentrate on preserving the stories and the language. Some research and write about the history of their people so that the events of the past will not be **irretrievably** lost.

As a poet who writes a verse in the sand watches the tide erase it forever, American Indians have watched the dreams and traditions of their grandparents fade into distant memories. Today, however, the Indian nations of Oklahoma struggle to regain their traditions and to make them meaningful in the present.

A *pronoun reference* is used here to provide a clue to the meaning of **fallacy**.

Note that a *coordinating conjunction* helps clarify the meaning of **reconcile**.

An *appositive* provides a clue to the meaning of **priority**.

The writer indicates the meaning of **reluctant** through a *cause-and-effect relationship*.

Note that a form of the verb *to be (are)* provides a clue to the meaning of **garb**.

Figurative language is the key to understanding the meaning of **irretrievably**.

A Final Note

How can you learn strategic reading? Practice is a great way to improve your ability. The following lessons will help you recognize the different context clues a writer uses. As you complete each lesson, you will become a more effective reader.

READING NEW WORDS IN CONTEXT

Lesson 1 | CONTEXT: Literary Figures

The passage gives you an opportunity to expand your vocabulary. Below are twenty Vocabulary Words that are used in the passage and in the exercises that follow it.

abject	distraught	lugubrious	propriety
admonish	euphemism	nebulous	prosaic
banal	finesse	nefarious	pseudonym
bellicose	glib	nemesis	purloin
commensurate	lampoon	phlegmatic	revile

Mary Shelley's Monster

Mr. Conlee said, "We've spent a few weeks studying the Gothic novel. By now, you probably have a good idea of the techniques that Gothic writers used. Can anyone give me some examples of Gothic conventions?"

Adam grinned and raised his hand. "Most of the stories have creepy settings—you know, like old castles full of cobwebs or dungeons with torture chambers."

"That's right. Writers of Gothic novels wanted to create an atmosphere of gloom or horror, and eerie settings helped establish the mood. Of course, the image of a dark, cobwebby castle or a chattering skeleton seems **banal** (1) to most readers today. But in the eighteenth and nineteenth centuries, such descriptions weren't yet stale from overuse; they were still quite effective. Yes, Dolores?"

"I notice that a lot of movies **lampoon** (2) those old Gothic novels—for example, I just saw one movie, *Young Frankenstein*, that satirized the original *Frankenstein*."

"Yes—Gothic tales are popular subjects for movie spoofs. Watching old film versions of the Frankenstein story, you may have difficulty appreciating how strange and horrifying the original novel was to nineteenth-century readers.

"And speaking of *Frankenstein*, I hope you all finished the book last night, because it's our next novel for discussion. Here's a tricky question: For two extra credit points, can anyone tell me whether Mary Shelley published *Frankenstein* under a **pseudonym** (3) or under her real name?"

One student piped up, "She didn't use any name! She published it anonymously in 1818."

"Emma is correct! Here's another question. What prompted Mary Shelley to write *Frankenstein*? I'm looking for a very specific reason, not a **nebulous** (4), or vague one."

Malcolm raised his hand. "Shelley and her husband, the poet Percy Bysshe Shelley, along with the poet Lord Byron and Mary's stepsister Claire, were staying in some villas in Switzerland. One night Byron suggested that they all write ghost stories, and Mary came up with the idea for *Frankenstein*."

Mr. Conlee nodded and picked up the story from there.

"Mary Shelley's thoughts turned to recent scientific discussions about the possibility of creating life. Such radical thoughts were not uncommon for Mary Shelley. She frequently disregarded conventional standards of acceptable behavior, what we call propriety (5). And there was nothing **prosaic** (6), or dull and ordinary, about her intellect and imagination."

The Creation of the Monster

"Can anyone explain how the young Dr. Frankenstein created his monster?" Mr. Conlee asked.

"He **purloined** (7), uh, remains from graveyards, and he also stole remains from dissecting rooms," Emma responded.

"That's right. But I think you're being rather careful in your choice of words, Emma. Can you be more direct?"

"You're right. I used the **euphemism** (8) *remains* because I thought the word *corpses* was too gross."

"Well, it's true that Dr. Frankenstein used rather gruesome materials. And, as a result of using parts of dead bodies, he produced a creature that was not too pleasing to look at. Shelley notes that he has yellow skin and a 'shrivelled complexion.'"

Good, Bad, or Unlucky?

"Now we must talk about the character of the creation," Mr. Conlee continued. "We usually think of Frankenstein's monster as a **nefarious** (9) character—a wicked villain, right? And we also tend to think of him as **bellicose** (10). He did, after all, wage war against his community, committing hostile acts such as killing innocent people. He even killed a child—Dr. Frankenstein's younger brother. The monster was so dangerous, in fact, that he became the **nemesis** (11) of his creator, inflicting punishment for what he saw as wrongs committed against him, like a Gothic Darth Vader. But is this the only impression the reader gets of the monster? Is he truly all evil?"

Dolores replied, "No. There actually is much sadness in his character. He wasn't bad to begin with."

"Yes, he is a **lugubrious** (12) character," Mr. Conlee agreed. "That he is deeply sad is evident in his question, 'Am I not alone, miserably alone?' He wants love but becomes **distraught** (13) when people flee from him in horror. Similarly, he wants acceptance but becomes agitated when he cannot find it.

"The creature tries to **admonish** (14) Dr. Frankenstein to let him know what he is becoming," Mr. Conlee continued, "but the doctor ignores the warning. In fact, the good doctor, unable to face his hideous creation, flees from it. He refuses to accept responsibility, and so ends up truly creating a monster, for his creation turns to evil out of bitterness.

"In probing the psychological aspects of both Dr. Frankenstein and his creation, Mary Shelley shows quite a bit of **finesse** (15)—that is, delicate skill and subtlety. She presents a haunting, heartbreaking story of an **abject** (16) creature. And his miserable condition is through no fault of his own; he didn't ask to be created and then abandoned. Throughout the novel, the tormented creature **reviles** (17) himself, cruelly attacking himself with such descriptions as 'deformed and loathsome.'"

"Mr. Conlee, do you think we are supposed to feel sorry for the monster?" Dolores asked.

"Yes, Dolores, I do. It certainly is difficult for a reader to have a **phlegmatic** (18) response toward him. In fact, I think Mary Shelley wanted us to be concerned and to feel the creature's misery."

Mr. Conlee concluded his introduction to *Frankenstein*. "Mary Shelley said she wanted to write a tale 'which would speak to the mysterious fears of our nature and awaken thrilling horror.' I think she was speaking sincerely, not **glibly** (19), because her *Frankenstein* is just such a tale. Her writing talent was **commensurate** (20) with her imagination—totally equal to it. I hope you'll see that as we discuss the novel."

EXERCISE 1   *Finding Synonyms*

Directions. Reread the preceding passage. Then write on the line provided a synonym for each of the words in boldface. If you cannot think of an exact synonym, you may write a brief definition of the word.

1. banal _____

2. lampoon _____

3. pseudonym _____

4. nebulous _____

5. propriety _____

6. prosaic _____

7. purloined _____

8. euphemism _____

9. nefarious _____

10. bellicose _____

11. nemesis _____

12. lugubrious _____

13. distraught _____

14. admonish _____

15. finesse _____

16. abject _____

17. reviles _____

18. phlegmatic _____

19. glibly _____

20. commensurate _____

EXERCISE 2 *Reading Strategically* 👉

Directions. Now that you have read the passage and thought about the words in boldface, circle the letter of the correct answer to each of the following items. The numbers of the items are the same as the numbers of the boldface Vocabulary Words in the passage.

1. According to the passage, a word, phrase, or image becomes **banal** when it
   (A) is no longer used
   (B) becomes a useful part of our language
   (C) is used in a book about a monster
   (D) is overused and becomes stale
   (E) is used only in special situations

2. In the passage, the word _____ provides a clue to the meaning of **lampoon**.
   (A) serialized
   (B) specialized
   (C) satirized
   (D) copied
   (E) immortalized

3. To provide a clue to the meaning of **pseudonym,** the writer
   (A) defines **pseudonym**
   (B) contrasts **pseudonym** with the words *real name*
   (C) uses an example of a **pseudonym**
   (D) gives a list of **pseudonyms**
   (E) contrasts **pseudonym** with the word *anonymously*

4. In the passage, **nebulous** means
   (A) specific
   (B) Romantic
   (C) lucky
   (D) vague
   (E) satirical

5. If Mary Shelley disregarded **propriety,** as the writer of the passage suggests, she
   (A) cared little about what others thought of her
   (B) was very concerned about proper behavior
   (C) conformed to the conventional standards
   (D) wrote stories everyone enjoys reading
   (E) depended on society for acceptance and approval

6. In the passage, why is there nothing **prosaic** about Mary Shelley's intellect and imagination?
   (A) Her intellect and imagination were extraordinary, not dull and ordinary.
   (B) She never used her intellect and imagination to write prose.
   (C) She was actually a rather dull person with an average intellect and imagination.
   (D) She used her intellect and imagination rarely.
   (E) Her intellect and imagination were used only in the pursuit of writing poetry.

7. We can tell from the passage that when Dr. Frankenstein **purloined** remains, he
   (A) stole them
   (B) destroyed them
   (C) made them
   (D) traded them
   (E) purchased them

8. In the passage, Emma uses the word _____ as a **euphemism** for the word *corpses.*
   (A) materials
   (B) monsters
   (C) bodies
   (D) people
   (E) remains

9. According to the passage, **nefarious** means to be
   (A) agreeable
   (B) kind and good
   (C) misunderstood
   (D) villainous
   (E) inexperienced

10. To tell us that **bellicose** is defined as "warlike and hostile," the writer
   (A) contrasts **bellicose** with an antonym
   (B) uses **bellicose** in a simile
   (C) says the monster was **bellicose** because he committed hostile acts
   (D) uses a metaphor as an example
   (E) uses **bellicose** in a series of words similar in meaning

11. Because the monster becomes Dr. Frankenstein's **nemesis** after Dr. Frankenstein rejects him, the writer compares the monster by simile to
   (A) a Gothic creator
   (B) a wicked stepsister
   (C) a Gothic Darth Vader
   (D) Boris Karloff
   (E) a Gothic avenging son

12. The word in the passage that provides a clue to the meaning of **lugubrious** is
   (A) alone
   (B) evident
   (C) character
   (D) question
   (E) sad

13. In the passage, if someone becomes **distraught** because of unfair treatment, we may expect the person to be
   (A) happy
   (B) hostile
   (C) free from pain
   (D) agitated
   (E) alone

14. In the passage, **admonish** means
  (A) blame
  (B) warn
  (C) destroy
  (D) accept
  (E) show

15. When we read in the passage that Mary Shelley shows **finesse** in probing the psychological aspects of Dr. Frankenstein and the monster, we should realize that she
  (A) shows delicate skill and subtlety
  (B) shows very little sympathy for either character
  (C) views the outcome as disastrous
  (D) does not focus on the thoughts and feelings of the characters
  (E) exaggerates the traits of the characters

16. In the passage, the word _____ provides a clue to the meaning of **abject**.
  (A) haunting
  (B) abandoned
  (C) fault
  (D) condition
  (E) miserable

17. In the passage, **reviles** means
  (A) compliments enthusiastically
  (B) reveals
  (C) attacks with cruel language
  (D) lives in fear of
  (E) shows fondness for

18. According to the passage, it is difficult to remain **phlegmatic** about the creature because
  (A) we don't understand him
  (B) we can identify with his pain and sadness
  (C) he is totally unlikeable
  (D) we are bored by the story
  (E) his behavior is unjustified

19. To let us know that **glibly** is defined as "in a way that is too smooth to be sincere," the writer
  (A) uses a synonym for **glibly**
  (B) contrasts **glibly** with the word *sincerely*
  (C) uses **glibly** in a metaphor
  (D) uses **glibly** in a series of words similar in meaning
  (E) links **glibly** to the words *thrilling horror*

20. We can tell from the passage that **commensurate** means
  (A) sincere
  (B) unrelated
  (C) equal
  (D) talented
  (E) imaginative

READING NEW WORDS IN CONTEXT

Lesson 2 | CONTEXT: Literary Figures

The passage gives you an opportunity to expand your vocabulary. Below are twenty Vocabulary Words that are used in the passage and in the exercises that follow it.

adroit	choleric	discursive	fortuitous
allay	cognizant	ennui	hyperbole
assimilate	colloquy	expatriate	incognito
blazon	despot	farcical	mesmerism
bravado	dirge	feign	omniscient

A Conference on Shakespeare

"All the world's a stage," William Shakespeare (1564–1616) wrote in *As You Like It*. For Shakespeare, all the world—at least the world of which he was **cognizant** (1)—was also a source of play material. One part of the world Shakespeare was aware of was the New World of the Americas, which was being explored by Europeans in the 1600s. You may be surprised to learn that Shakespeare **assimilated** (2) or absorbed knowledge about the New World and used what he had learned in his final play, *The Tempest* (1611).

My information about Shakespeare's "American" play came during a recent **colloquy** (3) of Shakespearean scholars, who were meeting to confer about the sources, characters, and themes of Shakespeare's plays. Since the conference was open to the public, I attended several of the meetings to earn extra credit in my senior English course.

In the program, the discussion about *The Tempest* was called "Shakespeare Discovers America!" I suspected that the title of the discussion was a **hyperbole** (4), an obvious exaggeration made for effect. It was designed to catch people's attention, and it certainly caught mine.

Waiting for the discussion to begin, I was intensely curious: What was Shakespeare's connection to the New World? The speaker was quick to **allay** (5) or lessen the suspense. He explained that *The Tempest* is not set in America and that Shakespeare did not write about New World explorations. However, the speaker said that Shakespeare must have read about the explorations and must have been inspired by them, for *The Tempest* is full of references to Renaissance exploration.

The Bermuda Connection

In particular, it is almost certain that Shakespeare knew about the adventures of a group of English sailors who were stranded on the Bermuda islands in 1609–1610. For nine months, the sailors thrived on these islands and experienced a kind of natural paradise. It is probable, some scholars say, that Shakespeare had read the published narratives of the sailors' adventures, as well as a letter from William Strachey, one of the seafarers. There is a deliberate connection between the Bermuda adventures and *The Tempest*, some scholars maintain. They say it is not just **fortuitous** (6) that *The Tempest* includes some details from the narratives, nor is it accidental that Shakespeare emphasized a sense of wonder connected with an island paradise.

Shakespeare very **adroitly** (7), or skillfully, captures the mystery and wonder of an island paradise in *The Tempest*. In the play, Prospero, the rightful duke of Milan, had been removed from power by a tyrant, his **despotic** (8) brother Antonio. Prospero and his daughter, Miranda, live on an enchanted island with the half-human Caliban and the sprite Ariel. The play includes **mesmerism** (9) in the hypnotic abilities of Prospero, a magician; **farcical** (10) incidents, such as the comical scene of the disappearing banquet; and **choleric** (11) characters whose bad tempers are no match for magic.

Caliban, scholars point out, is almost an anagram of the word *cannibal*. It is likely that the character Caliban represents the image of primitive people that was held by early New World adventurers. The conference speaker reminded us that today's scholars are not **omniscient** (12). They are not all-knowing, and thus cannot say for sure what source, if any, Shakespeare used for Caliban's character.

Other Shakespearean Topics

Some of the other meetings I attended were interesting; others were not. One meeting featured a **discursive** (13) speaker who rambled on for what seemed like hours about **blazons** (14) or coats of arms used on shields, flags, and pennants in Shakespeare's plays. I'm afraid my **ennui** (15) was obvious during that meeting. I experienced similar boredom during the lecture and demonstration by a Shakespearean director who incorporates **dirges** (16) into Shakespeare's tragedies. To me, listening to funeral hymns is like watching ice melt. Thank goodness some of the other sessions were more exciting.

I especially liked the talk titled "**Expatriates** (17) in Shakespeare's Plays." Several of Shakespeare's plays, it turns out, deal with a central character who is exiled or who has withdrawn from his or her native land. Another lively meeting was about Shakespearean characters who travel **incognito** (18), their true identities unknown to others. In *Twelfth Night*, for example, Viola disguises herself as a boy and **feigns** (19) being a duke's page. Such characters in Shakespeare's plays usually succeed quite well in pretending to be other people. Such disguises, the speaker said, sometimes give the characters an amusing air of **bravado** (20), like cartoon mice showing false bravery against stalking cats.

I suppose that Shakespeare has been written about and discussed more than any other writer in the English language. The conference I attended was only one of many such conferences held all over the world. It's easy to see why there's such enthusiasm for Shakespeare's works: He offers something for everyone. My only misgiving about the conference was that I missed a session with the most intriguing title of all: "Shakespeare in Outer Space."

EXERCISE 1 Finding Synonyms

Directions. Reread the preceding passage. Then write on the line provided a synonym for each of the words in boldface. If you cannot think of an exact synonym, you may write a brief definition of the word.

1. cognizant _____

2. assimilated _____

3. colloquy _____

4. hyperbole _____

150 LESSON 2

5. allay _____

6. fortuitous _____

7. adroit _____

8. despot _____

9. mesmerism _____

10. farcical _____

11. choleric _____

12. omniscient _____

13. discursive _____

14. blazons _____

15. ennui _____

16. dirges _____

17. expatriates _____

18. incognito _____

19. feigns _____

20. bravado _____

EXERCISE 2 *Reading Strategically* 👈

Directions. Now that you have read the passage and thought about the words in boldface, circle the letter of the correct answer to each of the following items. The numbers of the items are the same as the numbers of the boldface Vocabulary Words in the passage.

1. In the passage, the word that provides a clue to the meaning of **cognizant** is
   (A) explored
   (B) aware
   (C) world
   (D) stage
   (E) source

2. In the passage, the phrase "Shakespeare **assimilated** . . . knowledge" means that he
   (A) investigated it
   (B) absorbed it
   (C) explored it
   (D) rejected it
   (E) ignored it

3. In the passage, a **colloquy** is a
   (A) university
   (B) play
   (C) scholar
   (D) character
   (E) conference

4. In the passage, a **hyperbole** is an _____ exaggeration.
   (A) exciting
   (B) unintentional
   (C) overused
   (D) obvious
   (E) unpleasant

5. In the passage, **allay** means to
   (A) increase
   (B) activate
   (C) lessen
   (D) understand
   (E) question

6. To let us know that **fortuitous** means "accidental," the writer
   (A) defines **fortuitous** as being "a sense of wonder"
   (B) links **fortuitous** to the synonym *emphasized*
   (C) links **fortuitous** to the synonym *accidental*
   (D) uses **fortuitous** in a simile about an island paradise
   (E) uses **fortuitous** to describe a shipwreck

7. In the passage, **adroit** means
   (A) clever
   (B) mysterious
   (C) playful
   (D) dishonest
   (E) enchanting

8. In the passage, **despotic** means
   (A) like a sprite
   (B) tyrannical
   (C) like a duke
   (D) rightful
   (E) enchanted

9. In the passage, the word _____ provides a clue to the meaning of **mesmerism**.
   (A) mystery
   (B) hypnotic
   (C) paradise
   (D) comical
   (E) tempers

10. We can tell from the passage that **farcical** incidents are
   (A) serious
   (B) magical
   (C) comical
   (D) hypnotic
   (E) enchanted

11. According to the passage, magic can triumph over **choleric** characters because it
   (A) can make them more **choleric**
   (B) can make them feel guilty
   (C) is strong enough to defeat bad tempers
   (D) can destroy laughter
   (E) can make **choleric** characters even more angry

12. When we read in the passage that today's scholars are not **omniscient,** we should realize that they
   (A) know everything
   (B) question all theories
   (C) understand the sources
   (D) don't know everything
   (E) rely on anagrams

13. If someone is **discursive** about a subject, the writer of the passage suggests we may expect the person to
   (A) keep strictly to the subject at hand
   (B) speak loudly, clearly, and plainly
   (C) read the entire speech rapidly
   (D) present charts and graphs as examples
   (E) talk a lot and not get to the point

14. We can tell from the passage that **blazons** are
   (A) coats of arms
   (B) dull speakers
   (C) jackets
   (D) boring meetings
   (E) lectures

15. The writer provides a clue to the meaning of **ennui** by
   (A) praising a director's lecture
   (B) linking **ennui** to the word *boredom*
   (C) implying that **ennui** is excitement
   (D) giving an example of **ennui**
   (E) using a simile

16. The writer finds listening to **dirges** very boring and compares it by simile to
   (A) attending a funeral
   (B) watching a sad play
   (C) reading a dull book
   (D) watching ice melt
   (E) directing a Shakespearean tragedy

17. According to the passage, **expatriates** are people who no longer live in their _____ lands.

    (A) native

    (B) adopted

    (C) favorite

    (D) holy

    (E) underdeveloped

18. In the passage, people who travel **incognito** are

    (A) members of royalty

    (B) Shakespearean scholars

    (C) in disguise

    (D) exiles

    (E) wealthy

19. In the passage, when Viola **feigns** being a duke's page, it means that she

    (A) learns

    (B) refuses

    (C) faints

    (D) tries

    (E) pretends

20. Because some characters have an amusing **bravado,** the writer compares them by simile to

    (A) stalking cats disguised as mice

    (B) cats that are afraid of mice

    (C) mice and cats that travel in disguise

    (D) cartoon mice that show false bravery against cats

    (E) actors who portray brave cats and mice

READING NEW WORDS IN CONTEXT

Lesson 3 | CONTEXT: Literary Figures

The passage gives you an opportunity to expand your vocabulary. Below are twenty Vocabulary Words that are used in the passage and in the exercises that follow it.

amorphous	exhort	nondescript	sanguine
ascetic	facile	nonentity	scurrilous
decorum	guile	parsimonious	seraphic
doggerel	implicit	proffer	sundry
dogma	inveigle	protégé	vociferous

Christina Rossetti's Goblins

"Goblin Market" is a haunting narrative poem by Christina Rossetti (1830–1894), an English poet identified with the Pre-Raphaelites, members of an artistic movement of the mid-1800s. "Goblin Market," her most famous work, tells a fantastic story that is excitingly presented and easily understood. However, the poem also has **implicit** (1) meanings beyond the expressed story.

The Story of "Goblin Market"

In the poem, two sisters, Lizzie and Laura, pass the Goblin Market each day. The goblins' **sundry** (2) or varied offerings include dozens of fruits—apples, lemons, apricots, and strawberries. With much **guile** (3), or cunning, the goblins **exhort** (4) the young women to buy the fruit. The goblins are not subtle in their urgings. In fact, they are loud and demanding to the point of being **vociferous** (5). Yet as noisy as they are, the goblins are never **scurrilous** (6); they are far too sly to risk offending the girls with foul language.

Lizzie tells Laura, who is plainly curious, not to look at the goblins' wares: "Their offers should not charm us,/Their evil gifts would harm us." At first, neither sister is enticed by the goblins' continual cries of "Come buy, come buy." Finally, though, the tricky goblins

inveigle (7) Laura to buy fruit from them. She says she has no money, but the goblins aren't to be foiled. They are no doubt used to tricking both the poor and those people who have money but are too **parsimonious** (8) to spend any of it. The goblins offer to let Laura pay for the fruit with a golden curl of her hair. Laura accepts, and she **proffers** (9) a lock of her hair, offering it in exchange for the fruit.

Finding out what Laura has done, Lizzie becomes upset. She reminds Laura about a friend of theirs who ate the goblins' fruit and died because she wanted more but could not have it. People who have tasted the goblins' fruit once can thereafter no longer hear the goblins' calls or buy their fruits. Horribly, however, their cravings for the fruit grow ever stronger.

Lizzie's warning is well-founded, for soon, like the goblins' other victims, Laura begins to fade away. She starts to die slowly because she cannot taste the goblins' fruit a second time. Lizzie, who fortunately has a **sanguine** (10) temperament, is, as usual, optimistic and hopeful, even in the face of tragedy. She decides to go to the Goblin Market, confident that she can somehow save Laura's life.

Lizzie finds the goblins. Rossetti does not present these supernatural beings as

---

nondescript (11) creatures but describes them as "[c]at-like and rat-like." The goblins will not sell Lizzie any fruit to take back to Laura unless Lizzie herself will taste the fruit. Lizzie staunchly refuses the temptation. Her refusal makes the goblins angry, and they squeeze their fruits against Lizzie's face. Lizzie holds fast against the goblins' assault, and she avoids eating the fruit. The goblins finally give up, and Lizzie goes home. She lets Laura drink the fruit juices and eat the pulp remaining on her face. In this way, Lizzie saves Laura by letting her have a second taste of goblin fruit. Laura stops fading away and is restored to her former seraphic (12) appearance; she looks like an angel with "gleaming locks," sweet breath, and dancing eyes.

Lasting Appeal

Rossetti's poem, still the most famous of all her works, holds the reader's attention from beginning to end. One reason for the poem's appeal is that the story revolves around strange creatures and their magical abilities. The story thus appeals to the reader's interest in the unusual and fantastic. Of course, the reader knows that goblins, like ghosts and trolls, exist only in the imagination. Yet even though goblins are nonentities (13), they seem real enough in the fantastical world of Rossetti's poem.

Another reason for the poem's lasting appeal is its lively meter and inventive rhymes:

> Backwards up the mossy glen
> Turned and trooped the goblin men,
> With their shrill repeated cry,
> "Come buy, come buy."

Such lines are examples of very good poetry, not doggerel (14). It appears that Rossetti was a facile (15) writer, that she smoothly and easily fashioned her imaginings into concise, refined verse. "Goblin Market" is a well-organized narrative with a definite plot and structure, not an amorphous (16), rambling tale about mysterious creatures.

"Goblin Market" is more than an entertaining story, however. The poem may be viewed as a moralistic tale that warns people not to give in to evil or dangerous temptations. The poem may also be viewed as a religious story. Some critics have noted that the theme ties in with the biblical account of Eve because Laura eats the "fruit forbidden" that brings death. Some readers see the story as a Christian parable and point out that salvation from death, what Rossetti refers to in the poem as "life out of death," comes through love and suffering—Lizzie's sacrifice for Laura.

The Goblins' Creator

Such interpretations of "Goblin Market" seem consistent with its author's personality traits. Christina Rossetti was a very religious woman who believed in the teachings of the Church of England and strictly adhered to that dogma (17) all her life. She lived as an ascetic (18), denying herself fashionable clothes and other worldly pleasures and comforts. She was a shy, private person, raised in a loving, artistic household where decorum (19), or polite behavior, was stressed. It is perhaps hard to imagine that such a retiring person would have the courage to make her poetry—much of which involved themes of death and unfulfilled love—known to the outside world. In fact, some people credit her brother, the poet and painter Dante Gabriel Rossetti, with being her primary influence and critic, the one who helped her to create a bridge between her private world and the outer world. Still, she was far from being merely her brother's protégé (20). Although he did in many ways act as a mentor to her by promoting her career as a poet, Christina Rossetti had a firm grasp of her own talent and often disregarded her more famous brother's advice. Today, many critics regard her as the superior poet and see her talent as evidence not only of true originality but also of genius.

Name _____ Date _____ Class _____

EXERCISE 1 *Finding Synonyms*

Directions. Reread the preceding passage. Then write on the line provided a synonym for each of the words in boldface. If you cannot think of an exact synonym, you may write a brief definition of the word.

1. implicit _____
2. sundry _____
3. guile _____
4. exhort _____
5. vociferous _____
6. scurrilous _____
7. inveigle _____
8. parsimonious _____
9. proffers _____
10. sanguine _____
11. nondescript _____
12. seraphic _____
13. nonentities _____
14. doggerel _____
15. facile _____
16. amorphous _____
17. dogma _____
18. ascetic _____
19. decorum _____
20. protégé _____

Name _____ Date _____ Class _____

EXERCISE 2 *Reading Strategically* ✍

Directions. Now that you have read the passage and thought about the words in boldface, circle the letter of the correct answer to each of the following items. The numbers of the items are the same as the numbers of the boldface Vocabulary Words in the passage.

1. To tell us that **implicit** means "tacit, or understood without being expressed," the writer
   (A) refers to a fascinating, fantastic story
   (B) uses figurative language as an illustration
   (C) contrasts the words **implicit** *meanings* with the words *expressed story*
   (D) links **implicit** to a series of synonyms
   (E) gives a quotation from the poem as an example

2. In the passage, what does it mean that the goblins' offerings are **sundry**?
   (A) There is only one kind of offering.
   (B) The offerings are not clean.
   (C) There are only a few offerings.
   (D) The offerings are sold on Sunday.
   (E) There are a variety of offerings.

3. In the passage, the meaning of **guile** is
   (A) offerings
   (B) cunning
   (C) curious
   (D) urgings
   (E) untrustworthy

4. In the passage, when the goblins **exhort** people to buy the fruit, they strongly
   (A) expect people to buy it
   (B) warn people not to buy it
   (C) prevent people from buying it
   (D) urge people to buy it
   (E) praise people who buy it

5. If the goblins are always **vociferous** in their urgings, as the writer of the passage suggests, we may expect
   (A) the market always to be noisy with the goblins' loud demands
   (B) people to be unaware of the goblins' presence
   (C) the market to be very quiet and peaceful
   (D) the goblins to be quietly charming and rather humorous
   (E) the goblins to be quiet and undemanding

6. We can infer from the passage that if someone is **scurrilous**, that person
   (A) is trustworthy
   (B) moves around quickly
   (C) speaks softly and politely
   (D) uses foul language
   (E) is like a squirrel

7. In the passage, the words _____ provide a clue to the meaning of **inveigle**.

(A) *money* and *foiled*
(B) *offers* and *gifts*
(C) *curious* and *charm*
(D) *wares* and *buy*
(E) *enticed* and *tricky*

8. In the passage, **parsimonious** means to be

(A) generous
(B) poor
(C) stingy
(D) wealthy
(E) curious

9. In the passage, **proffers** means

(A) tricks
(B) offers
(C) steals
(D) takes away
(E) refuses

10. When we read in the passage that Lizzie has a **sanguine** temperament, we should realize that she is

(A) violent and dangerous
(B) optimistic and confident
(C) bossy and overbearing
(D) depressed and melancholy
(E) quiet and unconcerned

11. According to the passage, the goblins are not **nondescript** creatures because they

(A) are never described by Rossetti
(B) all look alike
(C) are angels in disguise
(D) are described as having distinctive qualities
(E) are imaginary and therefore have no qualities

12. When Laura is restored to her former **seraphic** appearance, the writer compares her by simile to

(A) a goblin
(B) a magician
(C) an angel
(D) fruit juice
(E) a sacrifice

13. In the passage, the "goblins are **nonentities**" means they are

(A) imaginary
(B) strange
(C) appealing
(D) popular
(E) real

14. We can infer from the passage that **doggerel** is
   (A) bad poetry
   (B) a quotation
   (C) rhyming poetry
   (D) a poem about dogs
   (E) a complex rhyme scheme

15. In the passage, **facile** means
   (A) influential
   (B) fake
   (C) easy
   (D) definite
   (E) religious

16. If a narrative is **amorphous,** as the writer of the passage says "Goblin Market" is not, we may expect it to be
   (A) well organized and concise
   (B) vague and rambling
   (C) interesting and imaginative
   (D) creepy and unsettling
   (E) mysterious and subtle

17. In the passage, Rossetti's adherence to the **dogma** of the Church of England shows that she believed in the _____ of the Church.
   (A) progress
   (B) poetry
   (C) teachings
   (D) restoration
   (E) formation

18. When we read in the passage that Rossetti was an **ascetic,** we should realize that she
   (A) practiced self-denial and self-discipline
   (B) wasted money
   (C) wore fancy clothes and shoes
   (D) was too poor to afford even necessities
   (E) had a biting wit and a bad temper

19. In the passage, **decorum** means
   (A) worldly possessions
   (B) strict discipline
   (C) shy, private person
   (D) artistic household
   (E) polite behavior

20. In the passage, why should we consider Christina Rossetti to be more than merely her brother Dante Gabriel's **protégé?**
   (A) Christina Rossetti never listened to or trusted her brother.
   (B) Dante Gabriel never cared about his sister's work.
   (C) Although in many ways he acted as her mentor, she often disregarded his advice.
   (D) Dante Gabriel was never her mentor in the first place.
   (E) Although Christina Rossetti was a poor poet, her brother Dante Gabriel promoted her work.

Name _____ Date _____ Class _____

Lesson 4 · CONTEXT: Literary Figures

The passage gives you an opportunity to expand your vocabulary. Below are twenty Vocabulary Words that are used in the passage and in the exercises that follow it.

absolve	erudite	indigent	retroactive
antipathy	etymology	infringe	specious
antipodes	extol	nettle	subjugate
broach	gratuitous	ostensible	truism
charlatan	immutable	predispose	venerate

Chinua Achebe: A Criticism of Joseph Conrad's Heart of Darkness

Renowned Nigerian author Chinua Achebe (b. 1930) finds little light in *Heart of Darkness,* the famous novella by Polish-born English novelist Joseph Conrad (1857–1924). Although Conrad's story about colonial exploitation of Africans in the Belgian Congo has been generally **venerated** (1) since its 1902 publication (it was, in fact, the inspiration for Francis Ford Coppola's famous film *Apocalypse Now*), Achebe does not regard the novella with respect. In fact, Achebe considers Conrad's viewpoint racist and believes *Heart of Darkness* reflects Conrad's strong **antipathy** (2) toward the African people.

To begin with, Achebe says, in *Heart of Darkness* Conrad uses Africa as a symbol of a primitive world in contrast to the civilized European world. Achebe maintains that in Conrad's mind Africa and Europe are opposites. As **antipodes** (3), the two worlds can never share a common ground. Conrad seems to think it is his exclusive privilege, as a "civilized" European, to look down on all that is African, Achebe asserts. Achebe believes that Conrad attempts to pass off a falsehood as a **truism** (4) to his readers: Conrad portrays

Africa as a primitive, uncivilized heart of darkness as if that view were obviously the true one. Achebe refutes Conrad's stand by pointing out the respected accomplishments of African artists at the time Conrad wrote his story.

Achebe on Conrad's Racial Bias

Even more disturbing to Achebe than Conrad's use of Africa as a symbol of a primitive world is Conrad's depiction of the African people. Some readers claim that Conrad should be declared blameless since the racially biased views expressed belong to the fictional narrator, not to Conrad himself. But Achebe is not willing to **absolve** (5) Conrad of responsibility for distorted portrayals of Africans. Achebe is irritated by Conrad's descriptions of Africans as a "prehistoric" people who have a "remote kinship" with Europeans. He is also **nettled** (6) by Conrad's depiction of most Africans as being incapable of speech and uttering instead "a violent babble of uncouth sounds" (evidently not worthy of any **etymological** (7) endeavor). Conrad apparently regards Africans as **immutable** (8) savages, unchanged since prehistoric times. Achebe notes that the

Africans in *Heart of Darkness* seem to have no function in their lives other than to plague Marlow, the European narrator.

Achebe indicates that he is not swayed in his opinion of *Heart of Darkness* by arguments that Conrad's apparent purpose was to show the terrible atrocities committed against the **indigent** (9) or poor people of the Congo by King Leopold II of Belgium. Leopold's goal was to **subjugate** (10) the Congo for its rich resources, to conquer the land and its people. In a trip to the Congo in 1890, Conrad saw firsthand how ruthlessly Leopold was **infringing** (11), or trespassing, on the rights of the Congo's inhabitants. For Achebe, however, this **ostensible** (12) purpose of Conrad's is overshadowed by what he regards as Conrad's hidden motive to dehumanize Africa and Africans. In Conrad's time, Africans were looked down upon, Achebe says, and this atmosphere of prejudice **predisposed** (13) Conrad, or made him susceptible, to a racist attitude toward Africans. Achebe also points out that Conrad had a personal obsession with issues of race and revealed a fixation with skin color that at times was irrational.

Are Achebe's Views Justified?

Achebe does admit that Conrad's story has some literary merit, and he praises Conrad's writing abilities. Yet Achebe says he cannot **extol** (14) the work as a whole because of its blatant racism. Achebe believes his attacks on *Heart of Darkness* are not **gratuitous** (15).

Rather, they are justified, he says, because Conrad's racism and stereotyped descriptions of Africa should be exposed and considered as central elements in the story.

Achebe introduced, or **broached** (16), the subject of Conrad's racism in an **erudite** (17), or scholarly, lecture in 1975. This lecture later was published in a scholarly review. As a result, writers and teachers took note of Achebe's comments about Conrad. They took his comments very seriously because they knew Achebe is not a literary **charlatan** (18); he possesses expert knowledge and skills. In fact, many critics rate him as Nigeria's greatest novelist and one of the finest English-language novelists in the world. His novels include *Things Fall Apart* and *Arrow of God*, both of which concern Nigeria's early colonization. Achebe has also been a professor, diplomat, and lecturer.

After reading Conrad's *Heart of Darkness*, you can decide for yourself whether you think Achebe's arguments are **specious** (19) or whether they actually are reasonable and true. Those who agree with Achebe may wish that his views could automatically become the accepted outlook of that time, like a **retroactive** (20) law that would go into effect in 1890. Of course, time travel is not possible, but there is still much today that can be done to reduce racial prejudice. Achebe, no doubt, would approve of any efforts to promote racial equality.

EXERCISE 1 *Finding Synonyms*

Directions. Reread the preceding passage. Then write on the line provided a synonym for each of the words in boldface. If you cannot think of an exact synonym, you may write a brief definition of the word.

1. venerated _____

2. antipathy _____

3. antipodes _____

4. truism _____

5. absolve _____

6. nettled _____

7. etymological _____

8. immutable _____

9. indigent _____

10. subjugate _____

11. infringing _____

12. ostensible _____

13. predisposed _____

14. extol _____

15. gratuitous _____

16. broached _____

17. erudite _____

18. charlatan _____

19. specious _____

20. retroactive _____

EXERCISE 2 Reading Strategically

Directions. Now that you have read the passage and thought about the words in boldface, circle the letter of the correct answer to each of the following items. The numbers of the items are the same as the numbers of the boldface Vocabulary Words in the passage.

1. In the passage, how does Achebe's opinion of Conrad's work differ from the opinions of those who have **venerated** Conrad?
   (A) Achebe highly respects Conrad's work.
   (B) Most people have little respect for *Heart of Darkness*.
   (C) Achebe dismisses Conrad's writing as unimportant.
   (D) Achebe thinks Conrad's work is not appreciated enough.
   (E) Achebe does not regard Conrad's work with respect.

2. In the passage, Conrad's feeling **antipathy** toward Africans means that he
   (A) respected them
   (B) strongly disliked them
   (C) had an understanding of them
   (D) was sympathetic to them
   (E) lived in Africa among them

3. In the passage, **antipodes** are
   (A) opposites
   (B) similarities
   (C) activities
   (D) assertions
   (E) symbols

4. To tell us that a **truism** is "a statement that is generally regarded as true," the writer
   (A) links **truism** with the synonym *falsehood*
   (B) gives a definition of **truism**
   (C) contrasts **truism** with the words *respected accomplishments*
   (D) uses figurative language to illustrate **truism**
   (E) uses a pronoun reference to explain **truism**

5. In the passage, Achebe is unwilling to **absolve** Conrad because he
   (A) believes Conrad has done nothing wrong
   (B) believes Conrad is guilty of racism
   (C) wants everyone to read and respect Conrad
   (D) does not feel justified in criticizing Conrad
   (E) does not feel any anger toward Conrad

6. In the passage, the word that provides a clue to the meaning of **nettled** is
   (A) depiction
   (B) violent
   (C) regarded
   (D) intentions
   (E) irritated

7. The writer tells us that **etymological** refers to the study of word origins by
   (A) using a synonym for **etymological**
   (B) contrasting **etymological** with the word *incapable*
   (C) using **etymological** in a metaphor
   (D) using **etymological** in a series of words similar in meaning
   (E) linking **etymology** to the words *speech* and *sounds*

8. In the passage, to be **immutable** means to
   (A) be unchangeable
   (B) be hard of hearing
   (C) live forever
   (D) have prehistoric traits
   (E) be bothersome

9. In the passage, **indigent** means
   (A) meek
   (B) tall
   (C) weak
   (D) poor
   (E) fast

10. In the passage, the word that provides a clue to the meaning of **subjugate** is
   (A) resources
   (B) atrocities
   (C) conquer
   (D) trespassing
   (E) rights

11. If Leopold was **infringing** on the rights of the Congo people, we may expect
   (A) the Congo's inhabitants to have had their rights supported
   (B) the Congo's inhabitants to have encouraged Leopold's efforts
   (C) Leopold to have improved the conditions of the Congo's inhabitants
   (D) the Congo's inhabitants to have lost many of their rights
   (E) Leopold not to have known about the rights of the Congo's inhabitants

12. To tell us that **ostensible** is defined as "apparent," the writer
   (A) uses **ostensible** with a series of synonyms
   (B) contrasts **ostensible** with the words *hidden motive*
   (C) uses a quotation as an example of **ostensible**
   (D) relates **ostensible** to the verb *dehumanize*
   (E) declares that all purposes are **ostensible**

13. When we read in the passage that the time in which Conrad lived **predisposed** him to racist attitudes, we should realize that
   (A) Conrad was in no way influenced by the thinking of the time
   (B) Conrad was his own person and formed his own conclusions
   (C) the thinking of the time made Conrad susceptible to racism
   (D) Conrad had to keep his motives hidden because he was sincere
   (E) other people were unable to understand Conrad's attitudes

14. We can infer from the passage that to **extol** is to
   (A) criticize
   (B) publicize
   (C) absorb
   (D) despise
   (E) praise

15. The writer provides a clue to the meaning of **gratuitous** by
   (A) linking it to the word *descriptions*
   (B) using the word *blatant* to describe racism
   (C) contrasting **gratuitous** with the word *justified*
   (D) using the word *stereotyped*
   (E) implying that **gratuitous** means "justified"

16. In the passage, **broached** means
   (A) introduced
   (B) learned
   (C) subjected
   (D) criticized
   (E) controlled

17. According to the passage, writers and teachers took note of Achebe's **erudite** lecture because he
(A) is very critical of Conrad
(B) is a very learned and scholarly person
(C) wrote only to offend other Conrad scholars
(D) is a very entertaining writer
(E) is too familiar with Conrad's writing

18. When we read in the passage that Achebe is not a literary **charlatan,** we should realize that
(A) a **charlatan** is a skilled and knowledgeable expert
(B) Achebe has never been a published author
(C) Achebe has expert knowledge and skills
(D) Achebe has learned to speak and write in English
(E) Achebe pretends to be something that he is not

19. We can tell from the passage that arguments that are **specious**
(A) are actually reasonable and true
(B) are never publicly written or spoken
(C) are made by suspicious people
(D) seem reasonable and true but are not
(E) can easily be proven to be acceptable

20. Because many people will agree with Achebe's views, they might wish his views could be **retroactive**. To reinforce this point, the writer uses a simile of
(A) the accepted outlook in 1890
(B) a law that is made now but goes into effect in the past
(C) a law that was established in 1890
(D) a person who dwells on historic facts
(E) time travel

READING NEW WORDS IN CONTEXT

Lesson 5 | CONTEXT: Literary Figures

The passage gives you an opportunity to expand your vocabulary. Below are twenty Vocabulary Words that are used in the passage and in the exercises that follow it.

abnegation	eulogy	humdrum	paragon
ascribe	euphony	idiosyncrasy	poignant
copious	extraneous	inconsequential	progeny
elegy	hackneyed	introvert	sonorous
engender	homily	mundane	tenure

The Journals of Dorothy Wordsworth

William Wordsworth (1770–1850) was one of the greatest of England's Romantic poets. Yet many people are unaware that the great poet owed much of his success to another talented member of the Wordsworth family, his sister Dorothy Wordsworth (1771–1855). Dorothy's role as her brother's "dearest Friend," as he described her in the poem "Tintern Abbey," and her contributions to his life and works are clearly seen in the journals Dorothy began keeping in 1797. Through these journals, we know that Dorothy helped produce a harmonious home life for William. We also discover that her journal writings helped **engender** (1) or bring about some of her brother's finest poetry.

Making the Most of a Quiet Life

Dorothy Wordsworth was a shy, quiet person, an **introvert** (2). Beginning at the age of six, she lived with various relatives after her mother died. **Abnegation** (3) was second nature to her; having little money, she became accustomed to self-denial. At an early age she chose to devote her life to her brother William. Her desire to set up a household with William was realized in 1795. Even when William married in 1802, Dorothy remained with him, living in the same house with the couple.

The journals that Dorothy kept about the Wordsworth households may be called **copious** (4) because they are filled with information. She recorded many details about the ordinary or **mundane** (5) activities of their lives in England's Lake District. She wrote, for example, of the simple pleasures of going for walks with her brother, attending to domestic chores, and talking to friends. "We had sunshine and showers, pleasant talk, love and cheerfulness," she wrote of one outing in 1802. She found poetry in all aspects of life. She could write of the **sonorous** (6) sounds of waves tumbling against a lake shore, calling forth their deep and rich tones with her well-chosen words. She could just as poetically write of baking pies and ironing clothes. Dorothy also enjoyed children and often cared for the **progeny** (7) of William and his wife, Mary. Some people might describe Dorothy's life as **humdrum** (8), but it apparently wasn't dull to her.

Dorothy's talents as a writer are evident in her journals. Her writing is admired for its vivid descriptions, rich details, frankness, and energy. Her style is fresh and original, not **hackneyed** (9). For example, you may note the absence of trite expressions in the following excerpt from a January 31, 1802, journal entry:

"I found a strawberry blossom in a rock. The little slender flower had more courage than the green leaves, for *they* were but half expanded and half grown, but the blossom was spread full out. I uprooted it rashly, and I felt as if I had been committing an outrage, so I planted it again. It will have but a stormy life of it, but let it live if it can."

Her journals show that Dorothy frequently took delight in happenings that might seem **inconsequential** (10) to someone else. To her they were not unimportant; they had great significance. Her writing is insightful but not overly sentimental. She was direct and to the point, and was not one to write a long, moralizing **homily** (11) where a brief description would do. She was not, after all, writing sermons for a Sunday service; she was recording the realities of everyday life.

In addition to her journals, Dorothy wrote poems, short stories, and letters. One of her works is a **eulogy** (12) to a couple who were killed in a snowstorm in 1808 and who left behind eight children. This tribute is a **poignant** (13) one, especially in its emotionally touching depiction of the eldest child, an eleven-year-old girl, who must become a mother to her younger siblings.

Dorothy's Influence on William Wordsworth

As you can imagine, Dorothy's writings are important sources of biographical information about her more famous brother, William Wordsworth. Through Dorothy's journals, we discover some details relating to William's personal peculiarities—his **idiosyncrasies** (14)—and to his writing habits.

Dorothy's journals were also valuable sources for William himself. When writing poems, he frequently consulted his sister's journals for details and descriptions. Some famous lines and images attributed to William actually should be **ascribed** (15) to Dorothy. For example, in her journal Dorothy wrote, "At once the clouds seemed to cleave asunder, and left her in the centre of a black-blue vault." In his poem "A Night-piece," William wrote, "—the clouds are split / Asunder,—and above his head he sees / The clear Moon, and the glory of the heavens." Both excerpts have an agreeable sound; their **euphony** (16) is, in fact, similar. Neither writer cluttered his or her thoughts with **extraneous** (17) words, but rather carefully chose only relevant, necessary words to evoke certain moods or images.

With Dorothy providing help and support in the background, William developed into one of England's foremost poets. Like a crown jewel among lesser stones, his writing is considered a **paragon** (18) of English Romantic poetry. Among these exemplary poems are lyrical ballads and **elegies** (19). (An **elegy** is a mournful poem, often about someone who is dead.) In 1843, William Wordsworth was made poet laureate of England. His **tenure** (20) in that office lasted until his death. Dorothy Wordsworth, on the other hand, knew no such earthly fame in her lifetime. For many decades, scholars, if they studied her writings at all, did so with an eye only to learning more about William Wordsworth. Today, however, an increasing number of scholars are finding much to admire in Dorothy's journals and letters. Even without the benefit of the kind of education her brother—and other male writers of the time—received, Dorothy managed to develop a perspective and a literary voice all her own.

From *Journals of Dorothy Wordsworth,* edited by E. de Selincourt. Published by Macmillan & Co. Ltd, London, England, 1941.

EXERCISE 1 *Finding Synonyms* 👆

Directions. Reread the preceding passage. Then write on the line provided a synonym for each of the words in boldface. If you cannot think of an exact synonym, you may write a brief definition of the word.

1. engender _____

2. introvert _____

3. abnegation _____

4. copious _____

5. mundane _____

6. sonorous _____

7. progeny _____

8. humdrum _____

9. hackneyed _____

10. inconsequential _____

11. homily _____

12. eulogy _____

13. poignant _____

14. idiosyncrasies _____

15. ascribed _____

16. euphony _____

17. extraneous _____

18. paragon _____

19. elegies _____

20. tenure _____

EXERCISE 2   *Reading Strategically* 👈

Directions. Now that you have read the passage and thought about the words in boldface, circle the letter of the correct answer to each of the following items. The numbers of the items are the same as the numbers of the boldface Vocabulary Words in the passage.

1. In the passage, the meaning of **engender** is
   (A) clearly seen
   (B) journal writings
   (C) bring about
   (D) finest poetry
   (E) harmonious home life

2. According to the passage, an **introvert** is
   (A) a social situation
   (B) a loud voice
   (C) a journalist
   (D) a shy, quiet person
   (E) an orphan

3. In the passage, **abnegation** means
   (A) appreciation
   (B) accommodation
   (C) selfishness
   (D) activity
   (E) self-denial

4. In the passage, **copious** means
   (A) without mistakes
   (B) domestic
   (C) full of information
   (D) unable to cope
   (E) disorganized

5. The writer provides a clue to the meaning of **mundane** by
   (A) linking **mundane** to two antonyms
   (B) using the prepositional phrase "of their lives"
   (C) using the simile of *simple pleasures*
   (D) relating **mundane** to the word *activities*
   (E) linking **mundane** to the synonym *ordinary*

6. In the passage, **sonorous** means
   (A) high and thin
   (B) deep and thin
   (C) high and loud
   (D) deep and rich
   (E) slow and loud

7. We can infer from the passage that Dorothy was well suited to caring for William and Mary Wordsworth's **progeny** because she
(A) baked pies
(B) liked children
(C) never did housework
(D) was rich
(E) had children of her own

8. In the passage, the word that provides a clue to the meaning of **humdrum** is
(A) dull
(B) life
(C) written
(D) enjoyed
(E) rich

9. According to the passage, a **hackneyed** style is characterized by
(A) vivid descriptions
(B) journals written by the sisters of poets
(C) frankness and energy
(D) stale writing and trite expressions
(E) writing that is obscure and difficult

10. In the passage, **inconsequential** happenings are
(A) important
(B) unimportant
(C) outdoors
(D) insightful
(E) frequent

11. Dorothy never wrote a **homily,** but the writer of the passage suggests that many **homilies** are
(A) lively, fresh, descriptive passages
(B) tightly written poems
(C) funny, cheerful, and short articles
(D) long and involved jokes
(E) long and moralizing pieces of writing

12. We can infer from the passage that a **eulogy** is a
(A) cheerful letter to a friend
(B) description of a family friend
(C) question about something
(D) tribute to someone who has died
(E) commentary on the meaning of life

13. When we read in the passage that Dorothy's tribute is a **poignant** one, we should realize that it is
(A) not well written
(B) a very famous poem
(C) the only thing she wrote
(D) emotionally touching
(E) emotionally detached

14. In the passage, **idiosyncrasies** are
  (A) personal details
  (B) religious practices
  (C) personal sleep habits
  (D) personal peculiarities
  (E) family members and friends

15. In the passage, the word that provides a clue to the meaning of **ascribed** is
  (A) valuable
  (B) attributed
  (C) consulted
  (D) sources
  (E) descriptions

16. Dorothy's journal writing and William's poetry have a **euphony** because they both have _____ sounds when read aloud.
  (A) noisy
  (B) sad
  (C) agreeable
  (D) unnatural
  (E) exciting

17. If the Wordsworths did not use **extraneous** words, as the writer of the passage suggests, we may expect
  (A) the words they used to be relevant and necessary to the subject
  (B) their writing to ramble on about uninteresting things
  (C) their writing to be very difficult to understand
  (D) their writing to be cluttered with unnecessary descriptions
  (E) the words they used to apply to all subjects

18. Because William Wordsworth's writing is regarded as a **paragon** of English Romantic poetry, the writer compares it by simile to
  (A) Dorothy Wordsworth's writing
  (B) the death of a loved one
  (C) a pyramid in the desert
  (D) a crown jewel among lesser stones
  (E) lyrical ballads written by Coleridge

19. To tell us the meaning of **elegies,** the writer
  (A) uses an example of an **elegy**
  (B) defines **elegy**
  (C) uses the synonym *ballad* for **elegy**
  (D) uses the antonym *mournful* for **elegy**
  (E) uses a simile about someone who is dead

20. When we read in the passage that William Wordsworth's **tenure** lasted until his death, we should realize that
  (A) **tenure** has to do with writing poetry
  (B) **tenure** is the length of time a position is held
  (C) a person has to die to obtain **tenure**
  (D) **tenure** always lasts multiples of ten years
  (E) people who write poetry lose **tenure** when they die

READING NEW WORDS IN CONTEXT

Lesson 6 | **CONTEXT:** History and Society

The passage gives you an opportunity to expand your vocabulary. Below are twenty Vocabulary Words that are used in the passage and in the exercises that follow it.

aberration	captivate	deduce	proponent
adjudge	chicanery	diurnal	refute
artifice	configuration	extant	retrospect
augury	corroborate	herculean	salient
candor	dearth	ludicrous	scrupulous

Two British Mysteries

The First Mystery: Stonehenge

You stand within a circle of massive stones and stare at a strange **configuration** (1), wondering why the stones are arranged to form such an outline. Many stones are capped with other stones, forming open doorway-like constructions. Beyond the giant stones you can see the rolling farmlands of the Salisbury Plain in southern England.

You are standing at Stonehenge, one of England's greatest mysteries and tourist attractions. Stonehenge is a **salient** (2) feature on the grassy plain, as noticeable and conspicuous as a house in the middle of an otherwise vacant field. The stones obviously are very ancient, and you are amazed that they have not been destroyed but are **extant** (3). When and how did these rugged, giant stones come to be placed here? Who placed them, and why?

In the twelfth century, British chronicler Geoffrey of Monmouth wrote that an ancient king erected Stonehenge as a monument. According to the story, the magician Merlin told the king to travel to Ireland and bring back a group of sacred stones. But it would have taken someone with the superhuman strength of the Greek hero Hercules to accomplish this feat; certainly the king's soldiers

were unable to carry out the **herculean** (4) task of moving the stones. Merlin came up with an alternative: He constructed magic machines that moved the stones across the water from Ireland.

Is this story ridiculous, merely a **ludicrous** (5) fairy tale? Perhaps, but in the 1950s, the researcher Richard J. C. Atkinson believed that he had identified Merlin's so-called magic machines. Reasoning from historical knowledge, Atkinson **deduced** (6) that the stones were transported on rafts along the west coast of Britain and then up rivers on canoes. Thus, Atkinson, in a sense, confirmed or **corroborated** (7) the tale of Merlin's magic machines.

Today, we know that the construction of Stonehenge began about 2800 B.C. No records of its construction were ever made, but there is no **dearth** (8), of speculations about the purposes for which Stonehenge was built.

Why Was Stonehenge Built?

Recent investigations have revealed that the stones were assembled by early peoples of Western Europe, not by visitors from foreign civilizations. But why was Stonehenge built? What possible purpose did it serve? One researcher, Professor Gerald S. Hawkins, believes he has the answer. In the early 1960s, he made **scrupulous** (9) calculations, as precise as those a computer could produce, to identify the positions of the sun and the moon during the period of Stonehenge's construction in 2800 B.C. From these exact calculations, he concluded that the monument was actually an observatory for studying the nocturnal, or nightly, cycles of the moon and the **diurnal** (10) cycles of the sun. Scholars have supposed that religious ceremonies tied to the summer and winter solstices were held by early British peoples at Stonehenge. Perhaps Stonehenge even functioned as a daily calendar.

The Second Mystery: Crop Circles

You are standing in a field located a few hours' drive from Stonehenge. It is summer, and you can hear the faint rumbling of farm equipment in the distance. Looking around, you notice that an eerily precise clearing has been made in a field of wheat four feet high. It looks as though someone has mown away part of the wheat field. If you could get a clear bird's-eye view, you would see that a circle with a circumference of almost one hundred feet has been made in the wheat. The wheat all around the circle is standing tall, as is the wheat in the middle of the circle. You glance over at your guide, who is standing on another flattened area that seems to be shaped like a key. "How did these get here?" you ask her. Her honest and direct answer reveals a welcomed **candor** (11). "We don't know," she says frankly, obviously as baffled as you are. "They appeared overnight."

You are in the middle of a crop circle. You have become totally **captivated** (12) by the mystery of your surroundings. Fascinated, you explore further and find other patterns in the wheat: rectangles, crosses, and bars. You notice that the crops were not destroyed when these strange patterns were made.

How Are Crop Circles Created?

From 1990 through 1991, more than six hundred examples of crop circles were found throughout Britain. They are definitely **aberrations** (13), deviations from the normal. But what caused them? Some people believe they were caused by swirling currents of electrically charged air. Other people, **proponents** (14) of the UFO theory, speculate that the crop circles were caused by extraterrestrial beings trying to communicate with us. The UFO theorists see the circles as omens, or **auguries** (15), that aliens eventually will make meaningful contact with humanity.

Time magazine discounted these explanations, however, after two men claimed that they had created the patterns at night by attaching wooden boards to their feet and moving about the fields. According to the article in *Time*, the **artifice** (16) of these men—their artful trick—was the explanation that would disprove or **refute** (17) all other theories.

Problems, however, remain with this explanation. How could these men, even if they were able to deceive many by their **chicanery** (18), have created six hundred patterns in a year? And how could they have extended their trickery to twenty-nine other countries, where similar crop-circle patterns have been discovered? Unfortunately, the answer to this mystery is not one that can be **adjudged** (19) in a law court; perhaps it cannot be decided by any law, natural or supernatural.

The creation of the crop circles remains a mystery. Perhaps, however, in 3,500 years our descendants will examine the past. In the same way that we have, in **retrospect** (20), developed plausible theories about the origin of Stonehenge, perhaps they will be able to offer satisfying explanations for the mystery of the crop circles.

EXERCISE 1 *Finding Synonyms* ✍

Directions. Reread the preceding passage. Then write on the line provided a synonym for each of the words in boldface. If you cannot think of an exact synonym, you may write a brief definition of the word.

1. configuration _____
2. salient _____
3. extant _____
4. herculean _____
5. ludicrous _____
6. deduced _____
7. corroborated _____
8. dearth _____
9. scrupulous _____
10. diurnal _____
11. candor _____
12. captivated _____
13. aberrations _____
14. proponents _____
15. auguries _____
16. artifice _____
17. refute _____
18. chicanery _____
19. adjudged _____
20. retrospect _____

EXERCISE 2 *Reading Strategically* ✍

Directions. Now that you have read the passage and thought about the words in boldface, circle the letter of the correct answer to each of the following items.

1. In the passage, the word that provides a clue to the meaning of **configuration** is
(A) massive
(B) strange
(C) stones
(D) outline
(E) wonder

2. To illustrate what a **salient** feature Stonehenge is, the writer compares it by simile to
(A) a house in the middle of an otherwise vacant field
(B) the rolling farmlands of the Salisbury Plain
(C) magic machines moving stones across the water
(D) rugged, giant stones in Ireland
(E) a circle of massive stones capped with smaller stones

3. According to the passage, it is amazing that Stonehenge is **extant** because
(A) Stonehenge no longer exists
(B) of the location of Stonehenge
(C) of the age of Stonehenge
(D) we know everything about it
(E) the rocks are not from the earth

4. According to the passage, a **herculean** job requires someone who is very _____.
(A) sacred
(B) honest
(C) ancient
(D) young
(E) strong

5. To tell us that **ludicrous** is defined as "laughable or absurd," the writer
(A) links **ludicrous** to the synonym *ridiculous*
(B) contrasts **ludicrous** with the words *fairy tale*
(C) defines **ludicrous** as "happy"
(D) describes a **ludicrous** machine
(E) compares **ludicrous** to the word *magical*

6. To tell us that **deduced** is defined as "concluded by means of logic," the writer
(A) describes the method used to transport the stones
(B) links **deduced** to the phrase "Reasoning from historical knowledge"
(C) uses an antonym for **deduced**
(D) uses a simile to describe Merlin's method of transporting the stones
(E) uses **deduced** to explain different theories

7. In the passage, **corroborated** means
- (A) refuted
- (B) praised
- (C) sensed
- (D) confirmed
- (E) disproved

8. We can infer from the passage that if there is no **dearth** of speculations, there are
- (A) only incorrect speculations
- (B) no speculations
- (C) many speculations
- (D) a few speculations
- (E) fewer than a hundred speculations

9. According to the passage, to be **scrupulous** means to
- (A) be careless
- (B) be electronic
- (C) be exact
- (D) produce
- (E) estimate

10. If the sun has **diurnal** cycles, as the writer of the passage says, we may expect them to be related to
- (A) the night
- (B) the tides
- (C) moonlight
- (D) the day
- (E) spring

11. According to the passage, to speak with **candor** means to
- (A) speak secretly
- (B) be misunderstood
- (C) tell a falsehood
- (D) speak quietly
- (E) speak frankly

12. In the passage, the word that provides a clue to the meaning of **captivated** is
- (A) totally
- (B) fascinated
- (C) surroundings
- (D) destroyed
- (E) patterns

13. In the passage, **aberrations** are
- (A) revelations of mysteries
- (B) deviations from the normal
- (C) usual circumstances
- (D) currents of electrically charged air
- (E) seasonal rotations of crops

14. According to the passage, the people who are **proponents** of the UFO theory _____ that the crop circles are caused by extraterrestrial beings.

   (A) believe
   (B) deny
   (C) question
   (D) fear
   (E) disproved

15. In the passage, **auguries** means

   (A) circles
   (B) extraterrestrial beings
   (C) omens, or signs
   (D) alien contact
   (E) natural events

16. If the two men are successful in their **artifice**, the writer of the passage suggests that they will have

   (A) honestly created art
   (B) explained ancient signs
   (C) harvested crops
   (D) artfully tricked people
   (E) questioned authorities

17. In the passage, the word that provides a clue to the meaning of **refute** is

   (A) answers
   (B) artful
   (C) convince
   (D) mystery
   (E) disprove

18. When we read in the passage that the men used **chicanery**, we should realize that they

   (A) honestly tried to solve the mystery
   (B) deliberately intended to deceive people
   (C) hoped to perfect their methods
   (D) became rich and famous for their work
   (E) used electronic devices to make the crop circles

19. We can infer from the passage that if the mystery could be **adjudged** in a law court, it could be

   (A) decided
   (B) tried
   (C) denied
   (D) confused
   (E) extended

20. The writer provides a clue to the meaning of **retrospect** by

   (A) describing the creation of the crop circles
   (B) using an antonym for **retrospect**
   (C) saying that "our descendants will examine the past"
   (D) linking **retrospect** to the origin of the circles
   (E) using the word *solve*

READING NEW WORDS IN CONTEXT

Lesson 7 | CONTEXT: History and Society

The passage gives you an opportunity to expand your vocabulary. Below are twenty Vocabulary Words that are used in the passage and in the exercises that follow it.

affront	exhilaration	incarcerate	patrimony
capitulate	foible	indulgent	precocious
civility	germane	magnanimous	propitious
connoisseur	gregarious	munificent	punctilious
effusion	guffaw	obsequious	querulous

Samuel Johnson: A Great Man of Letters

Samuel Johnson (1709–1784) was an expert in the English language as well as a **connoisseur** (1) of eighteenth-century English literature and culture. He is famous for a variety of writings, including *A Dictionary of the English Language*, which remained the definitive English dictionary for more than a century and a half.

A Witty Eccentric
Johnson was so popular in English society that many people wrote down their impressions of him. These accounts tell us that Johnson was not only a scholarly writer but also a lively conversationalist. When he conversed with equally witty friends, the **effusion** (2) of clever, amusing remarks was like water gushing from a fountain. The **exhilaration** (3) his listeners felt was no greater than the excitement Johnson himself experienced during such rapid-fire exchanges of wit. Johnson was **gregarious** (4) by nature; he always enjoyed the company of others. Although he definitely did not spend all his time clowning around, he was certain to **guffaw** (5) appreciatively at a clever joke. In fact, one of Johnson's friends wrote of him that "no man loved laughing better."

Of course, Johnson was not perfect; he had his **foibles** (6). For example, he could be abrupt or rude, and he sometimes grew impatient with the people who came to him for advice. Since Johnson did not like being fussed over and flattered, one can imagine that he had little tolerance for visitors who seemed **obsequious** (7). In addition, he no doubt offended some people with his casual attitude toward conventions of behavior. Johnson was no more **punctilious** (8) about details of etiquette than he was exact and careful about his personal appearance. Most people, though, overlooked his shortcomings, for they valued his kindness and generosity and admired his honesty, courage, and spirit.

A Self-Made Man
Although Johnson was unusually mature and intelligent as a young man, he apparently was not **precocious** (9) as a small child. He was extremely frail, and his first few years were dominated by illness. One incident from his childhood may be **germane** (10) to the development of Johnson's character. In Johnson's time, many people believed that the touch of a royal person could cure certain ailments. Seeking a cure for her son,

Johnson's mother took him to London, where he and two hundred other sick children were touched by Queen Anne. The queen showed great **civility** (11), courtesy, and respect to the children, and she gave the young Johnson a religious medal to wear on a ribbon around his neck. Perhaps this early experience helped shape Johnson's generous, noble spirit, his **magnanimous** (12) nature.

Johnson did not become rich and famous as soon as he set a pen to paper. Much of his life was a struggle for survival. His father, an unsuccessful bookstore owner, died poor and therefore left Johnson no **patrimony** (13). Yet Johnson was not **querulous** (14) or complaining about the lack of an inheritance. For many years he supported himself and his wife by writing articles for periodicals. Then, in the 1750s, he began publishing a highly successful series of essays on moral and religious themes. These and other essays eventually made Johnson famous throughout England. King George III recognized Johnson's literary achievements by awarding him a pension of three hundred pounds a year. This **propitious** (15) or favorable event ensured that Johnson would never have to worry about money again. **Munificent** (16) by nature, Johnson showed his extreme generosity by supporting several less-fortunate people and allowing them to live in his house. Some people may have thought that Johnson was too **indulgent** (17) with his guests. Yet it seems out of character for someone as direct and self-assured as Johnson to be overly kind or

lenient with others. Johnson no doubt simply treated them with the same kind of respect and kindness that he would have expected others to show him.

Johnson's Dictionary

Johnson may have been relaxed about social conventions, but he was never casual about scholarship. He spent nine years painstakingly compiling his definitive *Dictionary of the English Language*. (He must have been confined often during that lengthy time and, perhaps, felt **incarcerated** (18).) His dictionary included more than forty thousand words and many definitions. Reading some of the entries, one might conclude that Johnson took any misuse of the language as an **affront** (19), an intentional insult, to his person. For example, he expressed his disapproval for then-colloquial words such as *fun* and *slim*. Exacting a scholar as he was, Johnson could not resist the opportunity to add some humor to his dictionary. For example, he illustrated the meaning of the word *dull* by writing the sentence "To make dictionaries is dull work."

Johnson's dictionary remained the authoritative dictionary of the English language until 1928, when supporters of Johnson's book **capitulated** (20), or yielded, to the establishment of a new authority, now called the *Oxford English Dictionary*. Neither Johnson nor his works have faded into obscurity, however; he is still acknowledged as one of England's greatest literary figures and one of its most engaging characters.

EXERCISE 1 *Finding Synonyms*

Directions. Reread the preceding passage. Then write on the line provided a synonym for each of the words in boldface. If you cannot think of an exact synonym, you may write a brief definition of the word.

1. connoisseur _____

2. effusion _____

3. exhilaration _____

4. gregarious _____

5. guffaw _____

6. foibles _____

7. obsequious _____

8. punctilious _____

9. precocious _____

10. germane _____

11. civility _____

12. magnanimous _____

13. patrimony _____

14. querulous _____

15. propitious _____

16. munificent _____

17. indulgent _____

18. incarcerated _____

19. affront _____

20. capitulated _____

EXERCISE 2   Reading Strategically ✍

Directions. Now that you have read the passage and thought about the words in boldface, circle the letter of the correct answer to each of the following items. The numbers of the items are the same as the numbers of the boldface Vocabulary Words in the passage.

1. In the passage, the word that provides a clue to the meaning of **connoisseur** is
  (A) famous
  (B) expert
  (C) language
  (D) literature
  (E) culture

2. In the passage, the **effusion** of Johnson's clever remarks is compared by simile to
  (A) an explosion of fireworks
  (B) a radio broadcast
  (C) water gushing from a fountain
  (D) the sound of gunfire
  (E) water bursting from a broken dam

3. The writer provides a clue to the meaning of **exhilaration** by
  (A) linking **exhilaration** to the word *excitement*
  (B) linking **exhilaration** to the word *greater*
  (C) implying that it is a conversation
  (D) describing Johnson's remarks as clever and amusing
  (E) contrasting **exhilaration** with an antonym

4. We can infer from the passage that **gregarious** means
  (A) private
  (B) enjoyable
  (C) valuable
  (D) sociable
  (E) exciting

5. When we read in the passage that Johnson was known to **guffaw,** we should realize that he
  (A) probably laughed loudly
  (B) sometimes wrote about his friends
  (C) was very sarcastic to others
  (D) was well known for his temper
  (E) had no sense of humor

6. According to the passage, to have **foibles** means to
  (A) have a bad temper
  (B) be perfect
  (C) have many friends
  (D) have integrity
  (E) have shortcomings

7. In the passage, why would Johnson be irritated by **obsequious** visitors?
  (A) Johnson was too poor to have valets or other servants.
  (B) Johnson was known to prefer servants who were inefficient.
  (C) Johnson did not like to have people fussing over him and flattering him.
  (D) Johnson's friends were jealous of Johnson having a servant.
  (E) Johnson treated servants very harshly and drove them away.

8. If Johnson was not **punctilious,** as the writer of the passage states, we may expect that he
  (A) carefully followed etiquette and was careful about his appearance
  (B) hated visitors and let them know it
  (C) was never on time for anything
  (D) was not exact and careful about etiquette or his personal appearance
  (E) was very demanding of everyone except himself

9. According to the passage, to be **precocious** means to be
  (A) healthy
  (B) unusually mature
  (C) frail
  (D) very young
  (E) slow-witted

10. To tell us that **germane** is defined as "pertinent," the writer
(A) uses the word *or* to link **germane** to the word *pertinent*
(B) gives examples that illustrate the meaning of **germane**
(C) defines **germane** in an earlier paragraph
(D) uses **germane** in an extended metaphor
(E) contrasts **germane** with words of opposite meaning

11. According to the passage, to treat someone with **civility** means to
(A) treat them courteously
(B) be honest with them
(C) ignore them
(D) treat them with kindness
(E) be impolite to them

12. If Samuel Johnson had a **magnanimous** nature, as the writer of the passage suggests, we may expect him to be
(A) selfish and demanding
(B) argumentative and sarcastic
(C) a famous author
(D) frail and sickly
(E) kind and generous

13. According to the passage, to receive a **patrimony** means to
(A) support oneself
(B) leave great wealth
(C) inherit something from one's father
(D) dislike one's father
(E) receive money in a divorce settlement

14. We can tell from the passage that a **querulous** person
(A) complains
(B) questions
(C) struggles
(D) stumbles
(E) supports

15. In the passage, **propitious** means
(A) doubtful
(B) worrisome
(C) favorable
(D) proper
(E) unnatural

16. In the passage, the words that provide a clue to the meaning of **munificent** are
(A) less fortunate
(B) extreme generosity
(C) direct and self-assured
(D) favorable event
(E) out of character

17. According to the passage, Johnson may have seemed **indulgent** or _____ with his guests.
(A) overly kind
(B) self-assured
(C) too strict
(D) less fortunate
(E) very cruel

18. We can tell from the passage that **incarcerate** means
(A) many years
(B) scholarship
(C) lengthy time
(D) confined
(E) painstaking

19. In the passage, an **affront** is
(A) a compliment
(B) a scholarly work
(C) an intentional insult
(D) a colloquial expression
(E) an argument

20. When we read in the passage that users of Johnson's dictionary **capitulated** to the establishment of a new source, we should realize that they
(A) searched for a better dictionary
(B) hated Johnson's dictionary
(C) faded into obscurity
(D) insisted that Johnson's book was best
(E) yielded to a more definitive source

READING NEW WORDS IN CONTEXT

Lesson 8 | CONTEXT: History and Society

The passage gives you an opportunity to expand your vocabulary. Below are twenty Vocabulary Words that are used in the passage and in the exercises that follow it.

abeyance	discrepancy	inscrutable	perfidious
chastise	emanate	intercede	pervade
demagogue	harbinger	inundate	prevaricate
deplore	homogeneous	irrevocable	primordial
detriment	illicit	obnoxious	sumptuous

Tyranny in the Congo

As captain of a river steamer that journeyed to the Belgian Congo in 1890, adventurer and novelist Joseph Conrad (1857–1924) received an unsettling view of conditions there. The region was in turmoil, and conditions didn't improve until more than a decade later.

Conrad found the country **primordial** (1). He felt that sailing on the River Congo was like "traveling back to the earliest beginnings of the world." He later described the mysterious land and its equally **inscrutable** (2) atmosphere in his novella *Heart of Darkness*. Some readers object to Conrad's descriptions of the Congo and its people because they find these accounts offensive; but Conrad was not intentionally **obnoxious** (3) in his descriptions. He depicted the Congo as he perceived it.

The journey to the Congo was not a pleasant one for Conrad. His ship was a simple "tin-pot" steamer; it was not **sumptuous** (4) at all. Many of his crew members were sick, and Conrad himself later became ill and had to return home to England.

However, it was not the primitiveness of the land or of his sailing conditions that upset Conrad but rather what foreigners were doing to the land and the people. Conrad **deplored** (5) the looting of Africa's natural

riches by Europeans. His strong disapproval is evident in the harsh words he uses to describe the situation. He calls the exploitation of Africa "the vilest scramble for loot that ever disfigured the history of human conscience, a **detriment** (6) to the human race."

Leopold's Reign of Tyranny

The damage to Africa from European businesses and governments had begun about a decade before Conrad sailed. By 1900, most of Africa was **inundated** (7) by foreign imperialists. These outsiders overwhelmed the land like locusts. The country was eventually divided into European colonies. Because so many different races and cultures coexisted there after colonization, the Congo would never again be a **homogeneous** (8) area with a uniform population.

One greedy, power-hungry man—King Leopold II of Belgium—was the main force behind the early exploitation of the Congo. He founded the International Association for the Exploration and Civilization of Africa in 1876. His stated purposes were noble: to bring civilization to Africa and to stop the slave trade. But his true motive was far from noble. Leopold was a **demagogue** (9), a leader who stirred up people by appealing to their emotions. He persuaded other European powers to go along with him and to recognize him as ruler and owner of the Congo Free State. This action was only a **harbinger** (10), a forerunner, of trickery to come.

Leopold was actually interested in Africa's riches—ivory from elephant tusks and rubber from rubber trees. The new industrial Europe needed all the rubber it could get. Leopold did not have to worry about how he went about obtaining what he wanted. Were his actions **illicit** (11)? No, they were not forbidden by law because Leopold made the laws—and made them in his best interest. For example, in 1885, he decreed that all the Congo's "vacant" land was his own property; he then set about making the land vacant.

Leopold's power **pervaded** (12) the Congo. To help spread his power throughout the area, Leopold appointed explorer Henry Stanley as his chief agent in the Congo. Stanley set up garrisons and signed treaties with chiefs of African tribes. Leopold was particularly interested in improving transportation—steamship routes and railways—through Africa so that goods and troops could be moved faster. Leopold soon controlled the commercialization of rubber plantations.

Strict and cruel means of taxation **emanated** (13) or issued from Leopold's court. Government or company officials were required to collect taxes from the people of the Congo. Leopold established his own network of slavery in the Congo. Taxes had to be paid in labor or in flesh. Any African worker who did not bring in the established quota of ivory or rubber could lose a hand. Atrocities were commonplace. You can imagine what forms of punishment **perfidious** (14) acts would bring if merely failing to meet a quota resulted in maiming. Leopold most certainly would not have tolerated treachery.

Did He Get Away with It?

Eventually, the world became aware that there was a huge **discrepancy** (15) between Leopold's account of activities in the Congo and the actual conditions there. Roger Casement, appointed British Consul for the Congo Free State in 1898, investigated Leopold's methods and in 1904 published a report about Leopold's crimes. In his report, Casement did not **prevaricate** (16) but told the truth about Leopold's activities. Casement's report, documenting activities between 1901 and 1903, revealed cruelties that were highly objectionable to civilized people everywhere.

Leopold's cruelties so shocked the world that people demanded reforms in the Congo government. A Congo Reform Association was formed in England. Leopold himself was widely **chastised** (17). The severity of the criticisms made it obvious that more than a temporary suspension or **abeyance** (18) of Leopold's rule was needed. Of course, the cruelties inflicted during Leopold's rule of more than two decades in the Congo were **irrevocable** (19). However, Leopold's laws and methods, at least, could be reversed. A Belgian commission was formed to investigate the crimes described in Casement's report, and the commission agreed with Casement's findings. Apparently no one **interceded** (20) on Leopold's behalf, although Leopold did plead for himself. In 1906, the Belgian government voted to annex the Congo Free State. The Belgian government restored free trade to the area and brought an end to Leopold's tyrannical reign over the Congo.

EXERCISE 1 *Finding Synonyms* ✍

Directions. Reread the preceding passage. Then write on the line provided a synonym for each of the words in boldface. If you cannot think of an exact synonym, you may write a brief definition of the word.

1. primordial _____
2. inscrutable _____
3. obnoxious _____
4. sumptuous _____
5. deplored _____
6. detriment _____
7. inundated _____
8. homogeneous _____
9. demagogue _____
10. harbinger _____
11. illicit _____
12. pervaded _____
13. emanated _____
14. perfidious _____
15. discrepancy _____
16. prevaricate _____
17. chastised _____
18. abeyance _____
19. irrevocable _____
20. interceded _____

EXERCISE 2 *Reading Strategically* 👈

Directions. Now that you have read the passage and thought about the words in boldface, circle the letter of the correct answer to each of the following items. The numbers of the items are the same as the numbers of the boldface Vocabulary Words in the passage.

1. To tell us that **primordial** is defined as "primitive," the writer
  (A) uses the word *turmoil*
  (B) describes Conrad's ship
  (C) contrasts the word **primordial** with a series of antonyms
  (D) quotes Conrad's reference "to the earliest beginnings of the world"
  (E) uses synonyms in a series with **primordial**

2. If the land and its atmosphere are equally **inscrutable,** as the writer of the passage suggests, we may expect them to be
  (A) pleasant
  (B) rugged
  (C) mysterious
  (D) dangerous
  (E) easily described

3. When we read in the passage that Conrad was not intentionally **obnoxious,** we should realize that he did not
  (A) expect his views to be accepted
  (B) mean to be offensive
  (C) want to describe the Congo
  (D) mean to be mysterious
  (E) realize that people would read his descriptions

4. In the passage, to be **sumptuous** means to be
  (A) simple
  (B) luxurious
  (C) poor
  (D) mysterious
  (E) unpleasant

5. In the passage, the words that give a clue to the meaning of **deplored** are
  (A) the primitiveness
  (B) sailing conditions
  (C) disfigured the history
  (D) natural riches
  (E) strong disapproval

6. In the passage, **detriment** means
  (A) wealth
  (B) damage
  (C) decade
  (D) imperialism
  (E) benefit

7. Because imperialists **inundated** Africa, the writer compares the imperialists by simile to
   (A) governments
   (B) businesses
   (C) races
   (D) locusts
   (E) colonies

8. According to the passage, a country is **homogeneous** if it
   (A) contains similar races and cultures
   (B) contains different races and cultures
   (C) is uncivilized
   (D) is filled with imperialists
   (E) is divided into different regions

9. To tell us the meaning of **demagogue,** the writer
   (A) links **demagogue** to the synonym *stirred*
   (B) uses a series of adjectives
   (C) provides a definition of **demagogue**
   (D) compares **demagogue** by simile to locusts
   (E) links **demagogue** to the antonym *leader*

10. In the passage, **harbinger** means
   (A) follower
   (B) trickery
   (C) favorite
   (D) forerunner
   (E) ruler

11. We can infer from the passage that if something is **illicit** it is
   (A) illegal
   (B) vacant
   (C) industrial
   (D) legal
   (E) obtainable

12. The writer provides a clue to the meaning of **pervaded** by
   (A) telling about Henry Stanley
   (B) relating **pervaded** to the phrase "spread his power"
   (C) explaining the use of treaties in the Congo
   (D) providing a definition of **pervaded**
   (E) relating **pervaded** to the word *transportation*

13. In the passage, saying that tax measures **emanated** from Leopold's court means that
   (A) the government asked for voluntary tax donations
   (B) the Congolese had to bring their taxes directly to the court
   (C) the tax measures were kept secretly within the court
   (D) Leopold's court let the Congolese vote on the taxes
   (E) the tax measures issued from Leopold's court

14. In the passage, **perfidious** acts probably would bring about _____ punishment.
  (A) gentle
  (B) legal
  (C) severe
  (D) acceptable
  (E) fair

15. If there was a big **discrepancy** between what Leopold said he was doing and what he was actually doing, we may expect that
  (A) what he said he did and what he really did were the same
  (B) he had trouble carrying out his plans
  (C) he was telling the truth about actual conditions
  (D) there was a great difference between what he said and what he did
  (E) people around the world had access to the facts

16. We can infer from the passage that to **prevaricate** is to
  (A) lie
  (B) delay
  (C) spy
  (D) say
  (E) hesitate

17. In the passage, the words that provide a clue to the meaning of **chastised** are
  (A) reforms, government
  (B) temporary suspension
  (C) shocked, demanded
  (D) cruelties inflicted
  (E) severity, criticisms

18. According to the passage, an **abeyance** of Leopold's rule in the Congo would have
  (A) changed everything permanently
  (B) lasted too few years to do any good
  (C) rid the Congo of Leopold's laws
  (D) created more transportation routes
  (E) stopped the flow of information

19. When we read in the passage that the cruelties inflicted during Leopold's rule were **irrevocable,** we should realize that they could
  (A) be reversed
  (B) not be forgiven
  (C) not be reversed
  (D) not be repeated
  (E) be forgiven

20. According to the passage, **interceded** means
  (A) punished
  (B) agreed
  (C) pleaded
  (D) listened
  (E) traded

READING NEW WORDS IN CONTEXT

Lesson 9 CONTEXT: History and Society

The passage gives you an opportunity to expand your vocabulary. Below are twenty Vocabulary Words that are used in the passage and in the exercises that follow it.

anarchy	elocution	maim	promulgate
cadaverous	ethnology	menial	rampant
cajole	extricate	nadir	strident
commodious	impair	pestilence	subversion
consign	incorrigible	profuse	virulent

The English Slave Trade

Call him Jared. He was born in 1740 in a small village in West Africa. Eighteen years later, he, along with hundreds of other Africans, was captured by English slave traders. Jared had no chance to **extricate** (1) himself from the situation, just as a prisoner, chained hand and foot, has no chance to escape from his captors. A slave trader did not release his captives; they were worth far too much.

Jared had become a statistic in England's infamous era of slave trade. From 1690 to 1807, England imported an estimated 2,807,100 slaves. During the 1700s, England was the top carrier of slaves from Africa. Profit-hungry slave traders no doubt considered and proclaimed, or **promulgated** (2), this period as the zenith, or highest point, in England's commercial history. Yet people concerned with human rights must have held the opposite to be true: The era of slave trading was the **nadir** (3) of the country's history.

Many English shipping merchants and businesspeople spoke in favor of the slave trade, which uprooted the lives of such Africans as Jared. Some merchants were particularly adept at **elocution** (4); they argued **profusely** (5) and persuasively in their defense of the need for slaves to help England achieve commercial success in its colonial possessions. The ample, well-spoken words evidently had their effect: The British crown created slave-trading companies to gather slaves from its colonies in West Africa and to transport them to its colonies in the West Indies and North America. In addition, there were many independent slave traders.

Surviving the Journey

Jared and his companions were herded aboard a slave ship by a rough Englishman with a **strident** (6) voice. "Move on, move on!" the man yelled harshly. Jared was thrown into a room below deck that could hardly be considered **commodious** (7) for the number of people it held. In fact, the room had so little space that its one hundred occupants literally could not move. Africans of both sexes and of all ages were kept in the room and put into irons so they wouldn't escape.

The voyage was miserable. Rats scampered over Jared's legs. He thought his right leg would be permanently **maimed** (8) from the irons. He feared that his right arm might be similarly crippled from being crushed between two wooden posts. He had wedged himself between the posts to try to get some breathing room. The slave hold had little air, and its floors were cleaned rarely, if ever. The man next to Jared looked **cadaverous** (9) because he was so ill and gaunt; his deathlike face was sad and haunted. **Pestilences** (10), contagious and often fatal diseases that spread rapidly, were **rampant** (11) in the slave hold. The captives had no way to prevent the spread of **virulent** (12), or deadly, diseases. Many of the slaves who did not die aboard ship had their health **impaired** (13) for the rest of their lives by the illnesses they suffered aboard ship. Jared, fortunately, had only a minor illness that did not injure him permanently.

On Jared's ship, the captain did not enforce any laws or try to maintain order among his men. As a result, **anarchy** (14) prevailed; the ship was in a state of disorder, with no leadership. Some of the stronger slaves wanted to escape from their irons and overthrow the crew, but there was no way to manage such **subversion** (15).

The ship landed in the English West Indies, and agents on the islands arranged for the sale of the slaves. Strong slaves were especially needed to work the sugar plantations on islands such as Jamaica. Able slaves also were needed for the tobacco fields in England's North American colonies. Some weak, elderly, or very young slaves would be sold for **menial** (16), low-level work such as cleaning house and waiting on people.

Sold to the Highest Bidder

Jared was placed on a platform and examined by many buyers. He was sold to a large white-haired man and **consigned** (17) to one of the sugar plantations. Immediately, Jared was loaded onto a wagon and taken to his unpleasant assignment. About twenty other young men were put on the wagon, along with several older men who looked ill. The agent apparently had **cajoled** (18) or coaxed Jared's buyer into paying a reduced price for the older men. Perhaps after the buyer paid for the slaves he really wanted, he used his remaining funds to buy the less-desirable slaves. It would probably not have taken much in the way of leftover funds to purchase older people with health problems.

Jared lived the rest of his life, about thirty years, working on the plantation. He was one of thousands of slaves who helped feed England's "sweet tooth." (Sugar was England's most valuable colonial product.) In his first years on the plantation, Jared tried to rebel, but he reformed his ways after a few beatings. Some of his friends, however, refused to give in. They were considered **incorrigible** (19) because they made a habit of causing trouble for the cruel overseers. No matter how they were punished, these slaves persisted in their bid for freedom.

The British and American governments abolished the slave trade in 1808, but the damage had already been done. There could be no compensation for two centuries of disrupted and lost lives. How could governments ever compensate a people for such damage? How could anyone restore to the slaves all that they had lost?

Today, professors interested in the branch of anthropology known as **ethnology** (20) frequently go back to slave records to find information about the origins, cultures, and characteristics of Africans in the West Indies and in North America. Yet these records have little to say about the suffering of individual human beings, like Jared, whose lives were stolen from them by slave traders.

EXERCISE 1 *Finding Synonyms* 👈

Directions. Reread the preceding passage. Then write on the line provided a synonym for each of the words in boldface. If you cannot think of an exact synonym, you may write a brief definition of the word.

1. extricate _____

2. promulgated _____

3. nadir _____

4. elocution _____

5. profusely _____

6. strident _____

7. commodious _____

8. maimed _____

9. cadaverous _____

10. pestilences _____

11. rampant _____

12. virulent _____

13. impaired _____

14. anarchy _____

15. subversion _____

16. menial _____

17. consigned _____

18. cajoled _____

19. incorrigible _____

20. ethnology _____

EXERCISE 2   *Reading Strategically* 👈

Directions. Now that you have read the passage and thought about the words in boldface, circle the letter of the correct answer to each of the following items. The numbers of the items are the same as the numbers of the boldface Vocabulary Words in the passage.

1. Because Jared couldn't **extricate** himself from the clutches of slave traders, the writer compares Jared to
   (A) a statistic in England's history
   (B) a fish caught in a net
   (C) a prisoner chained by his captors
   (D) a boy about to become an adult
   (E) a village in West Africa

2. In the passage, to **promulgate** means to
   (A) desire
   (B) hope
   (C) create
   (D) declare
   (E) organize

3. In the passage, the era of slave trade might be considered the **nadir** of England's commercial history because it was
   (A) the time of England's greatest commercial success
   (B) the time when England was the top carrier of cargo
   (C) the time when England made very little money
   (D) England's lowest possible point for human rights
   (E) the time of great social upheaval and change

4. In the passage, merchants adept at **elocution** would have great influence because they would
   (A) write letters to newspapers supporting slavery
   (B) make persuasive speeches in support of slavery
   (C) make a great amount of money from selling slaves
   (D) be able to make changes in the laws
   (E) own most of the slave-trading companies

5. In the passage, the word that provides a clue to the meaning of **profusely** is
   (A) well-spoken
   (B) persuasively
   (C) ample
   (D) argued
   (E) defense

6. In the passage, to speak with a **strident** voice means to speak
   (A) softly
   (B) kindly
   (C) harshly
   (D) persuasively
   (E) continuously

7. We can infer from the passage that a **commodious** room is
  (A) very small
  (B) crowded
  (C) smaller than needed
  (D) commonly used
  (E) spacious

8. To provide a clue to the meaning of **maimed,** the writer
  (A) gives an explanation of the meaning of **maimed**
  (B) uses the word *permanently* to link **maimed** to the future
  (C) uses synonyms in a series to define **maimed**
  (D) links **maimed** to the word *crippled* by using the word *similarly*
  (E) implies that **maimed** has to do with a voyage

9. In the passage, to look **cadaverous** means to look
  (A) gaunt and corpselike
  (B) like caverns
  (C) strong and healthy
  (D) carefree and happy
  (E) kind and friendly

10. We can tell from the passage that **pestilences** means
  (A) deathlike
  (B) to spread
  (C) captives
  (D) slave hold
  (E) fatal disease

11. When we read in the passage that deaths were **rampant,** we should realize that
  (A) there were very few deaths
  (B) the death count was growing unchecked
  (C) deaths were usually avoided
  (D) deaths were instantaneous
  (E) deaths were due to unnatural causes

12. In the passage, **virulent** means
  (A) deadly
  (B) clean
  (C) captive
  (D) protected
  (E) healthy

13. In the passage, the word that provides a clue to the meaning of **impaired** is
  (A) health
  (B) minor
  (C) aboard
  (D) injure
  (E) deadly

14. In the passage, what does it·mean that **anarchy** prevailed on the ship?
   (A) It means that the captain laid down strict laws.
   (B) It means that the captain was rebelling.
   (C) It means that the ship was in disorder.
   (D) It means that most of the crew members were ill.
   (E) It means that the captain had stopped a rebellion.

15. In the passage, **subversion** by the slaves would have resulted in the _____ of the crew.
   (A) drowning
   (B) friendship
   (C) overthrow
   (D) understanding
   (E) orderliness

16. We can infer from the passage that **menial** work is
   (A) hard, physical field labor
   (B) done only by men
   (C) work that requires education
   (D) strictly mental exercise
   (E) done by or fit for servants

17. In the passage, the words that provide a clue to the meaning of **consigned** are
   (A) unpleasant assignment
   (B) loaded onto
   (C) sugar plantations
   (D) examined by many
   (E) large man

18. In the passage, **cajoled** means
   (A) reduced
   (B) worried
   (C) punished
   (D) coaxed
   (E) questioned

19. When we read in the passage that some of Jared's friends were considered **incorrigible,** we should realize that they
   (A) changed the way they behaved
   (B) continued to rebel and cause trouble
   (C) learned to get along with the overseers
   (D) acted the way Jared told them to act
   (E) were so weak from past illnesses that they could not work

20. In the passage, **ethnology** is
   (A) a branch of economics that deals with foreign cultures
   (B) the study of petroleum products
   (C) the study of logic and ethics
   (D) the study of the history of slavery
   (E) the study of the origins and characteristics of a culture

Lesson 10   CONTEXT: History and Society

The passage gives you an opportunity to expand your vocabulary. Below are twenty Vocabulary Words that are used in the passage and in the exercises that follow it.

auspices	foment	propensity	sedentary
calumny	hiatus	recant	solicitous
clandestine	impassive	repudiated	temerity
contingency	litigation	retaliate	vestige
fervid	mollify	reticent	vindicate

The British and Mahatma Gandhi

One person came to mind immediately when I was asked to write about my greatest hero: Mohandas K. Gandhi (1869–1948). A leader in India's fight for independence from Great Britain, Gandhi always tried to **circumvent** (1) violent demonstrations. He wanted to avoid violence, and indeed, he possessed a **propensity** (2) for seeking change through courageous, nonviolent action. Because his talents lay in this direction, he developed a philosophy of nonviolence that he called *satyagraha*, a Hindu word meaning "a grasping for truth."

Fighting for Indian Rights

Gandhi's civil rights work actually began in South Africa. Gandhi was trained as a lawyer in London and in 1893 went to South Africa to practice law. On a train in South Africa, Gandhi experienced racial discrimination. Because he was an Indian, Gandhi was ordered to leave his first-class compartment and go to the baggage car. In an act of **temerity** (3), Gandhi protested. However, his rashness only got him removed from the train. This incident led to his battle against discrimination. He handled the **litigations** (4), or lawsuits, of many Indians in South Africa and worked to obtain equal rights for them. During this time, Gandhi began forming his philosophy

of nonviolent action.

He returned to India in 1915 but stayed out of the public eye for a year. After this **hiatus** (5), in his public work, Gandhi became involved in various disputes on behalf of Indian workers. In 1920, Gandhi began a national campaign called the noncooperation movement to convince the people of India to resist British rule in nonviolent ways. For example, he was not **reticent** (6) in urging people to boycott British goods and jobs. His openness in speaking out began a unique political revolution that led in 1947 to Britain's decision to grant India independence. To thousands of people in India, Britain's exodus, or departure, **vindicated** (7) their faith in Gandhi and also justified the title they gave him—Mahatma, or "Great Soul."

Gandhi: A Moral Force in India

True, Gandhi's methods sometimes **fomented** (8) unrest despite his peaceful intentions. For stirring up trouble, he and his followers were often imprisoned. Still, Gandhi never **recanted** (9) his beliefs. He maintained that moral force, when used to defend truth, triumphs over physical force. Gandhi's efforts were under the **auspices** (10)—that is, with the approval and support—of the Indian National Congress, of which he was president for one year.

In 1929, after the Congress called for independence from Britain, Gandhi led a resistance campaign against the unpopular Salt Acts. These acts made it illegal for citizens to buy salt from any source other than the government. Gandhi led fifty thousand people on a two-hundred-mile march to the sea to make salt from sea water. In this way, the people could procure salt without paying a tax. Police attacked the marchers, but the marchers did not **retaliate** (11). Instead of returning the injuries, the marchers kept going until they were struck down. The police probably thought they had prepared for every **contingency** (12), but they had not prepared for the possible occurrence of passive resistance. The march attracted worldwide attention.

Although he might have seemed **impassive** (13), Gandhi was an emotional man who held **fervidly** (14) to his beliefs. He was so passionate about his convictions that he staged several long hunger strikes to protest various wrongs. In 1932–1933, for example, Gandhi fasted four times to protest discrimination against poor Indians known as "untouchables." During these fasts, his followers were greatly concerned about his welfare. He was mostly **sedentary** (15) during the fasts because he did not have the strength to move much.

Gandhi's Legacy

Gandhi lived a life of severe simplicity and harsh self-discipline. His austerity is seen in a lack of concern for, or interest in,

worldly pleasures and possessions. He dressed simply in hand-woven cloth made from hand-spun thread. Gandhi himself spun thread for cloth every day. Spinning was a very important activity for Gandhi because he considered it a symbol of India's self-sufficiency.

In the last years of his life, Gandhi worked to bring Hindus and Muslims together. He was always **solicitous** (16) of other people's opinions and beliefs, but he was also attentive to his own convictions and **repudiated** (17) the idea of dividing India into two nations. Although he strongly disapproved of the division, he supported a plan to create two nations, India and Pakistan, in order to insure independence. Gandhi was involved in both open and **clandestine** (18) meetings with Muslim leaders in an attempt to unite Hindus and Muslims. Right up until his death, Gandhi tried to **mollify** (19) or pacify the different factions within his beloved country.

Gandhi and his beliefs have continued to be a source of inspiration for people around the world—including the American civil rights leader Martin Luther King, Jr. In his fight against racial discrimination in the United States, King was greatly influenced by Gandhi's philosophy of nonviolent action. Thus, more than a trace, a **vestige** (20), of Gandhi's philosophy can be found in King's compelling speeches. Based on King's example, I am convinced that the world would be a better place if more leaders took Gandhi's words and actions to heart.

EXERCISE 1 *Finding Synonyms*

Directions. Reread the preceding passage. Then write on the line provided a synonym for each of the words in boldface. If you cannot think of an exact synonym, you may write a brief definition of the word.

1. circumvent _____

2. propensity _____

3. temerity _____

4. litigations _____

5. hiatus _____

6. reticent _____

7. vindicated _____

8. fomented _____

9. recanted _____

10. auspices _____

11. retaliate _____

12. contingency _____

13. impassive _____

14. fervidly _____

15. sedentary _____

16. solicitous _____

17. repudiated _____

18. clandestine _____

19. mollify _____

20. vestige _____

EXERCISE 2 *Reading Strategically* 👈

Directions. Now that you have read the passage and thought about the words in boldface, circle the letter of the correct answer to each of the following items. The numbers of the items are the same as the numbers of the boldface Vocabulary Words in the passage.

1. In the passage, the word that provides a clue to the meaning of **circumvent** is
  (A) violent
  (B) method
  (C) fight
  (D) change
  (E) avoid

2. We can tell from the passage that **propensity** means
  (A) nonviolence
  (B) desire
  (C) violence
  (D) talent
  (E) change

3. In the passage, the result of Gandhi's act of **temerity** on the train was that he
   (A) refused to ride the train
   (B) was removed from the train
   (C) wished he had spoken up
   (D) refused to protest his treatment
   (E) learned to accept discrimination

4. In the passage, **litigations** are
   (A) rights
   (B) protests
   (C) lawsuits
   (D) equalities
   (E) incidents

5. To let us know that **hiatus** is defined as "a break in continuity," the writer
   (A) uses figurative language
   (B) states that Ghandi "stayed out of the public eye for a year."
   (C) gives a series of synonyms for **hiatus**
   (D) uses an antonym
   (E) uses a metaphor

6. The writer tells us that **reticent** is defined as "inclined to silence" by
   (A) defining **reticent** as "openness"
   (B) using **reticent** with a series of synonyms
   (C) contrasting **reticent** with the word *urging*
   (D) describing a political revolution
   (E) using the antonym *openness*

7. In the passage, the word that provides a clue to the meaning of **vindicated** is
   (A) exodus
   (B) urged
   (C) boycotted
   (D) justified
   (E) involved

8. In the passage, what happened when Gandhi's methods **fomented** unrest?
   (A) Gandhi became tired of nonviolence and urged his followers to attack.
   (B) The authorities began to like the idea of nonviolence and started using it themselves.
   (C) Gandhi influenced the Indians to raise an army to defeat the British.
   (D) Gandhi's influence was so great that no one ever used any other method.
   (E) Trouble resulted and Gandhi and his followers were imprisoned.

9. In the passage, what does it mean that Gandhi never **recanted** his beliefs?
   (A) He continuously maintained his beliefs.
   (B) He frequently changed his opinions and goals.
   (C) Other people began believing what he believed.
   (D) He gave up his beliefs when they failed.
   (E) He refused to struggle to succeed.

10. According to the passage, Gandhi's efforts were under the **auspices** of the Indian National Congress. In other words, the Congress _____ what Gandhi was doing.
   (A) often questioned
   (B) complained about
   (C) approved of
   (D) voted on
   (E) did not like

11. In the passage, the marchers did not **retaliate** when they were attacked because
   (A) they did not understand why they were being attacked
   (B) they would not go against their belief in nonviolence
   (C) Gandhi told them to return violence with more violence
   (D) they were waiting until more people came to help fight
   (E) they wanted to anger the authorities and provoke a fight

12. To prepare for every **contingency** means to
   (A) be able to handle everything except nonviolence
   (B) have a plan for everything that might happen
   (C) ignore the possibilities you don't understand
   (D) be able to take care of only nonviolent events
   (E) be aware that there are people who disagree

13. We can tell from the passage that **impassive** means
   (A) wrong
   (B) unemotional
   (C) strong
   (D) hungry
   (E) weak

14. We can infer from the passage that **fervidly** means
   (A) closely
   (B) enduringly
   (C) passionately
   (D) weakly
   (E) angrily

15. In the passage, to be **sedentary** means to be
   (A) very active
   (B) strong
   (C) hungry
   (D) inactive
   (E) concerned

16. When we read in the passage that Gandhi was **solicitous** of other people's opinions and beliefs, we should realize that he
   (A) did not care about them
   (B) was attentive to them
   (C) was worried about them
   (D) misunderstood them
   (E) was secretive about his thoughts

17. The writer provides a clue to the meaning of **repudiated** by

(A) using the synonym *disapproved*
(B) giving Gandhi's position on dividing India
(C) assuming the reader knows that **repudiated** comes from a lack of concern
(D) explaining why Gandhi supported the plan to divide India into two nations
(E) describing Gandhi as "also attentive to his own convictions"

18. We can tell from the passage that **clandestine** meetings are

(A) open
(B) secret
(C) illegal
(D) legal
(E) violent

19. In the passage, **mollify** means

(A) anger
(B) destroy
(C) update
(D) pacify
(E) understand

20. In the passage, the word that provides a clue to the meaning of **vestige** is

(A) trace
(B) philosophy
(C) beliefs
(D) speeches
(E) actions

READING NEW WORDS IN CONTEXT

Lesson 11   **CONTEXT:** Science and Technology

The passage gives you an opportunity to expand your vocabulary. Below are twenty Vocabulary Words that are used in the passage and in the exercises that follow it.

chauvinism	empirical	officious	sagacity
cosmopolitan	epitome	quiescent	scathing
devoid	facetious	regimen	tenuous
differentiate	inexorable	renounce	testimonial
disparity	moot	repository	treatise

A Lesson from the Scientific Revolution

Gulliver's Travels, by Jonathan Swift (1667–1745), is today regarded as a literary classic. From the time it was first published in 1726, it was a great success. *Gulliver's Travels* was read, as the poet John Gay (1685–1732) wrote, "from the cabinet council to the nursery."

Swift's book is most often remembered for its description of the **officious** (1) Lilliputians, an overbearing race of people small in height but large in ego. Readers also often recall the giant inhabitants of Brobdingnag. Gulliver's third voyage, however, is often less memorable to readers, but it is very telling in its depiction of the scientific climate of Swift's era. In this voyage, Gulliver travels to the Grand Academy of Lagado, where all time and energy is devoted to useless scientific experiments. Gulliver discovers here a great **disparity** (2) between common sense and scientific practice. At the Academy of Projectors, for example, Gulliver finds men attempting such absurd experiments as trying to extract sunshine from cucumbers.

What readers often do not realize is that Gulliver's third voyage is a **scathing** (3), bitterly harsh satire of the Royal Society in London. This group was the very **epitome** (4) of science in Great Britain at the time, the

essence of the scientific community of the eighteenth century.

A Background to the Scientific Revolution

It would be impossible to isolate a single cause for the scientific revolution. Any single explanation would be simplistic and would do no more than inspire debates. Instead of pursuing such a **moot** (5) point, then, it is better to realize that the new worldview of the eighteenth century was a natural outgrowth of the work of philosophers and scientists during the Middle Ages.

Members of the Royal Society engaged in a new method of scientific inquiry that differed greatly from medieval scholarship, which emphasized philosophical or religious interpretations of the natural world. Indeed, the new science, argumentative in nature, would not produce scientists as **quiescent** (6) as those of the Middle Ages. Instead, it would produce thinkers who were bold, aggressive, and questioning.

Three basic characteristics of the new science produced this new breed of "show me" experimental investigators. First, the new science was **empirical** (7), relying on direct experience and observation rather than on hand-me-down ideas and assumptions. Scientists of the eighteenth century gave careful attention to what we now call the scientific method: stating an experimental aim, forming a hypothesis, conducting an experiment, gathering results, and drawing conclusions. The scientists' **regimen** (8) or routine of careful observation and meticulous attention to detail was at the heart of the scientific revolution.

Second, the new science relied on technological innovations. The telescope, for example, allowed people to **differentiate** (9) objects in the night sky that could not be detected by the unaided eye. Scientists thus were able to distinguish better than ever before the differences between celestial bodies such as stars and planets.

Third, the new science was **cosmopolitan** (10), rather than simply national. During the seventeenth century, universities throughout Europe had established centers for the study of science. Also, European governments established learned societies to foster scientific inquiry. The government of England, for example, formed the Royal Society that Swift satirized in *Gulliver's Travels*. This society and others like it printed journals to circulate information on scientific discoveries. *Philosophical Transactions,* begun in 1664, was the **repository** (11) of the ideas of the Royal Society: If the Royal Society thought it, this journal would print it. Such journals became forums for sometimes heated debates and allowed scientists both to voice their agreement with and on occasion to **renounce** (12) one another's work.

The Contributions of Sir Isaac Newton

In England, one name in particular continues to be associated with the scientific revolution: the mathematician Isaac Newton (1642–1727). Newton is best known for his work *Mathematical Principles of Natural Philosophy* (1687). Newton believed that the universe was a single uniform machine that operated according to **inexorable** (13) laws, laws that could not be altered or discontinued. Educated at Trinity College, Cambridge, Newton made his first contact with the Royal Society when he presented his theory of light and colors in 1672. In 1703, Newton was elected president

of the Royal Society and was reelected annually until his death. A statue was erected in his honor at Trinity College. On it are inscribed these lines by the poet William Wordsworth as a **testimonial** (14) to Newton's brilliance:

> The marble index of a mind for ever
> Voyaging through strange seas of Thought
> alone.

Women of the Scientific Revolution

During the Middle Ages, women who sought a life of learning were severely hampered because of the **chauvinism** (15) of the men who dominated society. These men, for the most part, believed that only men could fully benefit from formal education. In fact, during the scientific revolution, Benedict Spinoza (1632–1677) argued that an educated woman was similar to an antique gun "which one shows to the curious, but which has no use at all, any more than a carousel horse." Spinoza's comment was obviously based on **tenuous** (16) evidence, for women in science were in fact making important contributions.

Anna Maria Sibylla Merian (1647–1717), a contemporary of Newton's, established a reputation as an entomologist, or one who studies insects. Her studies resulted in her first **treatise** (17), *Wonderful Metamorphosis and Special Nourishment of Caterpillars,* an important book in her day. At the end of the seventeenth century, she made an expedition to the colony of Surinam to study insect and plant life. Her **sagacity** (18) as a scientist is revealed in the work for which she is best known, *Metamorphosis of the Insects of Surinam,* a penetrating and insightful work.

The Influence of the Scientific Revolution

Why, you might ask, did Swift satirize scientists such as Isaac Newton in *Gulliver's Travels*? Wasn't science improving the quality of life? Why then is Swift so **facetious** (19) in his description of the Academy of Projectors? Why does he make such obvious fun of scientists? While he recognized that science could be beneficial, Swift also recognized that science could be **devoid** (20) of practical concerns and completely lacking in ethics. Therefore, in its worst manifestations science was removed from the everyday lives of most people and was possibly even dangerous to society. As in Swift's time, many people today, having seen nuclear destruction and other examples of unchecked technology, find science terrifying in its implications.

What was Swift's message? How should we view science today? We should remember that, in the final analysis, science is a search for knowledge. That is the lesson we should learn from studying the scientific revolution. It is up to us to direct the use of science and to make sure that it does not dominate our world but instead is used to work for the common good.

EXERCISE 1 *Finding Synonyms*

Directions. Reread the preceding passage. Then write on the line provided a synonym for each of the words in boldface. If you cannot think of an exact synonym, you may write a brief definition of the word.

1. officious _____

2. disparity _____

3. scathing _____

4. epitome _____

5. moot _____

6. quiescent _____

7. empirical _____

8. regimen _____

9. differentiate _____

10. cosmopolitan _____

11. repository _____

12. renounce _____

13. inexorable _____

14. testimonial _____

15. chauvinism _____

16. tenuous _____

17. treatise _____

18. sagacity _____

19. facetious _____

20. devoid _____

EXERCISE 2 *Reading Strategically* 👈

Directions. Now that you have read the passage and thought about the words in boldface, circle the letter of the correct answer to each of the following items. The numbers of the items are the same as the numbers of the boldface Vocabulary Words in the passage.

1. To provide a clue to the meaning of **officious,** the writer
- (A) tells us that the Lilliputians are overbearing and small in height but large in ego
- (B) tells us that *Gulliver's Travels* was read "from the cabinet council to the nursery"
- (C) tells us that *Gulliver's Travels* was a great success when it was published in 1726
- (D) tells us that Gulliver visited the Grand Academy of Lagado
- (E) implies that Gulliver is, in fact, a spokesperson for Swift himself

2. The **disparity** between common sense and scientific practice may also be viewed as the _____ between the two.
- (A) commonality
- (B) equality
- (C) difference
- (D) correlation
- (E) equivalency

3. To let us know that a **scathing** satire may be defined as "an attack with cruel language," the writer
- (A) tells us that men in the Academy of Projectors attempted to extract sunshine from cucumbers
- (B) tells us that the Royal Society in London typified eighteenth-century science
- (C) implies that *Gulliver's Travels* is a satire
- (D) links the words *bitterly harsh* to **scathing**
- (E) uses alliteration to link **scathing** to the word *society*

4. In the passage, a synonym for **epitome** is
- (A) report
- (B) description
- (C) essence
- (D) satire
- (E) key

5. In the passage, it is a **moot** point to isolate a single cause of the scientific revolution because
- (A) there is no single cause of the scientific revolution
- (B) no one likes to discuss the scientific revolution
- (C) the single cause was so ridiculous that it is not worth discussing
- (D) since people already know what the single cause was, there is no point in discussing it
- (E) as far as anyone can tell, there were no causes at all of the scientific revolution

6. In the passage, a **quiescent** scientist might be described as
- (A) curious and probing
- (B) eccentric and suspicious
- (C) argumentative and aggressive
- (D) quiet and accepting
- (E) gullible and naive

7. According to the passage, an **empirical** science
- (A) is based on philosophical speculation
- (B) depends on government funding
- (C) disregards direct experience and observation
- (D) relies on direct experience and observation
- (E) does not follow the scientific method

8. To provide a clue to the meaning of **regimen,** the writer tells us that
- (A) the scientific method relies on direct experience
- (B) the scientists were careful
- (C) the scientific method allowed scientists to explore the earth
- (D) scientists during the scientific revolution adhered to a special routine
- (E) the new science relied on technology

9. In the passage, to **differentiate** objects in the universe means to
- (A) view by telescope
- (B) use empirical methods
- (C) perceive different objects
- (D) rely on technology
- (E) share technological innovations

10. When we are told that the new science was **cosmopolitan,** we should realize that it
- (A) was taught in universities
- (B) extended beyond national boundaries
- (C) was interested in the structure of the universe
- (D) was the object of satire
- (E) was empirical

11. A **repository** may be defined as a box, chest, or room where things are kept. How could *Philosophical Transactions* be a **repository** for the ideas of the Royal Society?
- (A) The Royal Society was, in reality, a library.
- (B) The Royal Society was, in reality, a journal.
- (C) The writer suggests that journals are places where ideas can be kept safely.
- (D) The writer suggests that ideas are like boxes, closets, or rooms.
- (E) The writer realizes readers know that scientific journals are printed.

12. Scientists who read journals such as the *Philosophical Transactions* **renounced** each other's work because they
- (A) would **renounce** work they did not agree with
- (B) would agree with the work they **renounced**
- (C) would either agree with each other or dispute each other's ideas
- (D) used direct observation and relied on technology to **renounce** each other's work
- (E) were influenced by the printing press

13. The writer provides a clue to the meaning of **inexorable** by
- (A) linking **inexorable** to the phrase "could not be altered or discontinued"
- (B) linking **inexorable** to Newton's *Mathematical Principles of Natural Philosophy*
- (C) linking **inexorable** to the words *operated according to*
- (D) using **inexorable** as an adverb
- (E) using **inexorable** as a synonym for *empirical*

14. Wordsworth's lines on Newton are a **testimonial** to the scientist's brilliance because they
  (A) are written by a poet
  (B) are a tribute to Newton's ideas
  (C) are a satire of modern science
  (D) remind us that Newton was English
  (E) are a bitter criticism

15. To let us know that **chauvinism** may be defined as "an unreasoning devotion to one's own country or group," the writer
  (A) tells us that men believed only other men could benefit from education
  (B) tells us that educated women were considered ridiculous
  (C) tells us that women made inroads into the scientific community
  (D) clearly defines **chauvinism** in the next three sentences
  (E) contrasts the Middle Ages with the eighteenth century

16. In the passage, a synonym for **tenuous** is
  (A) clear
  (B) strong
  (C) despicable
  (D) flimsy
  (E) warranted

17. According to the passage, Anna Maria Sibylla Merian's *Wonderful Metamorphosis and Special Nourishment of Caterpillars* is a **treatise** because it is
  (A) a formal, systematic discussion of a subject
  (B) a large, hard-to-read volume
  (C) the work of an entomologist
  (D) about insects
  (E) an unpublished manuscript

18. When we are told that Anna Maria Sibylla Merian demonstrated her **sagacity** as a scientist, we should realize that she
  (A) continued to write books throughout her life
  (B) used the scientific method
  (C) had sound judgment and a keen mind
  (D) had refined powers of observation
  (E) was very stubborn

19. Because Swift's description of the Academy of Projectors is **facetious,** the description is
  (A) vindictive
  (B) satirical
  (C) harsh
  (D) accurate
  (E) inaccurate

20. According to the passage, if science is **devoid** of practical concerns, it is
  (A) completely without practical concerns
  (B) absorbed in practical concerns to the exclusion of everything else
  (C) exempt from practical concerns because they are not relevant
  (D) the subject of harsh satire
  (E) part of the modern world

READING NEW WORDS IN CONTEXT

Lesson 12 · CONTEXT: Science and Technology

The passage gives you an opportunity to expand your vocabulary. Below are twenty Vocabulary Words that are used in the passage and in the exercises that follow it.

acrimonious	coerce	expound	mottled
anachronism	consternation	gauntlet	precursor
atrophy	desist	loquacious	terra firma
bode	enigma	mete	vantage point
burnish	esoteric	misnomer	voluminous

The Plow and the Stirrup: Technology in the Dark Ages

The Time: A.D. 899

The Place: The Anglo-Saxon Kingdom of Mercia

The lord looked out across his vast estate. It was sunset. Down long strips of fields, a farmer was forcing his oxen to pull a moldboard plow. He **coerced** (1) the reluctant beasts with a long whip.

"What an invention this plow is!" the lord remarked to his guest, a knight visiting from the neighboring shire of Lichfield. "See how it splits the soil with the front blade? Notice how the iron plowshare then cuts deeply down? See how the moldboard throws the soil to the side? Before, with the scratch plow, my farmers were barely able to break the surface of the solid earth. But this new moldboard plow cuts deeply into the **terra firma** (2). We shall have a rich harvest this year."

The guest smiled at the remarks of his **loquacious** (3) host. Although the knight himself was not usually given to conversation—he was certainly not as talkative as his host—he wanted his host to continue the conversation, for he enjoyed hearing about inventions. Glancing down at his stirrups, the knight discovered a new source of conversation.

"Indeed," the knight said, "inventions are wondrous! Why, my grandfather told me that

he had to be a foot soldier for most of his life. Why? Simply because it was impossible for him and many others to stay on the backs of their horses. With these stirrups, I can now stay safely mounted on my horse during an attack. Let no farmer ever fear for the safety of his family as they plow the fields. Steady on my horse, armed and armored, I will **mete** (4) out severe injury to any foe!" The thought of punishing his enemies made the Lichfield knight raise the **gauntlet** (5) on his hand in defiance. The metal-plated glove glistened in the sunlight. His manner and speech were **acrimonious** (6). He always became harsh and angry when he thought about threats to his land and people, for he had seen the deaths of many loved ones over the years. Lost in his angry imaginings, he reached instinctively for his sword.

For a moment, the host was filled with **consternation** (7) at his guest's behavior, but he soon controlled his bewilderment when he realized that the knight was merely momentarily overcome with emotion.

"**Desist** (8) from this rage. Stay your sword, my friend," said the host. "No threat is here."

The knight, rather embarrassed at his outburst, calmed down. "Yes," the host went on,

"I agree that these inventions are wondrous! With the plow and the stirrup, there is no telling how much our people can accomplish. Truly, God has blessed us with marvelous things."

The two nobles turned their horses and headed back to the dining hall. Both of the horses were **mottled** (9) like speckled marble against the evening landscape. The farmer, in the meantime, unhitched the eight oxen. Slowly, he led the oxen away into the rosy dusk. Before the next day's toil, he would **burnish** (10) the metal on the harnesses until it gleamed.

The Time: The Present

The Place: Where You Are

The scene just described is no **anachronism** (11); it could actually have taken place in the English kingdom of Mercia in the ninth century. The moldboard plow used by the farmer had been introduced in England by the ninth century. The stirrup had been introduced just one hundred years earlier. These two noblemen were just as fascinated with these technological innovations as you might be intrigued by laser discs or the possibilities of virtual-reality equipment.

Traditionally, historians have considered the period from A.D. 500 to 1000 to be the Dark Ages. During this period, Latin, once the standard language of scholarship, became a riddle, an **enigma** (12), as so few people were taught to speak and write it. As a result, classical texts became **esoteric** (13) documents that only a

few learned scholars could understand. During this time, the Church would traditionally allow schooling for only a privileged few; most people remained uneducated and illiterate. Circumstances did not **bode** (14) well for England. In fact, the situation foretold grim problems for the future of all of Western civilization.

Did civilization just **atrophy** (15) during the Dark Ages? Did it waste away as completely as the name of the period implies? No. Scholars have written many volumes indicating that the Dark Ages may not have been so dark after all. There is, in fact, **voluminous** (16) evidence that the Early Middle Ages may be seen as a **precursor** (17) to our own age. This ancient period is sometimes viewed as a forerunner to our modern age because it too was marked by exciting innovations and advances.

The historian L. S. Stavrianos **expounds** (18) this position in detail in his book *The Promise of the Coming Dark Age.* He has had the opportunity to research and study, and, from this **vantage point** (19), he explains that the Early Middle Ages were a time when Western European civilization was being born. To ignore the evidence of that birth in such innovations as the stirrup and the moldboard plow is to ignore this dynamic period of civilization. Have historians, then, incorrectly named this period? With Stavrianos's argument in mind, we may feel that the description of the Early Middle Ages as the Dark Ages is, indeed, a **misnomer** (20).

EXERCISE 1 *Finding Synonyms*

Directions. Reread the preceding passage. Then write on the line provided a synonym for each of the words in boldface. If you cannot think of an exact synonym, you may write a brief definition of the word.

1. coerced _____

2. terra firma _____

3. loquacious _____

4. mete _____

5. gauntlet _____

6. acrimonious _____

7. consternation _____

8. desist _____

9. mottled _____

10. burnish _____

11. anachronism _____

12. enigma _____

13. esoteric _____

14. bode _____

15. atrophy _____

16. voluminous _____

17. precursor _____

18. expounds _____

19. vantage point _____

20. misnomer _____

EXERCISE 2 *Reading Strategically*

Directions. Now that you have read the passage and thought about the words in boldface, circle the letter of the correct answer to each of the following items. The numbers of the items are the same as the numbers of the boldface Vocabulary Words in the passage.

1. In the passage, saying that the farmer **coerced** the oxen means he
(A) stopped them
(B) forced them
(C) bribed them
(D) turned them
(E) rode on them

2. In the passage, the words that provide a clue to the meaning of **terra firma** are
(A) scratch plow
(B) cuts deeply
(C) break the surface
(D) solid earth
(E) barely able

3. In the passage, the knight talks enthusiastically about stirrups, becoming as **loquacious,** or _____, as his host.
(A) talkative
(B) fearful
(C) defiant
(D) old
(E) remarkable

4. In the passage, the knight vows to **mete** out or _____ injury to his enemies.
(A) surrender
(B) give out
(C) decipher
(D) standardize
(E) forget about

5. According to the passage, a **gauntlet** is a
(A) sword
(B) drinking cup
(C) type of stirrup
(D) raised fist
(E) metal-plated glove

6. To tell us that **acrimonious** is defined as "bitter or sharp in language or manner," the writer
(A) describes the knight with a simile
(B) links **acrimonious** with the words _kind_ and _gentle_
(C) restates **acrimonious** with the word _harsh_
(D) provides an antonym for **acrimonious**
(E) compares riding a horse with plowing a field

7. When we read in the passage that the host was filled with **consternation,** we should realize that
(A) he fully expected his guest's response
(B) he was ready to fight his guest if necessary
(C) he agreed with his guest's remark
(D) he was confused by his guest's outburst
(E) he wanted to tell his guest to leave

8. According to the passage, why did the host say to his guest, "**Desist** from this rage"?
(A) The host hoped to make his guest even angrier.
(B) The guest obviously was only pretending to be angry.
(C) The host wanted his guest to stop being angry.
(D) The host wanted to have a sword fight with his guest.
(E) The host was pointing out a threatening situation.

9. To describe how the **mottled** horses look, the writer compares them by simile to
   (A) dining halls
   (B) spotted oxen
   (C) speckled marble
   (D) the evening landscape
   (E) shiny metal

10. According to the passage, to **burnish** metal means to
    (A) polish it
    (B) scratch it
    (C) reshape it
    (D) paint it
    (E) sharpen it

11. The writer tells us that **anachronism** is defined as something out of its proper time in history by
    (A) tying **anachronism** to technological innovations
    (B) contrasting **anachronism** to the phrase, "could actually have taken place"
    (C) using **anachronism** as a synonym for the *ninth century*
    (D) describing **anachronism** as a moldboard plow introduced in England in the ninth century
    (E) linking **anachronism** to the words *time period*

12. In the passage, the word that provides a clue to the meaning of **enigma** is
    (A) language
    (B) standard
    (C) period
    (D) riddle
    (E) classical

13. We can tell from the passage that something is **esoteric** if it is
    (A) widely taught and understood
    (B) part of common, everyday knowledge
    (C) from a traditional society
    (D) misunderstood by very few people
    (E) understood by only a few people

14. In the passage, **bode** means
    (A) foretell
    (B) listen
    (C) remember
    (D) abide
    (E) speak

15. According to the passage, what leads us to believe that civilization did not **atrophy** during the Dark Ages?
    (A) Virtually nothing changed during the Dark Ages.
    (B) Civilization wasted away completely during this time.
    (C) There were exciting innovations during this time.
    (D) There were many problems throughout the period.
    (E) It was a grim time.

16. According to the passage, there is **voluminous** evidence, enough to fill many _____, that the period known as the Dark Ages was not so dark.

(A) buildings
(B) civilizations
(C) ships
(D) volumes
(E) periods

17. In the passage, the word that provides a clue to the meaning of **precursor** is

(A) evidence
(B) forerunner
(C) innovations
(D) ancient
(E) problems

18. In the passage, **expounds** means

(A) positions
(B) explains
(C) questions
(D) ignores
(E) denies

19. When we read in the passage that historian L.S. Stavrianos has a **vantage point,** we should realize that he

(A) makes valid points in his book
(B) understands the Early Middle Ages
(C) gives much detail in his book
(D) ignores evidence of Western European civilization
(E) is speaking from an advantageous perspective

20. The writer provides a clue to the meaning of **misnomer** by

(A) relating **misnomer** to the Early Middle Ages
(B) describing the Dark Ages as truly dark
(C) comparing **misnomer** to a dynamic period of civilization
(D) linking **misnomer** to the words *incorrectly named*
(E) relating **misnomer** to historians

READING NEW WORDS IN CONTEXT

Lesson 13 | CONTEXT: Science and Technology

The passage gives you an opportunity to expand your vocabulary. Below are twenty Vocabulary Words that are used in the passage and in the exercises that follow it.

assiduous	corollary	extenuate	mercurial
avarice	denizen	fissure	pecuniary
aver	duress	impeccable	quell
cessation	equanimity	iniquity	rancor
conciliate	espouse	inordinate	tenable

Going Places: England's Railroads

Imagine a machine that could instantly take you anywhere in the world. One minute, you're standing in your swimsuit in sunny California. Two minutes later, you're freezing in Alaska. How do you feel about the power of this machine? At first you are thrilled. Then you begin to have doubts. Everything changes very quickly and unpredictably. You aren't at all sure if you can be as **mercurial** (1) as the technological world you live in.

The Coming of the Railroad

If you can imagine the impact of the machine described above, then you can get some idea of the impact of the railroad on Victorian England. The coming of the railroad changed almost every aspect of British life. Before the railroad, life was simple and familiar for the **denizens** (2) of England. Afterward, life was complex and strange for these same inhabitants.

The history of the steam locomotive began with the invention of the steam engine. By the early nineteenth century, a British mining engineer, Richard Trevithick, had built a small locomotive powered by a steam engine. Its job was to pull mining cars in Wales. By 1820, George Stephenson, a self-educated engineer, perfected steam-powered locomotives. He

had worked **assiduously** (3), and his perseverance was rewarded. He was given the task of building the Stockton and Darlington, the world's first public railroad. In 1829, Stephenson and his son designed the *Rocket,* which historians declare was the first practical locomotive. They also **aver** (4) that the *Rocket* was a symbol of a force that changed life in England forever.

Everything in Britain now seemed closer together. For travel, the railroad was the **tenable** (5) choice. It was reasonable for travelers to choose the railroad because it quickly covered distances once thought vast. To meet the growing demand for rapid travel, laborers laid over five thousand miles of railway line in Britain between 1830 and 1848. Train tracks, bridges, tunnels, viaducts, and train sheds checkered a countryside that had remained essentially unchanged since the Middle Ages.

The Railroad Changes the Face of Britain

Britain's countryside had always been divided by geographical barriers such as mountains and rivers. Each section of the country had developed its own dialect, cultural heritage, and even its own economy. The cracks in England's social structure were obvious. Indeed, England's social **fissures** (6) went as deep as the underground coal mines in Wales. Suddenly, however, all of England's people became neighbors because of the railroads. Regrettably, however, the **equanimity** (7) of the quiet country life was left behind with the introduction of the railroad. Such calmness and balance disappeared along with the horse-drawn coaches and the simple cottage industries. The railroad had come and it would not be stopped; there would be no **cessation** (8) of progress.

The railroads forced the Victorians to consider time and space in totally new, unfamiliar ways. For example, the railroads altered people's perceptions of time. Before the railways came, a person could travel only twelve to fifteen miles per hour by horse-drawn coach. Such speeds were tripled by railroad express trains. Moreover, travel by rail demanded **impeccable** (9) timekeeping. For example, people waiting for trains departing from London had to read exactly the same time on their watches as the train's engineers. Railroads and travelers alike depended on standardized clocks to time arrivals and departures. Travelers had to learn to be prompt. People who missed a scheduled departure could defend themselves by claiming **extenuating** (10) circumstances, but train schedules could not accommodate human excuses.

The Social Price of Progress

The railroad industry was greedy and intent on financial gain at almost any cost. Because of its **avarice** (11), the industry demanded immediate production of materials such as railroad ties, bridge materials, and other iron products. England's merchants saw great possibilities for **pecuniary** (12) gain with the railroads. Profit would come to those who could use the new technology to their advantage. Those who **espoused** (13) industry and progress began to realize profits; those who did not support the new technology were left far behind.

As demand and production grew, laborers began to move into England's most crowded spaces: the cities. The growth of the cities, therefore, was a definite **corollary** (14) to the growth of the railroad industry. The years from 1821 to 1831 saw a gain of 50 percent in the population of all major industrial cities in Britain. Never before had there been such rapid population growth. The cities were totally unprepared for such an **inordinate** (15), excessive influx of workers and their families.

Thus began the horrors of urban slums. **Iniquities** (16) against the poor were abundant because many employers, businesspeople, and property owners treated the poor in wicked and unrighteous ways. Ironically, because technology rendered their old economics obsolete, many country people were forced to leave their comfortable homes to make a living in the cities. The workers' spirits were **quelled** (17) by exhausting work, poor pay, and horrible living conditions. In addition, the workers were suppressed by the **duress** (18) that was frequently used by those in power. There was no real protection against the pressure to compel the weaker to serve the stronger. England's men, women, and children served the needs of industry, but their only reward, it seemed, was to have industry confine them even further. Industry did little to **conciliate** (19) the workers and make their lives easier. It can be reasonably assumed that **rancor** (20) built up in the hearts of the workers, because there were no friendly acts by industry to foster goodwill among the working class.

The railroad affected every aspect of life in Victorian England. It altered not only the geographical landscape but also the social landscape. It changed the way people thought about time. It brought people to the cities and affected living and working conditions. Who would have predicted that a simple steam engine would have such a wide-ranging effect?

EXERCISE 1 — *Finding Synonyms* ✍

Directions. Reread the preceding passage. Then write on the line provided a synonym for each of the words in boldface. If you cannot think of an exact synonym, you may write a brief definition of the word.

1. mercurial _____

2. denizens _____

3. assiduously _____

4. aver _____

5. tenable _____

6. fissures _____

7. equanimity _____

8. cessation _____

9. impeccable _____

10. extenuating _____

11. avarice _____

12. pecuniary _____

13. espoused _____

14. corollary _____

15. inordinate _____

16. iniquities _____

17. quelled _____

18. duress _____

19. conciliate _____

20. rancor _____

EXERCISE 2 *Reading Strategically* ✍️

Directions. Now that you have read the passage and thought about the words in boldface, circle the letter of the correct answer to each of the following items. The numbers of the items are the same as the numbers of the boldface words in the passage.

1. If the world continues to change in a **mercurial** way, as the writer of the passage suggests, we may expect
   (A) slow and predictable changes
   (B) change that results in benefits for everyone
   (C) a lack of progress and change
   (D) no growth in transportation
   (E) quick and unpredictable changes

2. In the passage, **denizens** are
   (A) transportations
   (B) newspapers
   (C) inhabitants
   (D) railroads
   (E) categories

3. To provide a clue to the meaning of **assiduously,** the writer
   (A) links **assiduously** to the word *perseverance*
   (B) relates **assiduously** to being self-educated
   (C) links **assiduously** to the first railroad
   (D) contrasts **assiduously** with an antonym
   (E) repeats **assiduously** in the next paragraph

4. According to the passage, to **aver** means to
   (A) deny
   (B) swerve
   (C) avoid
   (D) declare
   (E) question

5. To tell us that **tenable** is defined as "reasonable," the writer
   (A) uses figurative language to define **tenable**
   (B) says "it was reasonable for travelers to choose the railroad"
   (C) gives an example of travel by railroad
   (D) uses **tenable** to describe the growing demand for railway travel
   (E) lists a series of railroad properties

6. Because the **fissures** that separated the social classes in England were deep, the writer compares them by simile to
   (A) Britain's geographical barriers
   (B) the days of horse-drawn coaches
   (C) the simple cottage industries
   (D) train tracks that checkered Britain's countryside
   (E) underground coal mines in Wales

7. According to the passage, why was the **equanimity** of country life left behind?
  (A) The people who lived in the country preferred the excitement of the city.
  (B) "Calmness and balance disappeared along with horse-drawn carriages and simple cottage industries."
  (C) Horse-drawn coaches began racing about and competing with the railroads.
  (D) Neighbors began to argue over the depth of Welsh coal mines.
  (E) Simple cottage industries were boring.

8. According to the passage, if progress continues without **cessation,** we may expect
  (A) temporary progress
  (B) continuous progress
  (C) occasional progress
  (D) declining progress
  (E) an end to progress

9. When we read in the passage that travel by rail demanded **impeccable** timekeeping, we should realize that
  (A) trains always ran late
  (B) it never mattered what time it was
  (C) perfect time had to be kept
  (D) watches kept imperfect time
  (E) trains ran on random schedules

10. We can tell from the passage that **extenuating** circumstances are ones for which there are
  (A) solutions
  (B) excuses
  (C) limits
  (D) schedules
  (E) punishments

11. To tell us that **avarice** is defined as "an excessive desire for money," the writer
  (A) describes the railroad industry as greedy
  (B) gives an example of materials used in building railroads
  (C) contrasts **avarice** with financial losses
  (D) says the government is more generous than the railroad industry
  (E) implies that **avarice** is synonymous with progress

12. When we read in the passage that merchants saw great possibilities for **pecuniary** gain, we should realize that they
  (A) believed that the railroads would fail
  (B) were afraid of losing their money through the use of railroads
  (C) saw that they could make money through the use of railroads
  (D) wanted to maintain their simple country lifestyle
  (E) thought everyone was dishonest

13. According to the passage, those who **espoused** industry and progress _____ it.
  (A) stopped
  (B) changed
  (C) established
  (D) criticized
  (E) supported

14. According to the passage, why is the growth of the cities a **corollary** to the growth of the railroad industry?

(A) The growth of the cities declined as the growth of the railroad industry increased.
(B) The growth of the cities increased as the growth of the railroad industry declined.
(C) The railroads grew because the cities increased greatly in industry and population.
(D) The growth of the cities resulted directly from the growth of the railroad industry.
(E) A great amount of money could be made in the railroad industry and in cities that grew along the railways.

15. In the passage, the word that provides a clue to the meaning of **inordinate** is

(A) growth
(B) intense
(C) excessive
(D) influx
(E) unprepared

16. According to the passage, **iniquities** are

(A) buildings in an urban slum
(B) wicked and unrighteous acts
(C) jobs offered to the poor
(D) kindnesses done for poor people
(E) buildings of unequal size

17. In the passage, the word that provides a clue to the meaning of **quelled** is

(A) suppressed
(B) similarly
(C) compelled
(D) exhausting
(E) conditions

18. In the passage, **duress** is

(A) a common way of setting up a system
(B) a depressing way of combating technology
(C) hiring workers at high wages
(D) a term used by railroad engineers
(E) the use of force or threats

19. We can infer from the passage that because industry did little to **conciliate** the workers, industry

(A) was concerned about the workers
(B) cared very little about the workers
(C) was interested in improving conditions
(D) did everything it could to help
(E) preferred to hire good workers

20. To tell us that **rancor** is defined as "a bitter feeling of resentment," the writer

(A) contrasts **rancor** with the word *confine*
(B) provides the antonym *goodwill*
(C) tells us that the workers' lives were difficult
(D) tells us there were no friendly acts by industry
(E) provides the synonym *friendly*

Lesson 14 **CONTEXT:** Science and Technology

The passage gives you an opportunity to expand your vocabulary. Below are twenty Vocabulary Words that are used in the passage and in the exercises that follow it.

abstruse	caricature	frugal	pallor
apostasy	commiserate	gambol	promontory
bauble	evanescent	iridescent	remuneration
bullion	festoon	maudlin	usury
burgeoning	fresco	opulence	venal

England and the Industrial Revolution

Art can tell us a great deal about the values of a culture. Giotto di Bondone (c. 1267–1337) was one of Italy's greatest painters. In **frescoes** (1) such as *Flight into Egypt*, the images of the Virgin Mary and the Christ Child, painted on fresh plaster, reflect the period in which Giotto lived. In this painting, we see the first flowering of the humanitarian qualities that were part of the Italian Renaissance. Similarly, *Rain, Steam, and Speed: The Great Western Railway*, a dramatic painting by J.M.W. Turner (1775–1851), reflects the spirit of England at the beginning of the Industrial Revolution.

Considered by many to be Britain's greatest artist, Turner captured the coming industrialization of England in oil on canvas. In *Rain, Steam, and Speed*, a locomotive seems almost **evanescent** (2), a fleeting image speeding through the vapor of rain and wind across a viaduct. The scene seems to be observed from the perspective of a person standing on a **promontory** (3). Like the unseen observer, we look down from the headland at a landscape completely altered by the pale, swirling varied colors of the **iridescent** (4) rain. The misty rain has obscured the natural, deep colors of the landscape and makes it seem as washed-out and unnaturally pale as the **pallor** (5) of a sick person's flesh. The misty, hazy backdrop heightens the driving energy of the dark locomotive, making its speed even more apparent. If we compare Turner's painting to Giotto's much earlier religious fresco, we can see at a glance the stark contrast between the complex, sophisticated world of the Industrial Revolution and the simple, ingenuous world of the Italian Renaissance.

Britain was the first country in the world to experience the Industrial Revolution. As a historical period, the Industrial Revolution began in the 1780s and **burgeoned** (6). Its rapid development continued to overwhelm the British economic and social structures into the twentieth century. Some people considered the Industrial Revolution a time of **apostasy** (7); people abandoned age-old beliefs and principles as a result of their changing views of the world. During the Industrial Revolution, some people lived in **opulence** (8), while many others lived in poverty. The rich could afford to waste money on trinkets, or **baubles** (9); the poor could barely afford food. The homes of the wealthy were elaborately **festooned** (10); the homes of the poor remained virtually undecorated.

The Importance of Iron

No material played a more critical role in Britain's economic transformation than iron. This metal became one of Britain's most important natural resources because it was a source material for cast iron, wrought iron, and steel. To avoid **abstruse** (11) definitions of these terms, we can simply say that iron built the nineteenth century. Masses of the metal poured from Britain's foundries. The resulting iron bars could be regarded as the gold bars, or **bullion** (12), of the Industrial Revolution.

Britain made so much iron that British production surpassed that of the rest of the world in 1870. Ironworking began at the blast furnace. There, molten iron poured out of a blast furnace along a system of channels. At the end of the process, pig iron—iron in its crudest form—was taken to a foundry, remelted, and poured into molds that shaped the iron into needed products. This was a backbreaking process in which unskilled laborers, called *puddlers,* worked for far too little **remuneration** (13), or pay. The puddlers had the hardest job in the blast furnace, working in thirty-minute shifts to stir the molten iron. As the metal hardened, it became more and more difficult to stir; the puddlers had to work harder and harder.

The days of the puddlers were numbered, however, for new technologies were developed that allowed greater mechanization and less manual labor. Today, early blast furnace work seems like a **caricature** (14) of modern iron-production processes. The exertions of the puddlers seem satirically exaggerated when compared to the more modern Bessemer process, which employs chemists instead of puddlers.

It should be noted that England's production of iron paled once the United States's natural resources were unlocked. England's production of iron was almost insignificant when compared to the tremendous output of the factories of U.S. businessman Andrew Carnegie. Carnegie was known for his **frugality** (15). His devotion to economy made him among the world's richest men. Carnegie was never accused of being **maudlin** (16). In fact, his tough and practical approach often made him appear coldhearted, for he would scrap an entire manufacturing plant for profit.

A Difficult Time for the Working Class

During England's Industrial Revolution, merchants, landowners, and city authorities were not generally concerned with social responsibility and thus had little sympathy or compassion for workers. Consequently, they indulged in very little **commiseration** (17) with workers concerning the crowded and often unsanitary living conditions in the cities. Low-paid laborers were sometimes easy victims of corruption. For example, many were harmed by the practice of **usury** (18), in which some merchants and bankers charged excessively high interest rates on loans.

Of course, there were honest as well as **venal** (19) merchants and employers. Over time, employers and union officials in England collaborated to set wages and to maintain industrial relations. It would be incorrect and misleading to paint a whimsical picture of the relations between management and labor, however. The two factions were not like children **gamboling** (20) on a playground; there was little lighthearted frolicking and a great deal of interpersonal conflict. Nevertheless, conditions in England improved as employers increased safety measures for workers, provided insurance programs, and shortened the workday.

EXERCISE 1 *Finding Synonyms* 👉

Directions. Reread the preceding passage. Then write on the line provided a synonym for each of the words in boldface. If you cannot think of an exact synonym, you may write a brief definition of the word.

1. frescoes _____
2. evanescent _____
3. promontory _____
4. iridescent _____
5. pallor _____
6. burgeoned _____
7. apostasy _____
8. opulence _____
9. baubles _____
10. festooned _____
11. abstruse _____
12. bullion _____
13. remuneration _____
14. caricature _____
15. frugality _____
16. maudlin _____
17. commiseration _____
18. usury _____
19. venal _____
20. gamboling _____

EXERCISE 2 *Reading Strategically* 👉

Directions. Now that you have read the passage and thought about the words in boldface, circle the letter of the correct answer to each of the following items. The numbers of the items are the same as the numbers of the boldface Vocabulary Words in the passage.

1. In the passage, **frescoes** are
   (A) refreshing soft drinks
   (B) oil paintings done on stretched canvas
   (C) paintings done on fresh plaster
   (D) sculptures copied by Giotto di Bondone
   (E) paintings of industrialized society

2. Which word in the passage provides a clue to the meaning of **evanescent**?
   (A) painting
   (B) perspective
   (C) viaduct
   (D) fleeting
   (E) industrialization

3. According to the passage, why does it seem as though the painting is observed from the perspective of a person standing on a **promontory**?
   (A) We seem to be looking down at the scene.
   (B) The painting shows us standing on a **promontory**.
   (C) The locomotive is shown on a **promontory**.
   (D) We are forced to look up to see the painting.
   (E) We cannot see anything because of the rain.

4. In the passage, **iridescent** means
   (A) rain mixed with snow
   (B) heavy rain that causes floods
   (C) something dark that has faded
   (D) the darkness of nature
   (E) swirling varied colors

5. In the passage, the landscape is compared to the **pallor** of a sick person's flesh because
   (A) the misty rain makes the landscape seem pale and washed-out
   (B) the colors of the landscape are darker than normal
   (C) it is night and no color is visible on the landscape
   (D) the sun is bright enough to fade the colors of the landscape
   (E) the landscape is intensely colored like a person with a fever

6. In the passage, **burgeoned** means
   (A) failed to thrive
   (B) developed rapidly
   (C) experienced
   (D) social structures
   (E) overwhelmed

7. If the Industrial Revolution was a time of **apostasy,** as the writer of the passage suggests, we may expect other times of technological advance to
   (A) cause people to appreciate Italian art
   (B) bring about higher prices on new products
   (C) result in people abandoning long-held beliefs and principles
   (D) change the way people travel and communicate
   (E) force people to compete for new occupations

8. According to the passage, during the Industrial Revolution some people lived in **opulence** and therefore were _____ enough to spend money on elaborate decorations.
   (A) poor
   (B) educated
   (C) wealthy
   (D) resentful
   (E) overworked

9. In the passage, **baubles** are
   (A) changing views
   (B) trinkets
   (C) homes
   (D) festivals
   (E) age-old beliefs

10. In the passage, **festooned** homes points out the difference in the economic levels of the people by showing that
   (A) everyone during the Industrial Revolution had enough money to have parties, parades, and decorations
   (B) the Industrial Revolution produced new products that were used for decorations
   (C) the wealthy people were concerned about the poor and gave festivals for them
   (D) since all people had good jobs as a result of the Industrial Revolution, there were no longer economic differences
   (E) some people had money to spend on unnecessary decorative things, while many people struggled merely to exist

11. When we read in the passage that there are **abstruse** definitions, we should realize that
   (A) they are easily understood
   (B) they are detailed and hard to understand
   (C) they will not be avoided
   (D) the writer doesn't know them
   (E) they require little knowledge

12. Because the iron bars were a source of great wealth, they are compared by simile to **bullion,** which is
   (A) pig iron
   (B) molten iron
   (C) precious gems
   (D) gold bars
   (E) thin soup

13. To provide a clue to the meaning of **remuneration,** the writer
   (A) defines *puddlers*
   (B) links **remuneration** with the word *pay*
   (C) says the puddlers had the hardest job in the blast furnace
   (D) describes ironworking
   (E) explains that puddlers worked hard

14. The writer provides a clue to the meaning of **caricature** by
   (A) describing the Bessemer process
   (B) comparing the puddlers to a painting
   (C) linking **caricature** to the words *satirically exaggerated*
   (D) using an antonym for **caricature**
   (E) implying that **caricature** means "mechanization"

15. According to the passage, Carnegie's **frugality** meant that he was _____ with money.
   (A) generous
   (B) seldom
   (C) cursed
   (D) never
   (E) careful

16. In the passage, the writer provides a clue to the meaning of **maudlin** by
   (A) linking it to social responsibility
   (B) contrasting it with the words *tough* and *practical*
   (C) using a metaphor
   (D) contrasting it with the words *generally concerned*
   (E) describing an entire manufacturing plant

17. In the passage, **commiseration** is
   (A) a commission
   (B) living conditions
   (C) insincere concern
   (D) sympathy and compassion
   (E) an easy victim

18. We can infer from the passage that because of the practice of **usury,**
   (A) merchants and bankers never charged interest
   (B) some poor people had to pay too much interest
   (C) poor people were protected from paying too much interest
   (D) low-paid laborers sometimes turned to crime
   (E) poor people were lucky to be able to borrow money

19. To tell us that **venal** is defined as "dishonest," the writer
   (A) describes a **venal** employer
   (B) uses a synonym for **venal**
   (C) contrasts **venal** with the word *honest*
   (D) uses a metaphor for **venal**
   (E) includes **venal** in a series of synonyms

20. When we read in the passage that laborers and employers were not like children **gamboling** on a playground, we should realize that
   (A) laborers and employers were not getting along playfully and lightheartedly
   (B) laborers and employers fought like children on a playground
   (C) employers gambled with laborers' benefits
   (D) labor and management never collaborated and never reached any agreement
   (E) laborers and employers were too old to be considered children

READING NEW WORDS IN CONTEXT

Lesson 15 | CONTEXT: Science and Technology

The passage gives you an opportunity to expand your vocabulary. Below are twenty Vocabulary Words that are used in the passage and in the exercises that follow it.

abscond	circumvent	extort	malinger
adjure	elicit	fiasco	prognosis
aspersion	emaciate	ignominy	remonstrate
biennial	equivocal	longevity	reprisal
capricious	ethereal	malign	taciturn

Environmental Pollution in England

When it entered the Industrial Revolution, England also entered the age of pollution. In the nineteenth century, more and more people crowded into England's cities. Britain's industry was in full throttle, and no one had to **extort** (1) increased production from the manufacturers. It was the promise of profits, not the threat of harm, that motivated manufacturers.

Pollution problems arose on all fronts. Water supplies were contaminated, waste disposal was not regulated, and the air itself became polluted. Pollution actually began to negatively affect the people's **longevity** (2), or length of life. In London, citizens regularly fell prey to various diseases. An investigator in 1838 reported that of the six people occupying a single small room, two were ill and **emaciated** (3), wasting away with fever.

The story was the same throughout Britain. Although many employers accused their employees of **malingering** (4), the truth of the situation was that many workers were indeed sick. They had become ill from inhaling, drinking, or eating toxic substances. It takes little effort for us to **elicit** (5) the truth about the effects of industrial pollution. Research verifies that each technological advantage—railways, home coal furnaces, and industrial

chimneys—produced its own environmental problems. Under the pretense of increasing prosperity, industry had, like a thief in the night, **absconded** (6) with the clean environment.

At the height of the Industrial Revolution, however, the forecast for Britain's ailing environment was guardedly optimistic. This improved **prognosis** (7) came about because the nation had at last begun to deal with the reality of its environmental problems. The Town Improvement Act of 1847, for example, required railroad engines to consume their own smoke. Further legislation in the mid-1920s attempted to regulate industrial pollution. Still, environmental pollution remained severe in spite of these measures.

Damage to the Air and the Land

In 1952, air pollution reached a crisis point in London. Even usually **taciturn** (8) or uncommunicative people began remarking on the unhealthy haze that hung over London. The haze resulted from a combination of industrial pollutants, London's natural fog, and the burning of home fuels—wood, coal, and peat. In an effort to **circumvent** (9) continued problems, the British government introduced a preventive measure, the Clean Air Act, in

1956. This act forbade the emission of smoke and soot in areas designated as smokeless zones.

Not only the air, but the land itself, sustained great damage from industry. Sensitive to their surroundings, England's poets often celebrated the **ethereal** (10) as well as the earthly beauties of the countryside before the Industrial Revolution. For example, in 1807 William Wordsworth (1770 –1850) wrote of wandering "lonely as a cloud / That floats on high o'er vales and hills." But a little more than a century and a half later, Wordsworth's lovely vales and hills had changed. No longer were they crowded with yellow daffodils or the **biennial** (11) thistles that once could be counted on to bloom every second year. Instead, the countryside was littered with mass-produced farm equipment and showed evidence of the damage that could be inflicted by harmful chemical methods of soil nourishment. In a 1974 poem titled "Going, Going," poet Philip Larkin (1922–1985) **remonstrated** (12) against the lack of environmental planning. He warned that one day all of the countryside would be covered with concrete.

A Response to the Problem

In response to the industrialization of the countryside, a massive conservationist movement arose in England. This movement refused to be **equivocal** (13) about environmental protection. Because of the movement's decided stand, there was rapid growth in the Council for the Preservation of Rural England (and Wales). There was nothing **capricious** (14) about Britain's decision to save the environment; they decided to take a firm stand on environmental concerns. They unswervingly pursued measures that would cut down on pollution and conserve natural resources. In 1982, for instance, Britain passed the Wildlife and Countryside Act. This law states that it is best to have local management set its own environmental provisions rather than to command or **adjure** (15) the national government to make environmental laws.

Today in England, the environment is not treated carelessly, as it was during so many decades of the Industrial Revolution. If pollution has not disappeared completely, it has at least faded measurably. There is even a political party—the Green Party—founded on environmental concerns.

The Future of Britain's Environment

Many in Britain believe that the environment suffered under the conservative Prime Minister Margaret Thatcher (b. 1925). A common complaint is that Thatcher's allegiance to industry compromised her devotion to the environment. Some people label this charge a political **aspersion** (16), or slander. However, the loss of confidence in Mrs. Thatcher by her own party, which forced her resignation in 1989, may be viewed in some ways as a **reprisal** (17) concerning her environmental record. In other words, members of Britain's growing "green" movement injured Mrs. Thatcher politically because they believed she had injured the environment.

What does the future hold for Britain's environment? It is clear that current and future governments must address environmental concerns or run the risk of creating a **fiasco** (18). The situation is hopeful because politicians want to avoid public disgrace and save their reputations; they do not want to suffer **ignominy** (19). If they are to avoid being **maligned** (20) or slandered by an aggressive British press for taking a passive position on the environment, British leaders must make sure that environmental issues remain high on the nation's agenda.

EXERCISE 1 *Finding Synonyms* ✍️

Directions. Reread the preceding passage. Then write on the line provided a synonym for each of the words in boldface. If you cannot think of an exact synonym, you may write a brief definition of the word.

1. extort _____

2. longevity _____

3. emaciated _____

4. malingering _____

5. elicit _____

6. absconded _____

7. prognosis _____

8. taciturn _____

9. circumvent _____

10. ethereal _____

11. biennial _____

12. remonstrated _____

13. equivocal _____

14. capricious _____

15. adjure _____

16. aspersion _____

17. reprisal _____

18. fiasco _____

19. ignominy _____

20. maligned _____

EXERCISE 2 *Reading Strategically* 👈

Directions. Now that you have read the passage and thought about the words in boldface, circle the letter of the correct answer to each of the following items. The numbers of the items are the same as the numbers of the boldface Vocabulary Words in the passage.

1. In the passage, **extort** means
  (A) threaten
  (B) prevent
  (C) coax
  (D) shout at
  (E) argue with

2. If pollution negatively affects people's **longevity,** as the writer of the passage suggests, we may expect people
  (A) to live longer
  (B) to get taller each year
  (C) to lose their patience
  (D) to learn to live with pollution
  (E) not to live as long

3. To provide a clue to the meaning of **emaciated,** the writer
  (A) describes different kinds of pollution
  (B) blames London for being polluted
  (C) says six people lived in a small room
  (D) links **emaciated** to the words *wasting away*
  (E) provides an antonym for **emaciated**

4. When we read in the passage that employees were not **malingering,** we should realize that they
  (A) were pretending to be sick
  (B) were not patient enough to stay with their jobs
  (C) really were sick
  (D) were hoping to become sick
  (E) were unable to live in a single room

5. In the passage, to **elicit** the truth means to
  (A) bring forth the truth
  (B) cover up the truth
  (C) avoid the truth
  (D) change the truth
  (E) repeat the truth

6. Because industry **absconded** with the clean environment, it is compared by simile to
  (A) increasing prosperity
  (B) a thief in the night
  (C) industrial chimneys for manufacturing
  (D) a coal furnace in the home
  (E) an optimistic forecast

7. In the passage, the word _____ provides a clue to the meaning of **prognosis**.

    (A) problems
    (B) forecast
    (C) example
    (D) environment
    (E) legislation

8. In the passage, **taciturn** means

    (A) communicative
    (B) polluted
    (C) unpolluted
    (D) remarkable
    (E) uncommunicative

9. To tell us that **circumvent** is defined as "avoid or prevent," the writer

    (A) explains what the government did to **circumvent** environmental problems
    (B) uses a synonym for **circumvent**
    (C) contrasts **circumvent** with the antonym *continued*
    (D) uses a simile to describe what the government did to **circumvent** environmental problems
    (E) uses a series of words that have similar meanings to **circumvent**

10. In the passage, poets celebrated **ethereal** or _____ as well as earthly beauties of the countryside.

    (A) natural
    (B) unlikeable
    (C) heavenly
    (D) agricultural
    (E) foreign

11. We can infer from the passage that a **biennial** plant blooms

    (A) every four years
    (B) only in late summer
    (C) in two-year cycles
    (D) in the countryside
    (E) in vales

12. In the passage, the word _____ provides a clue to the meaning of **remonstrated**.

    (A) reminded
    (B) production
    (C) countryside
    (D) inorganic
    (E) protested

13. If people continue to refuse to be **equivocal** on their stand, as the writer of the passage suggests, we may expect

    (A) their undecided natures to give in easily to pressure
    (B) their lack of interest in the environment to be obvious
    (C) their refusal to express an opinion to hurt their cause
    (D) their determination to continue to have an effect
    (E) them never to stick to a single decision or idea

14. In the passage, why is there nothing **capricious** about Britain's decision to save the environment?

(A) All of the environmental problems in Britain have been completely solved.

(B) Since deciding to save their environment, the British have taken a firm stand on environmental concerns.

(C) The Industrial Revolution was over a long time ago.

(D) Since deciding to save their environment, the British have wavered in their decision.

(E) No one in Britain is concerned enough to bother with the environment.

15. In the passage, **adjure** means

(A) hurt

(B) treat

(C) command

(D) restore

(E) require

16. To cast an **aspersion** means to

(A) make a damaging, slanderous remark

(B) tell the truth about someone

(C) doubt someone's actions

(D) make a political statement that has a positive impact

(E) make a choice

17. In the passage, a **reprisal** is shown to be a(n) _____ done in response to an injury received.

(A) second chance

(B) appeal

(C) injury

(D) healing

(E) unnecessary job

18. In the passage, why does no government want to ignore environmental concerns and create a **fiasco**?

(A) Governments can easily solve environmental problems.

(B) Governments are strong enough to ignore such concerns.

(C) No government wants local agencies to set environmental standards.

(D) No government wants to be responsible for creating a complete failure.

(E) It is possible to run a successful government.

19. When we read in the passage that politicians do not want such **ignominy**, we should realize that they

(A) enjoy even negative publicity

(B) do not want public disgrace

(C) are mostly interested in laws

(D) don't like many publications

(E) would rather ignore the issues

20. In the passage, the word _____ provides a clue to the meaning of **maligned**.

(A) aggressive

(B) hopeful

(C) passive

(D) remained

(E) slandered

Vocabulary Words

aberration
abeyance
abject
abnegation
abscond
absolve
abstruse
acrimonious
adjudge
adjure
admonish
adroit
affront
allay
amorphous
anachronism
anarchy
antipathy
antipodes
apostasy
artifice
ascetic
ascribe
aspersion
assiduous
assimilate
atrophy
augury
auspices
avarice
aver

banal
bauble
bellicose
biennial
blazon
bode
bravado
broach
bullion
burgeoning
burnish

cadaverous
cajole
calumny

candor
capitulate
capricious
captivate
caricature
cessation
charlatan
chastise
chauvinism
chicanery
choleric
circumvent
civility
clandestine
coerce
cognizant
colloquy
commensurate
commiserate
commodious
conciliate
configuration
connoisseur
consign
consternation
contingency
copious
corollary
corroborate
cosmopolitan

dearth
decorum
deduce
demagogue
denizen
deplore
desist
despot
detriment
devoid
differentiate
dirge
discrepancy
discursive
disparity
distraught

diurnal
doggerel
dogma
duress

effusion
elegy
elicit
elocution
emaciate
emanate
empirical
engender
enigma
ennui
epitome
equanimity
equivocal
erudite
esoteric
espouse
ethereal
ethnology
etymology
eulogy
euphemism
euphony
evanescent
exhilaration
exhort
expatriate
expound
extant
extenuate
extol
extort
extraneous
extricate

facetious
facile
farcical
feign
fervid
festoon
fiasco
finesse

fissure
foible
foment
fortuitous
fresco
frugal

gambol
gauntlet
germane
glib
gratuitous
gregarious
guffaw
guile

hackneyed
harbinger
herculean
hiatus
homily
homogeneous
humdrum
hyperbole

idiosyncrasy
ignominy
illicit
immutable
impair
impassive
impeccable
implicit
incarcerate
incognito
inconsequential
incorrigible
indigent
indulgent
inexorable
infringe
iniquity
inordinate
inscrutable
intercede
introvert
inundate

Vocabulary Words *(continued)*

inveigle
iridescent
irrevocable

lampoon
litigation
longevity
loquacious
ludicrous
lugubrious

magnanimous
maim
malign
malinger
maudlin
menial
mercurial
mesmerism
mete
misnomer
mollify
moot
mottled
mundane
munificent

nadir
nebulous
nefarious
nemesis
nettle
nondescript
nonentity

obnoxious
obsequious
officious
omniscient
opulence
ostensible

pallor
paragon
parsimonious
patrimony
pecuniary
perfidious
pervade
pestilence
phlegmatic
poignant
precocious
precursor
predispose
prevaricate
primordial
proffer
profuse
progeny
prognosis
promontory
promulgate
propensity
propitious
proponent
propriety
prosaic
protégé

pseudonym
punctilious
purloin

quell
querulous
quiescent

rampant
rancor
recant
refute
regimen
remonstrate
remuneration
renounce
repository
reprisal
repudiate
retaliate
reticent
retroactive
retrospect
revile

sagacity
salient
sanguine
scathing
scrupulous
scurrilous
sedentary
seraphic
solicitous

sonorous
specious
strident
subjugate
subversion
sumptuous
sundry

taciturn
temerity
tenable
tenuous
tenure
terra firma
testimonial
treatise
truism

usury

vantage point
venal
venerate
vestige
vindicate
virulent
vociferous
voluminous

NOTES

NOTES

Curr Text Language H7422 Grade 12
Odell, Lee
Elements of language Sixth Course